Advances in Gerontological Nursing

1996
Issues for the 21st Century
Elizabeth A. Swanson, PhD, RN, and
Toni Tripp-Reimer, PhD, RN, FAAN, Editors

1997
Chronic Illness and the Older Adult
Elizabeth A. Swanson, PhD, RN, and
Toni Tripp-Reimer, PhD, RN, FAAN, Editors

1999
Life Transitions in the Older Adult:
Issues for Nurses and Other Health Professionals
Elizabeth A. Swanson, PhD, RN, and
Toni Tripp-Reimer, PhD, RN, FAAN, Editors
Winner, *American Journal of Nursing* Book-of-the-Year A ward

2001
Health Promotion and Disease Prevention in the Older Adult:
Interventions and Recommendations
Elizabeth A. Swanson, PhD, RN, Toni Tripp-Reimer, PhD, RN, FAAN, and
Kathleen C. Buckwalter, PhD, RN, FAAN, Editors

Elizabeth A. Swanson, PhD, RN, is an Associate Professor in the College of Nursing at The University of Iowa, in Iowa City, Iowa. Dr. Swanson received a BS in Nursing and an MA from The University of Iowa, College of Nursing, as well as a PhD from the College of Education

Her research ranges from health-promotion to the effects of nursing interventions on individuals with Alzheimer's disease and their caregivers. Current NINR funding includes Co-investigator on "Classification of Nurse Sensitive Patient Outcomes." She also is working on examining the perceptions of health and knowledge of health risks in older adults in the former Soviet Union.

Toni Tripp-Reimer, PhD, RN, FAAN, is Professor and Associate Dean for Research at the College of Nursing and Professor of Anthropology in the College of Liberal Arts at the University of Iowa in Iowa City, Iowa. Dr. Tripp-Reimer received a BSN from the University of Maryland. She holds a MS in Nursing and a MA and PhD in Anthropology from The Ohio State University. She also is director (or PI) of the NIH-funded Center for Gerontological Nursing Interventions Research (P30), the Institutional NRSA Training Program in Gerontological Nursing Research (T32), the Iowa-Veterans Affairs Nursing Research Consortium, and the Ethnogeriatric Core of the DHHS-funded Iowa Geriatric Education Center.

Her work has concerned the health behaviors of ethnic older persons for the past 20 years through a series of eleven funded projects. Her current work focuses on issues of bilingual access for minority elders; diabetes and end-of-life issues for Native American elders; and representational models of illness.

Kathleen C. Buckwalter, PhD, RN, FAAN, is Associate Provost for Health Sciences, and University of Iowa Foundation Distinguished Professor of Nursing at The University of Iowa, in Iowa City, Iowa. In addition, she is Associate Director of the Gerontological Nursing Interventions Research Center and Director of the UI Center on Aging, and also holds joint appointments in the College of Medicine's Department of Psychiatry and Internal Medicine. Dr. Buckwalter received a BS in Nursing and an MA in Psychiatric/Mental Health Nursing from The University of Iowa, College of Nursing. She received her PhD in Nursing from the University of Illinois, Chicago.

A prolific researcher and author, Dr. Buckwalter's work has been on improving mental health services and providing community-based care for chronically ill older adults. She has helped advance the knowledge base in both areas through more than a dozen funded research projects and training grants, thus stimulating promising new areas of research. Her most recent research includes "Evaluation of Special Care Units for Alzheimer's Disease," funded by the Alzheimer's Association, and the NINR-funded study, "PLST Model: Effectiveness for Rural ADRD Caregivers."

Health Promotion and Disease Prevention in the Older Adult

Interventions and Recommendations

Elizabeth A. Swanson, PhD, RN,
Toni Tripp-Reimer, PhD, RN, FAAN,
and **Kathleen Buckwalter,** RN, PhD,
Editors

 Springer Publishing Company

Springer Publishing Company, Inc.
536 Broadway
New York, NY 10012-3955

Acquisitions Editor: Ruth Chasek
Production Editor: Janice Stangel
Cover design by Susan Hauley

01 02 03 04 05 / 5 4 3 2 1

ISBN 0-8261-1376-1
ISSN 1083-8708

Printed in the United States of America

Contents

Contributors

Dorothy I. Baker, PhD, RNCS
Research Scientist
Yale University School of Medicine
New Haven, Connecticut

Diane M. Becker, RN, ScD, MPH
Associate Professor
Director, Center for Health Promotion
The Johns Hopkins University
Baltimore, Maryland

Ronni Chernoff, PhD, RD, FADA
Associate Director for Education/Evaluation
Geriatric Research Education and Clinical Center
John L. McClellan Memorial Veterans Hospital
and
Professor, College of Health Related Professions
University of Arkansas for Medical Sciences
Little Rock, Arkansas

Ronald L. Ettinger, BDS, MDS, DDSc
Professor
Department of Prosthodontics and Dows Institute
  for Dental Research
The University of Iowa
Iowa City, Iowa

Barbara A. Given, PhD, RN, FAAN
Professor, College of Nursing
Associate Director, Institute for Managed Care
Michigan State University
East Lansing, Michigan

Charles W. Given, PhD
Professor and Associate Chair, Department of Family Practice
College of Human Medicine
Michigan State University
East Lansing, Michigan

Barbara Holder, PhD, RN, FAAN
Associate Professor
School of Nursing
Clemson University
Clemson, South Carolina

Robert L. Kane, MD
School of Public Health
University of Minnesota
Minneapolis, Minnesota

Jurgis Karuza, PhD
Western New York Geriatric Education Center
University at Buffalo
Buffalo, New York

Kate Lorig, DrPH, RN
Stanford University School of Medicine
Palo Alto, California

Kathleen A. O'Connell, PhD, RN, FAAN
Professor of Nursing
Teachers College, Columbia University
New York, New York

Mary H. Palmer, PhD, RNC, FAAN
Associate Professor and Director
Office of Research
The State University of New Jersey-Rutgers
College of Nursing
Newark, New Jersey

Robert B. Wallace, MD
Professor
Department of Preventive Medicine and Environmental Health
The University of Iowa
Iowa City, Iowa

Jean F. Wyman, PhD, RN,CS, FAAN
Professor and Cora Meidl Siehl Chair in Nursing Research
School of Nursing
University of Minnesota
Minneapolis, Minnesota

Raphael Yook, MSPH
Research Analyst
The Johns Hopkins University
Baltimore, Maryland

National Advisory Panel

Ivo L. Abraham, PhD, CS, RN, FAAN
Professor
Schools of Nursing and Medicine
Charlottesville, Virginia
and
Catholic University of Leuven
Leuven, Belgium

Patricia G. Archbold, RN, DNSc, FAAN
Professor, School of Nursing
Oregon Health Sciences University
Portland, Oregon

Cornelia M. Beck, PhD, RN, FAAN
Professor and Associate Dean for Research and Evaluation
College of Nursing
University of Arkansas for Medical Sciences
Little Rock, Arkansas

Barbara A. Given, PhD, RN, FAAN
Professor and Director of Research
College of Nursing
Michigan State University
East Lansing, Michigan

Virgene Kayser-Jones, PhD, RN, FAAN
Professor
School of Nursing
University of California-San Francisco
San Francisco, California

Preface

The critical importance of health promotion efforts for older adults is increasingly recognized (Rakowski, 1997), despite the initial neglect of elders as targeted populations. Evidence for the central importance of health promotion and disease prevention research is found prominently in the recommendations of the U.S. Surgeon General's 1988 workshop on Health Promotion and Aging (USDHHS, 1988), the explication of the National Health Promotion and Disease Prevention Objectives for the year 2000, and the Institute of Medicine's call (Berg & Cassells, 1990) for health providers to look beyond curing and preventing disease to promoting health and preventing disability in the second half of life.

The Healthy People initiative which began in 1979, sets forth national health goals for every decade and then reviews the health of Americans against those goals (AAMC Reporter, 2000). The Healthy People 2000 National Objectives listed nine health status aims specific to the elderly, such as reducing suicide among white males and reducing significant visual impairment. It listed three objectives related to risk reduction, such as increasing the percentage of individuals who regularly participate in light to moderate activity for at least 30 minutes per day; and eight objectives targeting services and protection, including increasing the use of the oral care system and increasing the percentage of recipients of home food services. The Healthy People 2010 component was launched in late January 2000. Some important differences between the 2010 goals and those of previous decades include addressing the health needs of a larger, more diverse, and older population.

According to the U.S. DHHS Public Health Service (1991), in the first two decades of the health promotion and disease prevention campaign, 13% of the 319 objectives reached or exceeded their targets and significant progress has been achieved in another 43% of the goals. Unfortunately, that leaves 44% of the goals in which unsatisfactory progress was made (Buckwalter, 1999).

At present, health promotion is viewed as a right for all people, regardless of age. Yet, much of the nation's health care costs focus on illness and disease treatment rather than proactive strategies for health care (Maddox, 1999). This is particularly true for older adults, despite evidence that health promotion behaviors increase longevity, independence, and quality of life.

Other information supports the need to support proactive strategies in the form of intervention research. National Center for Health Statistics data on the functional status and health of older Americans indicate key potential areas for intervention research (Van Nostrand, Furner, & Suzman, 1993). They indicate that nearly 75% of persons aged 80 and older identify one or more problems in performing activities of daily living. Further, although elders experience a decline in acute health problems, chronic conditions are common with more than 80% of older adults reporting one or more chronic health problems. Ischemic heart disease, hypertension, vision impairment, hearing impairment, musculoskeletal impairment, and diabetes are the major conditions experienced by older adults. One must also note that the prevalence of chronic conditions increases with increasing age, as heart disease, cancer, and cerebrovascular disease account for 70% of deaths in those individuals 65 and older (Bureau of the Census, 1993).

The need for systematic gerontological research in health promotion/disease prevention is evident since gerontological nurses in a variety of practice settings will be called upon to engage older adults in health promotion and disease prevention activities. The rapid growth of the older adult population, the diversity of this population, and economic imperatives in the U.S. health care system indicate that these needs must be addressed with urgency.

While scientists have reached consensus on general recommendations regarding immunizations, regular exercise, dietary patterns, self-care practices, smoking cessation, and alcohol moderation, there is far less agreement on the best methods of promoting and maintaining those behavioral changes. This premise was the driving force behind a conference entitled Vitality Throughout the Adult Lifecycle: Interventions to Promote Health at The University of Iowa, College of Nursing, co-sponsored by The University of Iowa

Gerontological Nursing Interventions Research Center [funded by the National Institute of Nursing Research], American Academy of Nursing, and The University of Iowa College of Medicine. This book is derived from this conference.

In the first chapter, Wyman focuses on exercise, a structured regimen of physical activity, performed for the purpose of increasing health-related physical fitness. She provides a brief overview of national exercise guidelines and exercise prescription, reviews published studies on the effectiveness of exercise in healthy and impaired older populations, and formulates evidence-based recommendations for clinical practice. Areas for future research are also discussed.

Chernoff, in the second chapter, discusses strategies in health promotion, disease prevention, and disease treatment related to nutrition. Primary prevention approaches focusing on nutrition education and secondary prevention procedures relating to assessment and screening initiatives are presented. The chapter continues with suggested interventions related to tertiary prevention, which uses medical nutrition therapy as an integral part of disease treatment or amelioration. Challenges to these approaches are identified as well as suggestions to address them. Chernoff concludes the chapter with a series of health recommendations for older adults.

The third chapter presents the evolution of a single chronic disease patient education program, the Arthritis Self-Management Program (ASMP), also known as the Arthritis Self-Help (ASH) Course. Lorig includes a brief synopsis of previously published ASMP studies. She also discusses elements of self-management interventions, offers selected case histories of how ASMP has been disseminated, and concludes with a discussion of future self-management directions.

In the next chapter, the focus is oral health. Dental and oral diseases may be the most prevalent and the most preventable conditions affecting older Americans. Ettinger expands the health professionals' knowledge of oral health in older adults through addressing their utilization of oral health services, oral health problems, and treatment needs. He also offers suggestions for oral health education programs for all health care professionals working with the elderly.

The following chapter addresses smoking cessation among older clients. In this chapter O'Connell discusses issues in smoking and smoking cessation relevant to older smokers. Suggested interventions are discussed. Then a theoretical basis for under-standing smoking, the attraction of cigarettes despite the health risks, and the difficulties of smoking cessation are presented.

The focus of the next chapter is the serious public health prob-lem of falls in older adults. Baker discusses the Yale Frailty and Injuries: Cooperative Studies of Intervention Trials (Yale FICSIT), a randomized clinical trial comparing the effectiveness of usual health care and social visits to a home-based multifactorial, targeted risk factor abatement intervention in decreasing falls among at-risk community living older adults. The Yale FICSIT interventions are discussed and results are presented that suggest they are effective, feasible, safe, and cost-effective in reducing falls.

As Palmer acknowledges in chapter seven, urinary incontinence is a symptom, not a disease. She furthers the discussion by pre-senting an updated continence promotion model and information on the most recent research efforts to prevent or reverse urinary incontinence. Barriers to the development and implementation of prevention-focused interventions specific to older adults are reviewed. Palmer concludes the chapter by making recommenda-tions for nursing research and practice.

In the next chapter, Wallace acknowledges that cancer is a dis-ease of older people, noting the relationship of aging and the biol-ogy of cancer. The importance of primary prevention of cancer incorporating the significance of nutrition is set forth. He also notes the controversial area of secondary prevention due to the lack of evidence for efficacy of various cancer screening proce-dures for older adults, although evidence does exist for other pop-ulations. Wallace continues by identifying factors associated with underutilization of screening services and concludes with a dis-cussion of the tertiary prevention of cancer in the older population.

Becker and her co-author, Yook emphasize the familial nature of premature coronary heart disease. They focus on coronary heart disease (CHD), its risk factors, and the impact of risk factor modi-fication. Reviews of their studies on premature familial-aggregated CHD conclude the chapter.

Chapter 10 targets the topic of immunizations in the elderly. Karuza deals with the major topic areas of effectiveness of immu-nizations for the diseases of adulthood, current immunization rates in adults, barriers, and facilitating factors that influence adult immunization rates and outcomes of interventions that have improved rates. The thrust of the chapter is on influenza and pneumonia vaccinations of older adults. Immunization patterns for tetanus and hepatitis B are also discussed.

In Chapter 11, Holder summarizes the research literature on interventions for African American diabetics by emphasizing the effect of diabetic education and family-focused strategies. She also presents a summary of an ongoing longitudinal study with elderly African American diabetics and their families. Discussion of this study focuses on implications of the findings for nursing practice and research.

With the Given and Given chapter, the focal point is on the organization of health care for older adults. The authors discuss the characteristics of managed care organizations, provide descriptions and examine published research on health-oriented programs, and offer suggestions for opportunities to incorporate health promotion for the elderly into managed care organizations.

In the final chapter, Kane challenges the reader to focus on interventions based on conceptual and empirically verified models. In addition, he contends that these interventions need to be translated to the general population and applied to everyday practice.

Health promotion and disease prevention activities will continue to be of importance to individuals and their families in the 21st century. It will be critical for older adults as the research continues to convey the relevance of these activities to enhancing the quality of life. Through the contributions of these authors, it is our intent to promote evidence-based recommendations for older adults that health practitioners in a variety of settings can use. It is also hoped that the research and practice ideas related to health promotion and disease prevention for older adults suggested by these authors, be the building blocks for research projects examining approaches for meeting the needs of this unique population.

REFERENCES

Association of American Medical Colleges Reporter (2000). The nation's prevention agenda for 2010, 9(4), 2–3.

Berg, R. L., & Cassells, J. S. (Eds.) (1990). *Institute of Medicine, Division of Health Promotion and Disease Prevention—The second fifty years: Promoting health and prevention disability.* Washington, DC: National Academy Press.

Buckwalter, K. C. (1999). There's good news and bad news. *Journal of Gerontological Nursing, 25*(10), 6.

Bureau of the Census (1993). Statistical abstract of the United States 1993: The national data book. Washington D.C.: U.S. Government Printing Office.

Maddox, M. (1999). Older women and the meaning of health. *Journal of Gerontological Nursing, 25*(12), 26–33.

Rakowski, W. (1997). Health behavior in the elderly. In S. S. Gochman (Ed), *Handbook of health behavior research III: Demography, development, and diversity* (pp. 97–117). New York: Plenum.

U.S. Department of Health and Human Services (1988). Proceedings of the Surgeon General's workshop, health promotion and aging. Washington, DC: US Government Printing Office.

Van Nostrand, J., Furner, S., & Suzman, R. (Eds.) (1993). *Health data on older Americans: United States, 1992.* National Center for Health Statistics, Vital Health Statistics, 3, 27.

CHAPTER 1

Exercise Interventions

Jean F. Wyman

Exercise has an important role in promoting good health, functional independence, and quality of life in older adults. Beneficial effects of regular exercise may slow the physiological decline associated with aging, reverse consequences associated with disuse; prevent, reduce, or modify disease effects, reduce falls and disability; and decrease all-cause mortality (Elward & Larson, 1992; Pate, Pratt, Blair, Haskell, Macera et al., 1995; U.S. Department of Health and Human Services, 1996). Although there are well-established guidelines on the type and amount of exercise and physical activity that is recommended for adults, these are based on research conducted in healthy young and middle-aged adults. Are these exercise guidelines safe for the elderly? Do they provide the right dose to achieve the desired response in older adults, especially the frail elderly? How much exercise is necessary to improve or maintain functional performance? How should exercise be prescribed for different subgroups of elderly ranging from the healthy to the very frail?

The focus in this chapter will be on exercise, a structured regimen of physical activity, performed for the purpose of increasing health-related physical fitness (e.g., cardiorespiratory endurance, muscular endurance, muscular strength, flexibility, and body composition). This chapter will provide a brief overview of national exercise guidelines and exercise prescription, review published studies on the effectiveness of exercise in healthy and impaired older populations, and derive evidence-based recommendations for clinical practice. Areas for future research will also be discussed.

EXERCISE TRAINING

Exercise Types

Exercise studies in the elderly can be categorized based upon their primary functional goal: flexibility, strength, endurance, and balance training. An additional category, combination training, which incorporates two or more of the four basic types of exercise is frequently used in research and practice to achieve multiple goals. Flexibility or stretching exercises are designed to increase the length of muscles and ligaments and the range of motion available at a particular joint or group of joints. Active or passive range of motion exercise and yoga are examples of flexibility training. Strength or resistance training is aimed at increasing muscular strength, power, and endurance. Resistance may be provided by body weight, free weights, elastic bands, pneumatic, or hydraulic devices. Endurance or aerobic training is targeted towards improving cardiorespiratory endurance, and involves continuous movement of large muscle groups through activities such as running, cycling, swimming, brisk walking, rowing, or stair climbing. Balance training is designed to improve postural control mechanisms through a variety of static and dynamic exercises. Tai Chi is considered a form of balance training. Specialized balance training might involve the use of computerized force platforms.

National Exercise Guidelines

A number of groups such as the American Heart Association, National Institutes of Health, Centers for Disease Control, and American College of Sports Medicine have issued exercise recommendations (Table 1.1). The most recent guidelines issued by the Surgeon General (U.S. Department of Health and Human Services, 1996) indicates that moderate physical activity at least 30 minutes per day for 5 days per week will result in health benefits. Examples of moderate physical activity are listed in Table 1.2. For more vigorous physical activities, less time will be required to achieve health benefits. Conversely, the less vigorous the activity, the more time that will be needed to achieve exercise effects.

Although strength training is mentioned in several exercise recommendations, few guidelines provide specific details other than to mention that frequency should be twice a week. None of the

TABLE 1.1 Recommendations for Physical Activity and Exercise

Type of training	AHA 1995	NIH 1995	CDC/ACSM 1995	Surgeon General 1996
Endurance training				
Intensity	50–60% VO_2 max or HR max reserve	Moderate; Vigorous for those meeting standard	Moderate	Moderate
Duration	30 minutes	30 minutes/day; Intermittent bouts of activity (at least 10 min)	≥ 30 min/day in bouts of at least 8–10 mins	≥ 30 minutes
Frequency	≥ 3 days/week	All or most days of the week	All or most days of the week	All or most days of the week
Strength training	1 set, 10–15 reps, 8–10 exercises	Not specified	Addressed but not specified	Not specified
Frequency	2 days/week	Not specified	Not specified	≥ 2 days/week

AHA = American Heart Association
NIH = National Institutes of Health
CDC = Centers for Disease Control
ACSM = American College of Sports Medicine

TABLE 1.2   Moderate Intensity Exercise

Walking or waxing a car (45–50 mins)
Washing windows or floors (45–50 mins)
Gardening (30–45 mins)
Wheeling self in wheelchair (30–40 mins)

Less Vigorous, More Time
Walking 1 3/4 miles in 35 mins
Bicycling 5 miles in 30 mins
Dancing fast (30 mins)
Raking leaves (30 mins)
Walking 2 miles in 30 mins
Water aerobics (30 mins)

More Vigorous, Less Time
Swimming laps (30 mins)
Bicycling 4 miles in 15 mins
Jumping rope (15 mins)
Shoveling snow (15 mins)
Stairwalking (15 mins)

Adapted from Surgeon General's Report on Physical Activity and Health, 1996.

exercise guidelines mention flexibility and balance exercises which become more essential as one ages.

Exercise Prescription

Key principles of exercise training which should be considered in designing an exercise program include individuality, specificity, and progressive overload. According to the principle of individuality, individuals adapt to a training stimulus at different rates and with different outcomes. For example, a person's fitness level is an important consideration at the beginning of training. Optimal training responses occur when the exercise program is planned to meet individual needs and functional capacities. The principle of specificity indicates that training must be specifically matched to the type of activity that will produce the desired outcome. Thus, to develop cardiorespiratory endurance, the training program should select exercises designed to produce an aerobic response. The principle of progressive overload states that training must involve working the body (e.g., muscles, cardiorespiratory system) harder than normal to achieve a training response. As the body adapts to a particular exercise stimulus, training will need to progress to a higher work level to bring about a desired response. Achieving the appropriate overload for an individual requires manipulation of the exercise prescription with specific consideration given to the type of exercise.

An exercise prescription includes the following components: mode, frequency, duration, and intensity. Mode refers to the type of exercise such as endurance, flexibility, strength, and so on. Frequency refers to how often the exercise should be performed, for example, multiple daily sessions, daily, or several times per week. Duration is how long an exercise session should be conducted which is usually characterized in minutes. Intensity or how hard the exercise should be performed is typically described in how much energy or exertion is needed to perform the exercise. It is often categorized in aerobic capacity, for example, maximum oxygen uptake (VO_2), maximum heart rate, relative perceived exertion (RPE) using the Borg or modified Borg scale, or by energy consumption, for example, calorie counts or metabolic equivalent units (Mets). As a general rule, as one ages, it takes less intense activity to generate a higher RPE. The exercise prescription in terms of frequency, intensity, and duration of physical activity varies depending on the benefits that are desired. The minimum amount of exercise required to achieve a training effect (i.e., threshold of training) differs for people depending on their current fitness and activity levels and the desired benefits.

The exercise prescription should be based upon the individual's goals, and include three consecutive periods: warm-up, conditioning, and cool-down. The warm-up period consists of 5–10 minutes of light to moderate activities such as flexibility exercises performed for the purposes of reducing injury risk and soreness, minimizing venous pooling and hypotension, and possibly improving performance. The conditioning period follows with 20–60 minutes of more intense activities, usually cardiovascular endurance and strengthening exercises. The cool-down period of 5–10 minutes allows for tapering off with similar light to moderate activities as the warm-up period.

Depending on the exercise goal, it will take 4–12 weeks for initial conditioning to occur. Generally, older adults take longer to achieve a training response than younger adults. It is important to note that most exercise studies only report on the results of exercise following this initial conditioning period. However, continued improvement may be noted for up to 2 years following the initiation of an exercise program in the elderly (McCartney, Hicks, Martin, & Webber, 1996; Morey, Cowper, Feussner, DiPasquale, Crowley et al., 1991).

EXERCISE TRAINING IN OLDER ADULTS

This section presents a review of the research on each of the five types of exercise which have been conducted in adults age 60 years and over. Because of the heterogeneity of the elderly population and the varying target study populations, the literature was reviewed separately for healthy and impaired populations. Given the prevalence of chronic disease in the elderly, the grouping of studies based upon whether the samples were healthy or impaired was somewhat arbitrary. Sample selection criteria assisted in the grouping of the studies. The selection of studies with impaired older adults were based upon eligibility criteria such as residential status (e.g., nursing home) and/or disability status (e.g., self-reported disability). Research reports on exercise with specific patient populations other than those with osteoarthritis and specific rehabilitation programs such as cardiac or hip fracture rehabilitation were excluded from the analyses. Those studies categorized as having primarily a healthy older population used community-based samples and did not include eligibility criteria related to functional limitation or self-reported disability. In the majority of strength and endurance training studies, some flexibility or stretching exercises were included as part of a warm-up and/or cool-down period. These studies were categorized as primarily strength or endurance training according to the study's stated purpose rather than classifying them as combination training.

Following a strategy similar to that used by the Agency for Health Care Policy and Research in their formulation of clinical practice guidelines, this review also considered the type of study design and methodology in determining the strength of the evidence supporting a training effect for a particular exercise category in both healthy and impaired older populations. Studies were divided on the type of research design into three groups: a) randomized, clinical trials (RCTs); b) nonrandomed controlled trials; and c) observational studies employing a pre/post test design on the same cohort of individuals. Those studies that used a randomized controlled or a well-controlled, nonrandomized study design with statistically significant results were given the greatest weight in determining the strength of the evidence. Because a number of the RCTs incorporated more than one treatment group (e.g., strength training and endurance training), these studies are discussed in more than one section of the literature review. Thus, a study comparing two treatment groups against an untreated control group are discussed as separate studies under a specific type of training if data were available on the comparison of the one treatment group against an untreated control group. Although several studies compared different types of training against each other, the comparative outcomes of two types of training are beyond the scope of this review.

When data were available, adverse effects resulting from the exercise intervention are summarized. However, many research reports fail to include adverse effects associated with the conduct of the trial.

The number of studies conducted with elderly populations within the five categories of exercise along with space constraints for this chapter precluded presenting a summary table outlining the elements of individual studies. Instead, readers are referred to several excellent reviews on exercise interventions which include summary tables (Chandler & Hadley, 1996; Judge, 1997; Whipple, 1997). A listing of studies included in this chapter's review is summarized in the Appendix.

Flexibility Training

Flexibility training is particularly important in the elderly because of normal aging changes, disuse consequences, and disease effects such as those associated with arthritis. Flexibility or range of motion exercises are usually performed as part of the warm-up period. Typically, they are done in combination with other types of exercise rather than as the sole exercise, or they are used as a control condition in a randomized exercise trial. As a result, there are few reported studies investigating flexibility training alone. Often, flexibility training is selected as a control condition in studies focused on one of the other major types of exercise.

Several principles guide flexibility training. First, flexibility is specific to each joint of the body. Thus, no single test will give an indication of overall flexibility, nor will one type of exercise increase flexibility to all joints of the body. To increase flexibility in a particular joint, that joint must be exercised. Second, to increase flexibility, the muscle must be stretched (overload) beyond its normal length. Three types of flexibility exercise are used: static stretch, ballistic stretch, and proprioceptive neuromuscular facilitation. Static stretching which can be performed as an active or passive stretch is a slow stretch that is held for a specific time. This form of stretching is the most widely recommended because it tends to cause less injury in beginners, in those who have a history or are at risk of muscle and joint injury, and for those such as the elderly who do not need the exceptional levels of flexibility which are required for athletic performance (Corbin & Lindsey, 1997). Ballistic or bouncing stretching which uses momentum to achieve a stretch should be avoided in older adults because of its high potential for injury. Proprioceptive neuromuscular facilitation (PNF) consists of several techniques to stimulate muscles to contract more strongly or to relax more fully so they can be stretched. PNF which is used primarily during rehabilitation programs is considered the most effective method of improving flexibility (Corbin & Lindsey, 1997).

Exercise physiologists recommend that flexibility training programs should be conducted at a minimum of 3 days per week, with daily being the ideal (Corbin & Lindsey, 1997). Given the loss of flexibility associated with disuse and disease in older adults, it seems prudent to recommend that elders should perform flexibility exercises using all major muscle groups at least 3 days per week, and on a daily basis if possible. All major joints should be exercised. Individuals should be encouraged or assisted to slowly stretch as far as possible without pain. The stretch should be held for 15 seconds with a 15 to 30 seconds minimum rest period between stretches. At least three repetitions should be performed for each joint.

Strength Training

Loss of muscle strength and mass are key features of the aging process with losses of strength averaging 1 to 2% per year

(Aniansson, Sperling, Rundgren, & Lehnberg, 1983; Larson, Grimby, & Karlsson, 1979). Lower extremity muscles appear to be more affected than the upper extremity muscles (Aniansson et al., 1983). Adequate muscle strength is an important characteristic underlying mobility and the performance of daily activities. Thus, strength training either to maintain or regain strength would seem essential for the elderly to maintain functional independence.

Literature Review

Strength training has been extensively studied in the elderly. Thirty-five studies on strength training were reviewed; 29 studies were conducted in the healthy elderly, and six studies in the impaired elderly. In the healthy elderly category, there were 21 RCTs (Ades, Ballor, Ashikaga, Utton, & Nair, 1996; Buchner, Cress, de Lateur, Esselman, Margherita et al., 1997; Charette, McEvoy, Dyka, Snow-Harter, Guido et al., 1991; Era, 1988; Hagberg, Graves, Limacher, Woods, Leggett et al., 1989; Hanson, Agostinucci, Dasler, & Creel, 1992; Jette, Harris, Sleeper, Lachman, Heiskin et al., 1996; McCartney et al., 1995; Mills, 1994; Nichols, Omizo, Peterson, & Nelson, 1993; Panton, Graves, Pollock, Hagberg, & Chen, 1990; Rall, Meydani, Kehayias, Dawson-Hughes, & Roubenoff, 1996; Rooks, Kiel, Parsons, & Hayes, 1997; Singh, Clements, & Fiatarone, 1997; Sipila & Suominen, 1995; Skelton & McLaughlin, 1996; Skelton, Young, Greig, & Malbut, 1995; Topp, Mikesky, Dayhoff, & Holt, 1996; Topp, Mikesky, Wigglesworth, Holt, & Edwards, 1993; Wolfson, Whipple, Derby, Judge, King et al., 1996); 1 nonrandomized trial (Hartard, Haber, Illieva, Preisinger, Seidl et al., 1996) and eight observational studies (Aniansson & Gustafsson, 1981; Bassett, McClamrock, & Schmelzer, 1982; Brown & Holloszy, 1991; Frontera, Meredith, O'Reilly, Knuttgen, & Evans, 1988, 1990; Grimby, Aniansson, Hedberg, Henning, Grangard et al., 1992; Hunter, Treuth, Weinsier, Kekes-Szabo, Kell et al., 1995); involving over 925 participants (608 women, 317 men) ranging in age from 60 to 93 years. Sample sizes ranged from 14 (Hanson et al., 1992; Rall et al., 1996) to 142 (McCartney, Hicks, Martin, & Webber, 1995). Seven of the 20 RCTs had intervention groups containing 25 or more participants (Buchner et al., 1997; Jette et al., 1996; McCartney et al., 1995; Rooks et al., 1997; Topp et al., 1993; Topp et al., 1996; Wolfson et al., 1996).

The exercise prescriptions were quite variable. The mode of training involved individual or group-based instruction. With the exception of two studies (Hartard et al., 1996; Mills, 1994), most studies used a progressive resistance training protocol. Resistance was provided by pneumatic devices, free weights, elastic bands, or body weight. Training varied from a frequency of 2 to 3 days per week, with the majority of studies (23 studies) using 3 days per week. The duration of the exercise ranged from 20 to 60 minutes per exercise session. The length of the training program varied from 6 to 42 weeks. Exercise intensity ranged from low to high intensity (50–90% 1-RM—heaviest amount of weight that the individual can lift for one complete repetition of an exercise using correct technique). Each exercise was performed for 4 to 15 repetitions, with most studies using 8 to 12 repetitions, in one to four exercise sets.

In the impaired elderly category, there were three RCTs (Fiatarone, O'Neill, Ryan, Clements, Solares et al., 1994; McMurdo & Johnstone, 1995; McMurdo & Rennie, 1993) and three observational studies (Connelly & Vandervoort, 1995; Fiatarone, Marks, Ryan, Meredith, Lipsitz et al., 1990; Fisher, Pendergast, & Calkins, 1991) involving over 227 participants (160 women, 58 men) ranging in age from 63 to 98. Sample sizes ranged 10 (Fiatarone et al., 1990) to 100 (Fiatarone et al., 1994). Only one of the three RCTs had an intervention group of 25 participants or more (Fiatarone et al., 1994). All studies used progressive resistance exercise. The frequency of training varied from two times a week to daily with the majority of studies using three times per week (four studies). The length of the training protocol ranged from 6 to 28 weeks. Exercise intensity ranged from low to high (50–80% 1-RM). The number of repetitions varied from 5 to 12 which were performed in one to three exercise sets.

The trends and strength of the evidence on selected training outcomes are presented in Table 1.3. With the exception of four studies (Bassett et al., 1982; Hanson et al., 1992; McMurdo & Johnstone, 1995; Mills, 1994), all studies conducted in the healthy and impaired populations reported statistically significant improvements in muscle strength. Short-term strength training results in muscle strength gains from the young old who are relatively healthy (Charette et al., 1991; Frontera et al., 1988) to the very old with severe functional impairments (Fiatarone et al., 1990, 1994). The magnitude of the improvement (9 to 200%) varied according to the muscle group tested, type of measurement, the initial fitness level, and the intensity of the exercise. Strength evaluated by isokinetic measurements was less than that when 1-RM measurements are used (Judge,

TABLE 1.3 Strength Training Outcomes

	Trends & Strength of Evidence		References
	Healthy elderly	*Impaired elderly*	
Cardiovascular fitness	↔	↔	*Healthy:* Hagberg et al., 1989; Panton et al., 1990; Frontera et al., 1990; Rall et al., 1996; Ades et al., 1996; Rooks et al., 1997
			Impaired: Ettinger et al., 1997
Muscle strength	↑↑↑	↑↑	*Healthy:* Aniansson & Gustafsson, 1981; Bassett et al., 1982; Hagberg et al., 1989; Frontera et al., 1988; 1990; Era, 1988; Brown & Holloszy, 1991; Panton et al., 1990; Charette et al., 1991; Grimby et al., 1992; Hanson et al., 1992; Nichols et al., 1993; Mills, 1994; Judge et al., 1994; Hunter et al., 1995; Skelton et al., 1995; Sipila & Suominen, 1995; Ades et al., 1996; Jette et al., 1996; Wolfson et al., 1996; Rall et al., 1996; Topp et al., 1996; Hartard et al., 1996; Singh et al., 1997; Rooks et al., 1997; Buchner et al., 1997
			Impaired: Fiatarone et al., 1990; 1994; Fisher et al., 1991; Connelly & Vandervoort, 1995; McMurdo & Johnstone, 1995

TABLE 1.3 Strength Training Outcomes (Continued)

	Trends & Strength of Evidence		References
	Healthy elderly	Impaired elderly	
Muscle size	↑	↔	*Healthy:* Frontera et al., 1988; Brown & Holloszy, 1991; Grimby et al., 1992; McCartney et al., 1995, 1996; Skelton & McLaughlin, 1996; Sipila & Suominen, 1995
			Impaired: Fiatarone et al., 1990, 1994
Balance	↔	↔	*Healthy:* Bassett et al., 1982; Era, 1988; Topp et al., 1993; Skelton & McLaughlin, 1996; Wolfson et al., 1996; Rooks et al., 1997; Buchner et al., 1997
			Impaired: McMurdo & Johnstone, 1995
Gait velocity / time/distance	↑↑	↑↑	*Healthy:* Topp et al., 1993; 1996; Judge et al., 1993a, 1993b, 1994; Hunter et al., 1995; Skelton et al., 1995; Ades et al., 1996; McCartney et al., 1995; Buchner et al., 1997
			Impaired: Sauvage et al., 1992; Fiatarone et al., 1990, 1995; Fisher et al., 1991; Ettinger et al., 1997

TABLE 1.3 *(Continued)*

	Trends & Strength of Evidence		References
	Healthy elderly	*Impaired elderly*	
Mobility	↑	↔	*Healthy*: Skelton & McLaughlin, 1996 *Impaired*: Connelly & Vandervoort, 1995; McMurdo & Johnstone, 1995
Chair rise or stair climb time	↑	↑↑	*Healthy*: McCartney et al., 1995; Skelton et al., 1995; Skelton & McLaughlin, 1996; Rooks et al., 1997 *Impaired*: McMurdo & Rennie, 1993; Fiatarone et al., 1994; Ettinger et al., 1997
Body composition	↑	↔	*Healthy*: Nichols et al., 1993; Sipila & Suominen, 1995 *Impaired*: Fiatarone et al., 1994
Falls	↔	NR	*Healthy*: Buchner et al., 1997

Note: Up arrows indicate improvement in the expected direction. Side arrows indicate inconsistent findings among studies or no improvement. The more arrows, the stronger the evidence.

Whipple, & Wolfson, 1994). The training regimen in the three studies that did not report significant strength gains tended to be of lower intensity, fewer days per week, shorter duration, and/or less supervision (Bassett et al., 1982; Hanson et al., 1992; McMurdo & Johnstone, 1995; Mills, 1994). In general, the impaired elderly with the weakest muscles were more likely to achieve higher percentage strength gains than those whose muscles were stronger. The specificity of the training and its relationship to outcome measurement was an important factor in interpreting study results. In general, studies using different resistance machines in the training than what was used to measure the outcome of the intervention had lower improvement rates (Fiatrarone et al., 1990; Frontera et al., 1988; Judge et al., 1994). The greatest improvements in strength were seen in studies that trained at 70 to 80% 1-RM.

Similar to studies in younger populations, the greatest gains in muscle strength occurred during the first few weeks of training in older adults. Research findings in the elderly support the theoretical view that initial strength gains reflect neural adaptation rather than true muscle strength change. Thirty percent of the 1-RM occurs after 6 weeks of training, and 50% of the 1-RM by 12 weeks (Fiatarone et al., 1990; Frontera et al, 1988; McCartney et al., 1995; Nichols et al., 1993). Some muscle groups such as the hip abductors and ankle dorsiflexors may need a longer period to achieve a training effect (Wolfson et al., 1996). Long-term follow-up (94 weeks) of a twice a week resistance training program in the healthy elderly demonstrated that strength gains continue over time without any well-defined plateaus (McCartney et al., 1996). McCartney and his colleagues (1996) found that the proportion of strength gains in each year of a 2-year weight training program were comparable (63% versus 61%).

Although smaller than strength gains, there appears to be a corresponding increase in muscle mass in those studies who used measures of muscle hypertrophy in both healthy (Ades et al., 1996; Frontera et al., 1988; McCarney et al., 1995; Rooks et al., 1997; Sipila & Suominen, 1995) and impaired populations (Fiatarone et al., 1990, 1994).

Older men and women have similar short- and long-term training responses (McCartney et al., 1996). Training responsiveness continues through all decades of life (Fiatarone et al., 1990; McCartney et al., 1996), although young-old men may progress more than old-old men (Judge et al., 1994; McCartney et al., 1996).

There is good evidence that moderate intensity strength training in both healthy and impaired older adults results in increased flexibility (McMurdo & Rennie, 1993; Mills, 1994) improved gait speed or walking time (Ades et al., 1996; Fiatarone et al., 1994; Hunter et al., 1995; Judge et al., 1994; McCartney et al., 1995; Skelton & McLaughlin, 1996; Topp et al., 1996), time to rise from the floor or chair, and stair climbing time (Rooks et al., 1997). The evidence is not as clear related to the relationship between improved muscle strength to improvement in mobility and other functional performance variables (Ades et al., 1996; Judge et al, 1994; Skelton et al., 1995). This lack of a clear relationship might be explained in part by the ceiling effects on functional performance variables in the healthy elderly. However, training that was specific to particular functional tasks was more likely to result in a clear relationship between strength gain and improved functional status (McCartney et al., 1995; Skelton & McLaughlin, 1996). Impaired elderly were more likely to improve in functional status (Fisher et al., 1991; McMurdo & Johnstone, 1995; McMurdo & Rennie, 1993). Differences between the healthy and impaired population were seen with respect to balance in which there is some evidence that strength training can improve balance in healthy populations (Skelton & McLaughlin, 1996; Wolfson et al., 1996) but may not in impaired populations (McMurdo & Johnstone, 1995).

The effect of strength training on cardiorespiratory variables in the healthy elderly was inconclusive (Ades et al., 1996; Frontera et al., 1990; McCartney et al., 1995; Rooks et al., 1997). Improvement in body composition was inconsistent between populations. The healthy elderly were more likely to show an improvement in body composition (Nichols et al., 1993; Siplia & Suominen, 1995), whereas, the evidence in impaired elderly was mixed (Fiatarone et al., 1990, 1994).

Few studies reported an adverse affect rate associated with strength training. Nine of the 11 studies that reported on an adverse effect rate had no injuries (Buchner et al., 1997; Judge et al., 1994; McCartney et al., 1995; McMurdo & Rennie, 1993; Nichols et al., 1993; Singh et al., 1997; Sipila & Suominen, 1995; Skelton & McLaughlin, 1996). In two of the impaired elderly studies, 12 to 26% of participants experienced minor to moderate musculoskeletal complaints. One study in the healthy elderly reported exercise-induced syncope precipitated by an arrhythmia (Skelton & McLaughlin, 1996). No serious injuries or exercise-related deaths were reported.

Several conclusions about strength training are warranted. First, strength training in a program that is carefully tailored to the individual's ability and is well-monitored appears safe in the elderly. Second, age-related changes in muscle strength are partially reversible with exercise in both healthy and impaired older populations. However, strength gains vary in magnitude based upon initial fitness (strength) level, which muscle group was measured, how strength was measured, and the exercise intensity. For example, a particular training regimen can result in larger percentage changes in one-repetition maximum (1-RM) strength as measured in kilograms than in isokinetic strength (Frontera et al., 1990). A caveat should be noted when comparing strength improvements across studies. Although 100% improvement may be statistically significant, in a frail individual with severe muscle weakness it may not represent a clinically significant improvement. Another caveat in interpreting study results is to examine the testing procedure in light of the training protocol. It is best to test an individual using methodology that is not incorporated into the training regimen to eliminate the threat of contamination.

Third, progressive resistance exercise using a maximum load that increases with improvement in strength appears to be the ideal strength training program. Programs that trained to 70–80% of 1-RM achieved the greatest benefits. Fourth, although few studies have examined the relationship between improved strength and its effect on functional status, those that have report inconsistent results. Whether muscle strength gains lead to meaningful functional improvement is unclear. Future research is needed to clarify this relationship, and to delineate what is considered a clinically significant strength improvement.

Exercise Recommendations

A warm-up period (5–10 minutes) of stretching the muscles that will be focused on during a strength training program should precede any exercise session. In the healthy elderly, strength training at least three times per week, with eight to twelve repetitions for each major muscle group, in two to three exercise sets should be sufficient to achieve a training response. A rest period between repetitions and exercise sets should be provided. Frailer adults should start with fewer repetitions, perform only one exercise set initially, and gradually progress upwards. In general, progression

in a strength training program should be done by first adding repetitions and then exercise sets to achieve the desired training
response. For programs using weights or pneumatic devices, it is
recommended to start the individual at 50% 1-RM and then slowly progress to 70–80% 1-RM. Frailer adults may need more frequent but less intense sessions.

Endurance Training

Aerobic capacity regardless of activity level tends to decline with
age (Astrand, 1960; Astrand, Astrand, Hallback, & Kilbom, 1973).
Endurance training to maintain or improve cardiovascular functioning is the basis for all exercise recommendations. There have
been fewer studies examining the effect of endurance training
alone in adults over the age of 65 years. Rather, endurance training
is typically used in conjunction with flexibility, strength, and/or
balance training making it difficult to discern the health benefits of
endurance training alone. Also, implementing and interpreting
endurance training studies in the elderly, particularly in those who
are impaired or residing in nursing homes, is complex because of
the prevalence of interrupted training as a result of illness.

Literature Review

Twenty-eight studies were reviewed on endurance training; of
these, 22 studies were conducted with the healthy elderly, and six
studies were in the impaired elderly. In the healthy elderly category, there were 12 RCTs (Badenhop, Cleary, Schaal, Schaal, Fox
et al., 1983; Blumenthal, Emery, Madden, George, Coleman et al.,
1989; Buchner et al., 1997; Cunningham, Rechnitzer, Howard, &
Donner, 1987; Hamdorf, Withers, Penhall, & Haslan, 1992; Panton
et al., 1990; Posner, German, Windsor-Landsberg, Larsen, Bleiman
et al., 1992; Rooks et al.,1997; Sipilia & Suominen, 1995; Thomas,
Cunningham, Thompson, & Rechnitzer, 1985; Vitello, Wilkinson,
Merriam, Moe, Prinze et al., 1997; Warren, Nieman, Dotson, Adkins,
O'Donnell et al., 1993); eight nonrandomized controlled trials (Adams
& de Vries, 1973; Brown, Birge, & Kohrt, 1997; Brown & Holloszy,
1991; de Vries, 1970; Foster, Hume, Byrnes, Dickinson, & Chatfield,
1989; Roberts, 1989; Seals, Hagberg, Hurley, Ehsani, & Holloszy,
1984; Sidney & Shephard, 1978); and two observational studies
(Buccola & Stone, 1975; de Vries, 1971) involving over 1,422 participants (588+ women, 704+ men) ranging in age from 62 to 84

years. Sample sizes ranged from 11 (Seals, Hagberg, Hurley, Ehsani, & Holloszy, 1984) to 204 (Posner et al., 1992). Eight of the 12 RCTs had exercise groups containing 25 or more participants (Blumenthal et al., 1989; Cunningham et al., 1987; Posner et al., 1992; Rooks et al., 1997; Thomas et al., 1985; Vitello et al., 1997; Warren et al., 1993).

The mode of exercise in the healthy elderly involved walking, jogging, and cycling, with a combination of walking and jogging (eight studies) and walking alone (seven studies) being the most common modes. All studies employed supervised group-based programs. The training frequency was 2 to 5 times per week, with 3 days per week being the most common frequency (15 studies). The length of training varied from 10 weeks to 12 months. Typically, exercise sessions included warm-up and cool-down periods using flexibility exercise and some calisthenics. Although the duration of the exercise sessions ranged from 30 to 90 minutes, the actual duration of endurance activities during the session ranged from 10 to 45 minutes, with a mean duration of 35 minutes. The intensity of the exercise varied from low to high, with moderate intensity training (60–70% of peak heart rate) being the most frequently studied.

In the impaired elderly category, there were four RCTS (Ettinger, Burns, Messier, Applegate, Rejeski et al., 1997; Naso, Carner, Blankfort-Doyle, & Coughey, 1990; Schnelle, MacRae, Giacobassi, MacRae, Simmons et al., 1996; Stamford, 1972); one nonrandomized controlled trial (MacRae, Asplund, Schnelle, Ouslander, Abrahams et al. 1996); and one observational study (Koroknay, Werner, Cohen-Mansfield, & Braun, 1995) involving 608 participants (421+ women, 176+ men) ranging in age from 63 to 98 years.

The most frequent mode of exercise was walking, followed by cycling and upper and lower body conditioning such as rowing or wheelchair wheeling. Training varied from 3 to 7 days per week, with 3 days the most common (three studies). The duration of the exercise session ranged from 20 to 60 minutes. Follow-up ranged from 9 weeks to 18 months. Similar to studies in the healthy elderly, exercise intensity varied from low to high (80% maximum heart rate). Attrition varied from 17% in arthritic patients (Ettinger et al., 1997) to 54% in nursing home elderly (Schnelle et al., 1996).

Few studies (N = 10) reported on adverse effects associated with endurance training. Of the six studies reporting adverse effects, the complication rate ranged from 3% to 36% which consisted of two falls (Ettinger et al., 1997) and musculoskeletal injuries such as bursitis, sprains, and one foot fracture (Brown & Holloszy, 1993; Cunningham et al., 1987; Ettinger et al., 1997; Hamdorf et al., 1992; Naso et al., 1990). One study reported that 74% of subjects experienced hip, knee, or back pain which was counteracted by stretching prior to exercising (Brown & Holloszy, 1993). No exercise-related deaths were reported.

The trends and strength of the evidence on several training outcomes are presented in Table 1.4. There is good evidence that endurance training of low to high intensity for a minimum of 3 times a week results in a variety of health benefits. In the healthy elderly, there is consistent and strong evidence for improvement in cardiovascular fitness whether measured by VO_2 max or resting heart rate. Healthy older adults tend to achieve similar training gains in aerobic capacity as younger adults (Adams & de Vries, 1973; Buccola & Stone, 1975; de Vries, 1970; Hagberg et al., 1989; Sidney & Shephard, 1978), although one study suggested the pattern of adaptation to exercise may differ (Posner, Gorman, Gitlin, Sands, Kleban et al., 1990). Although men have greater aerobic capacity at baseline, both men and women show comparable improvements with endurance training (Blumenthal et al., 1989; Brown & Holloszy, 1993). Although there has been less research conducted, there is evidence indicating that the impaired elderly also show improvement in cardiovascular fitness with endurance training (Ettinger et al., 1997; Naso et al., 1990; Stanford, 1972).

The greatest gains in cardiovascular fitness may occur in the first 6–7 weeks of training (deVries, 1970; Sidney & Shephard, 1978) but training effects continue to accumulate over a full year of training (Hagberg et al., 1989). Increases in maximum attained oxygen uptake (VO_2 max) vary based on initial fitness level, intensity and length of training, as well as research design with controlled designs showing lower improvement rates. Improvements of 8 to 24% of VO_2 max are reported after 12–16 weeks of training (Blumenthal et al., 1989; Brown & Holloszy, 1993; Hagberg et al., 1989; Posner et al., 1992; Warren et al., 1993), and 10 to 30% after 6–12 months of training (Cunningham et al., 1987; Hagberg et al., 1989; Seals et al., 1984; Thomas et al., 1985). Although some studies suggest that improvements are most marked with moderately high to high intensity training (70% or maximum heart rate reserve

TABLE 1.4 Endurance Training Outcomes

	Trends & Strength of Evidence		References
	Healthy elderly	Impaired elderly	
Cardiovascular fitness	↑↑	↑	*Healthy:* de Vries, 1970; Adams & de Vries, 1973; Buccola & Stone, 1975; Badenhop et al., 1983; Seals et al., 1984; Thomas et al., 1985; Cunningham et al., 1987; Blumenthal et al., 1989; Foster et al., 1989; Hagberg et al., 1989; Posner et al., 1992; Panton et al., 1990; Hamdorf et al., 1992; Brown & Holloszy, 1993; Warren et al., 1993; Brown et al., 1997; Buchner et al., 1997; Vitello et al., 1997 *Impaired:* Ettinger et al., 1997; Naso et al., 1990; Stanford et al., 1972
Blood pressure	↑	↑	*Healthy:* Adams & deVries, 1973; Buccola & Stone, 1975; Posner et al., 1992 *Impaired:* Stamford, 1972
Endurance	muscular ↑	wheelchair and rowing ↔ standing ↑	*Healthy:* Brown & Holloszy, 1993 *Impaired:* Schnelle et al., 1996; Ettinger et al., 1997; Naso et al., 1990
Strength	↔	↑	*Healthy:* Hagberg et al., 1989; Buchner et al., 1997; Rooks et al., 1997
Reaction time	↑	NR	*Healthy:* Panton et al., 1990; Rooks et al., 1997

TABLE 1.4 (Continued)

	Trends & Strength of Evidence		References
	Healthy elderly	Impaired elderly	
Walking time/ distance	NR	↑ arthritic & NH pts	*Impaired:* Ettinger et al., 1997; Koroknay et al., 1995; MacRae et al., 1996; Schnelle et al., 1996
Balance	↔	NR	*Healthy:* Roberts, 1989; Brown & Holloszy, 1993; Buchner et al., 1997; Rooks et al., 1997
Falls	↔	↔	*Healthy:* Buchner et al., 1997 *Impaired:* Koroknay et al., 1995
Body weight/ composition	↑	NR	*Healthy:* deVries, 1970; Buccola & Stone, 1975; Thomas et al., 1985; Posner et al., 1992; Hamdorf et al., 1992; Sipila & Suominen, 1995; Brown et al., 1997; Vitello et al., 1997
Functional status	NR	↑ arthritic pts ↔ NH pts	*Impaired:* Koroknay et al., 1995; Ettinger et al., 1997; MacRae et al., 1996
Self-reported physical disability	NR	↑ arthritic pts	*Impaired:* Ettinger et al., 1997

NR = Data not collected and/or reported.

Note: Up arrows indicate improvement in the expected direction. Side arrows indicate inconsistent findings among studies or no improvement. The more arrows, the stronger the evidence.

21

or 129–156 beats per minute (Foster et al., 1989; Seals et al., 1984; Sidney & Shephard, 1978), several studies indicate that lower intensity exercise (30–40% of maximum heart rate reserve) is an adequate training stimulus in sedentary older adults and produces changes comparable to that by higher intensity training (60–70% of maximum heart rate reserve (Badenhop et al. 1983; de Vries, 1971; Posner et al., 1992; Warren et al., 1993). Adherence to low to moderate intensity exercise programs is higher than for high intensity programs (Hamdorf, Withers, Penhall, & Plummer, 1993; King, Haskell, Taylor, Kraemer, & DeBusk, 1991).

Depending on how it is measured, muscular endurance also appears to improve in both healthy (Brown & Holloszy, 1993) and impaired populations (Schnelle et al., 1996). However, studies examining standing endurance in the impaired elderly reported inconsistent findings (Schnelle et al., 1996). The distance walked and walking speed improves in arthritic patients (Ettinger et al., 1997) and nursing home patients (Koroknay et al., 1995; MacRae et al., 1996). Endurance training does not appear to affect muscle strength significantly in healthy elderly (Brown & Holloszy, 1993). There are inconclusive findings related to the effect of endurance training alone on balance and falls in both healthy (Brown & Holloszy, 1993; Buchner et al., 1997; Roberts, 1989) and impaired populations (Koroknay et al., 1995). There is good evidence that functional status in arthritic patients improves with training (Ettinger et al., 1997) but a lack of supporting evidence for improvement in nursing home residents.

In summary, the evidence supports that age-related changes in cardiovascular functioning are partially reversible in women and men, and that training gains are comparable to those achieved in younger adults. However, the stimulus for achieving a training response is lower than that required in younger adults.

Exercise Recommendations

Older adults adapt to low and high intensity endurance training with significant changes in cardiovascular fitness. The modes of endurance training that may be more suitable for the elderly given the incidence of arthritis are brisk walking, stationary cycling, water exercises, and armchair rowing. Research-based recommendations on endurance training for the elderly are consistent with the guidelines established by the Surgeon General (U.S. Department of Health and Human Services, 1996), American College of Sports Medicine (1995a, b), the Center for Disease Control (Pate, Pratt, Blair, Haskell, Macera, Bauchard et al., 1995), and the American Heart Association (1995). Training should be conducted on a graded basis working up to at least 30 minutes per day for a minimum of 5 days per week, at a low to moderate intensity level. Untrained adults should begin at 40 to 50% VO_2 maximum or heart rate reserve, and gradually progress to 60 to 75%. Very deconditioned elderly may need to start at 30 to 40% VO_2 maximum (Sidney & Shephard, 1978). Previous studies in younger populations have documented the effectiveness of shorter bouts (10–15 minutes) of exercise in young and middle aged adults but the value of breaking up the training period has not yet been evaluated in the elderly.

Balance Training

Aging is associated with changes in the sensory and motor systems that influence the postural control or balance mechanism leading to an increased risk of falls (Wolfson et al., 1996). The interest in balance training was heightened through the National Institute of Aging sponsorship of the Frailty and Injuries: Cooperative Studies of Intervention Techniques (FICSIT), which examined a variety of techniques to improve balance.

The majority of balance interventions designed to improved balance have included a combination approach incorporating strength and endurance training. These are reviewed in the next section. Research using dynamic or static exercises that are more specific to the balance response has been conducted primarily in the healthy elderly; thus, no studies from the impaired elderly group will be discussed.

Literature Review

In the healthy elderly category, seven studies were reviewed. Of these, six were RCTs (Hu & Woollacott, 1994a, 1994b; Johannson & Jarnlo, 1991; Judge et al., 1994; Lichenstein, Shields, Shiavi, & Burger, 1989 (same sample as Wolfson et al, 1996); Simmons & Hanson, 1996; Wolf, Barnhart, Kutner, McNeely, Googlen et al., 1996; Wolfson et al., 1996); and one was a nonrandomized controlled trial (Schaller, 1996) involving over 448 participants (303+ women, 76+ men; one study not reporting gender) with an age range of 55 to 90 years.

The mode of training included static and dynamic balance training with varying interventions such as floor exercises, water exercises, Tai chi, and computerized force platforms. Examples of static floor exercises used in the various protocols included standing on one leg with eyes open and eyes closed and tandem stance. Examples of dynamic floor exercises that were used included walking on different surface conditions, at different speeds, on a line or balance beam, and using a tandem heel/toe gait; maneuvering according to changing color signals; combining arm movement and dance steps in weight transfers; reacting to perturbations; and maintaining balance while sitting on a large rubber ball. The frequency of intervention varied from 1 to 7 days per week, with exercise sessions lasting 45 to 60 minutes. The length of the training ranged from 15 days to 16 weeks, with most studies using a training period between 10 to 16 weeks (four studies). Exercise intensity varied from low to moderate.

The Connecticut FICSIT group (Judge et al., 1994; Wolfson et al., 1996) evaluated the effectiveness of a static and dynamic exercise program against an educational control group in healthy community-dwelling adults age 75 years and over. Balance training consisted of three 45-minute exercise sessions using floor exercises (single leg stance and walking in different directions on carpet and foam, tandem gait, walking on a balance beam, sitting on a 14-cm rubber ball, and reacting to perturbations in balance) and a computerized moving platform in which subjects had to adjust their center of pressure with eyes open and closed. Participants in the balance intervention significantly improved their scores on all balance tests (loss of balance on the Sensory Organization Test, single-leg stance time, and functional base of support) with improvement rates similar to the rates of loss expected with normal aging. No strength gains were observed. Following a 6-month balance intervention using Tai chi, all participants maintained their improvements although not at the original level.

The Atlanta FICSIT trial (Wolf et al., 1996) compared the efficacy of a 15-week static versus dynamic balance training program which was provided 1 day per week in a supervised session involving either Tai chi or a computerized force platform. Although no exercise logs were kept, participants in the Tai chi group were encouraged to practice daily at home. Participants in Tai chi had a lower fear of falling, incidence of falls, and a lower multiple fall rate as compared to those in the control group. No strength or flexibility changes were observed.

Simmons and Hanson (1996) evaluated a 2-day per week, 5 week program of water exercises that included walking in different directions with different knee positions, doing standing partial squats, toe raises, heel kicks, and twisting. They found the program was effective in increasing functional reach.

The trends and significance of the balance training outcomes are illustrated in Table 1.5. Static and dynamic balance training does lead to improvements in balance such as single leg stance with eyes open (Johansson & Jarnlo, 1991; Schaller, 1996), functional reach (Simmons & Hanson, 1996), number of losses of balance during a computerized moving platform test (Wolfson et al., 1996); and reduction in falls and fear of falling (Wolf et al., 1996). However, the evidence on balance outcomes was not consistent across all measures and all studies. Evidence on single leg stance and sway area was equivocal (Lichtenstein et al., 1989; Schaller, 1996).

In summary, the evidence supports that age-related changes in balance are partially reversible. The improvements observed in balance are influenced by the mode and length of training as well as which particular balance outcome measure was used.

Exercise Recommendations

Recommendations for balance training in the elderly depend on what outcome is desired. The exercise prescription should be tailored to the individual's goals and specific deficits. For example, if lower extremity weakness is associated with balance difficulties, then the training program should focused on those exercises with a strengthening component. In general, integrated dynamic training such as Tai chi may be the most beneficial in reducing falls and fear of falling in the healthy elderly. To be effective, balance training should be performed at least 5 days per week.

Combination Training

Combination exercise programs incorporating flexibility, strength, endurance, and/or balance training are the most common type of exercise used in practice. Twenty-nine studies were reviewed. Of these, 20 studies were conducted in a healthy elderly population, and nine studies in an impaired population. In the healthy elderly

TABLE 1.5   Balance Training Outcomes in Healthy Elderly

	Trends & *Significance*	*References*
Single leg stance, eyes open	↑	Johansson & Jarnlo, 1991; Schaller, 1996; Wolfson et al., 1996; Lichenstein et al., 1989
Single leg stance, eyes closed	↔	Wolfson et al., 1996; Schaller, 1996; Johansson & Jarnlo, 1991; Lichenstein et al., 1989
Functional reach	↑	Simmons & Hanson, 1996
Sway area	↔	Lichenstein et al., 1989; Schaller, 1996
Loss of balance on Sensory Organization Test	↑	Wolfson et al., 1996
Muscle latency	↔	Hu & Woollacott, 1994a, 1994b
Flexibility	↔	Wolf et al., 1996; Schaller, 1996; Judge et al., 1994
Strength	↔	Wolfson et al., 1996; Wolf et al., 1996
Gait velocity	↔	Judge et al., 1994; Johansson & Jarnlo, 1991
Chair rise	↔	Judge et al., 1994
Falls	↑	Wolf et al., 1996
Fear of falling	↑	Wolf et al., 1996

NR = Data not collected and/or reported.
Note: Up arrows indicate improvement in the expected direction. Side arrows indicate inconsistent findings among studies or no improvement. The more arrows, the stronger the evidence.

category, there were 13 RCTs (Buchner et al., 1997; Campbell, Robertson, Gardner, Norton, Tilyard et al., 1997; Hornbrook, Stevens, Wingfield, Hollis, Greenlick et al., 1994; Judge et al., 1994; Judge, Lindsey, Underwood, & Winsemius, 1993a; Judge, Underwood, & Genosa, 1993b; Lord, Ward, & Williams, 1996; Lord, Ward, Williams, & Strudwick, 1995; Okumiya, Matsubayashi, Wada, Kimura, Doi et al., 1996; Reinsch, MacRae, Lachebruch, & Tobis, 1992; Stevenson

& Topp, 1990; Taunton, Rhodes, Wolski, Donelly, Warren et al, 1996; Wolfson et al., 1996); six nonrandomized controlled trials (Agre, Pierce, Raab, McAdams, & Smith, 1988; Amundsen, DeVahl, & Ellingham, 1989; Aniansson & Gustafsson, 1981; Lord & Castell, 1994; Rikli & Edwards, 1991); and one observational study (Morey, Cowper, Feussner, DiPasquale, Crowley, Kitzman et al., 1989) involving over 3,488 participants (3,036 women, 452 men) ranging in age from 60 to 97 years. Sample sizes ranged from 14 (Aniansson & Gustafsson, 1989) to 3,182 (Hornbrook et al., 1994). Eight of the 13 RCTs had intervention groups containing 25 or more participants (Buchner et al., 1997; Campbell et al., 1997; Hornbrook et al., 1994; Lord et al., 1995; Reinsch et al., 1992; Stevenson & Topp, 1990; Topp, Mikesky, Dayhoff, & Holt, 1996; Wolfson et al., 1996).

Both individual and group-based approaches were used. One study used a protocol of endurance training and calisthenics (Rikli & Edwards, 1991); two studies used strength, endurance, and balance exercise (Campbell et al., 1997; Judge et al., 1993); two studies used flexibility, strength, and balance exercise (Buchner et al., 1997; Wolfson et al., 1996;), four studies used flexibility, strength, and endurance exercise (Agre et al., 1988; Hamdorf et al., 1992, 1993; Lord & Castell, 1994; Morey et al., 1989, 1991); and three studies used protocols consisting of flexibility, strength, endurance, and balance training (Judge et al., 1993; Lord et al., 1995, 1996; Okumiya et al., 1996).

The frequency of combination training ranged 2 to 6 days per week with 3 days used in the majority of studies (10 studies). Exercise duration lasted from 30 to 95 minutes per exercise session with 60 minutes used in most studies (10 studies). The length of training ranged from 8 weeks to 12 months; two studies reporting long-term results from their initial conditioning study (Hamdorf et al., 1993; Morey et al., 1991). Most studies used a moderate exercise intensity.

In the impaired elderly category, there were seven RCTs (Crilly, Willems, Trenholm, Hayes, & Delaquerriere-Richardson, 1989; Mulrow, Gerety, Kanten, DeNino, & Cornell, 1994; Means, Rodell, O'Sullivan, & Cranford, 1996; Molloy, Delaquerriere-Richardson, & Crilly, 1988; Mulrow, Gerety, Kanten, DeNino, & Cornell, 1994; Sauvage, Myklebust, Crow-Pan, Novak, Millington et al., 1992; Thompson, Crist, Marsh, & Rosenthall, 1988; Tinetti et al., 1994; Weiner, Bongiorni, Studenski, Duncan, & Kochersberger, 1993); and one observational study (Harada, Chiu, Fowler, Lee, & Reuben, 1995) involving over 702 participants (410+ women, 200+ men) ranging in age from 40 to 105. Sample sizes ranged from 14 (Sauvage et al., 1992) to 301 (Tinetti et al., 1994). Four of the seven RCTs had intervention groups containing 25 or more participants (Crilly et al., 1989; Means et al., 1996; Mulrow, Gerety, Kanten, DeNino, & Cornel et al., 1994; Tinetti et al., 1994). Three studies examined one-to-one physical therapy (Harada et al., 1995; Mulrow et al., 1994; Weiner et al., 1993); two studies used a strength and endurance training (Sauvage et al., 1992; Thompson et al., 1988); one study used strength and balance training (Crilly et al., 1989); one study used flexibility, endurance, and balance training (Means et al., 1996); and one study used strength and mobility training (Tinetti et al., 1994).

All studies used an individualized training approach. The frequency of training ranged from 2 to 7 days per week with 3 days used in the majority of studies (six studies). Exercise duration was either not specified (one study) or lasted from 15 to 60 minutes per exercise session which was variable among studies. The length of training ranged from 4 to 52 weeks, with most studies using a 12–16 week training period (four studies). With the exception of two studies (Sauvage et al., 1992; Thompson et al., 1988) which used a moderate to high intensity training regimen, the remaining studies used low to moderate intensity regimens.

Table 1.6 summarizes the outcomes of combination training. Because of the diversity of the training protocols, it is difficult to generalize from the findings. There is good evidence that combination training resulted in muscle strength improvements in both healthy and impaired elderly populations. However, in most other outcomes such as cardiovascular fitness, balance, flexibility, gait velocity/time, mobility, and functional status, there were no consistent findings across healthy and impaired populations. In the healthy elderly, there is good evidence that combination training improves balance (Campbell et al., 1997; Judge et al., 1993a, 1993b; Lord et al., 1995; Morey et al., 1989; Okumiya et al., 1996; Rikli & Edwards, 1991; Wolfson et al., 1996), and fair evidence that it increases cardiovascular fitness in the healthy elderly (Amundsen et al., 1989; Aniansson & Gustafsson, 1981; Buchner et al., 1997; Morey et al., 1989). The lack of supporting evidence in impaired elderly may be related to the low intensity of the training regimen or the significant comorbidity of the population. There is preliminary

TABLE 1.6 Combination Training Outcomes

	Trends & Strength of Evidence		References
	Healthy elderly	*Impaired elderly*	*References*
Cardiovascular fitness	↑	↔	*Healthy:* Aniansson & Gustafson, 1981; Amundsen et al., 1989; Morey et al., 1991; Taunton et al., 1996; Buchner et al., 1997 *Impaired:* Thompson et al., 1988; Crilly et al., 1989; Sauvage et al., 1992
Muscle strength	↑	↑↑	*Healthy:* Aniansson & Gustafson, 1981; Agre et al., 1988; Morey et al., 1989; Rikli & Edwards, 1991; Morey et al., 1991; Judge et al., 1993a, 1993b; Reinsch et al., 1992; Lord et al., 1995; Wolfson et al., 1996; Taunton et al., 1996; Buchner et al., 1997 *Impaired:* Thompson et al., 1988; Crilly et al., 1989; Harada et al., 1995
Balance	↑↑	↑	*Healthy:* Morey et al., 1989; Rikli & Edwards, 1991; Judge et al., 1993a, 1993b, 1994; Lord et al., 1995; Okumiya et al., 1996; Wolfson et al., 1996; Campbell et al., 1997 *Impaired:* Thompson et al., 1988; Crilly et al., 1989, Harada et al., 1995

TABLE 1.6 Combination Training Outcomes (Continued)

	Trends & Strength of Evidence		References
	Healthy elderly	Impaired elderly	
Flexibility	↔	↔	*Healthy:* Raab et al., 1988; Morey et al., 1989; Rikli & Edwards, 1991; Lord et al., 1996; Taunton et al., 1996 *Impaired:* Mulrow et al., 1994; Means et al., 1996
Gait velocity/time	↔	↑↑	*Healthy:* Judge et al., 1993a, 1993b, 1994; Wolfson et al., 1996; Buchner et al., 1997 *Impaired:* Sauvage et al., 1992; Mulrow et al., 1994; Harada et al., 1995
Mobility	↔	↑	*Healthy:* Okumiya et al., 1996; Buchner et al., 1997 *Impaired:* Sauvage et al., 1992; Mulrow et al., 1994
Functional status	↔	↔	*Healthy:* Campbell et al., 1997 *Impaired:* Mulrow et al., 1994; Means et al., 1996
Falls	↑	↑	*Healthy:* Reinsch et al., 1992; Lord et al., 1995; Hornbrook et al., 1994; Campbell et al., 1997; Buchner et al., 1997 *Impaired:* Tinetti et al., 1994; Means et al., 1996

Note: Up arrows indicate improvement in the expected direction. Side arrows indicate inconsistent findings among studies or no improvement. The more arrows, the stronger the evidence.

30

evidence to suggest that combination training may contribute to a modest reduction in fall rates in community-dwelling elderly populations (Buchner et al., 1997; Campbell et al., 1997; Hornbrook et al., 1994; Tinetti et al., 1994). However, in two studies (Hornbrook et al., 1994; Tinetti et al., 1994), it is difficult to discern the relative contribution of the exercise program vis-a-vis the other interventions used in these trials such as medication reduction and fall prevention education.

In summary, because of the great diversity in training protocols and study populations, it is difficult to derive meaningful conclusions. Combination therapy appears to improve multiple training outcomes in both healthy and impaired populations. The magnitude of this effect varies by the intensity, frequency, and type of the training protocol as well as the characteristics of the study population. In comparing the outcomes from the individual types of training to those achieved with combination training, there does not appear to be an additive effect. Rather, the effects may influence a broader range of outcome variables.

Exercise Recommendations

Because of its focus on achieving multiple training outcomes, combination training is probably the most beneficial for achieving and/or maintaining overall health-related physical fitness in the healthy and the less severely impaired elderly. The exercise prescription should be tailored to the older adult's goals, and include elements of flexibility, strength, endurance, and balance training. In severely impaired elderly, a more targeted approach using flexibility, strength, and endurance training that is geared at correcting or improving specific deficits that underlie functional performance may be more worthwhile.

CONCLUSION

Exercise in the elderly who have been screened for medical contraindications is relatively safe with a low incidence of reported serious adverse effects. Although endurance training is associated with the highest and most serious adverse effects such as fracture, no exercise-related deaths have been reported in supervised programs. The elderly can achieve a training response with each of the different types of exercise training (e.g., flexibility, strength, endurance, balance, and combination); although differential effects are noted based on the individual's initial fitness level; the exercise intensity, frequency, and duration; and the outcome measured. Older adults at any age and at any level of impairment can benefit from exercise. In general, the Surgeon General's (1996) recommendations for moderate physical activity appear appropriate for the healthy elderly. In view of the losses in flexibility and strength especially in the lower extremities that occur with aging and their importance for the maintenance of functional independence, it would be advisable to add specific recommendations on both flexibility and strength training. Sedentary and frailer older individuals appear to achieve substantial benefit from lower intensity endurance training but may require more intense strength training programs. Exercise programs should be tailored to the individual's fitness level and properly monitored to prevent negative consequences.

Interpreting the exercise literature is difficult due to the variations in exercise protocols and lack of standardization of outcome variables. Although the scientific literature clearly shows the benefit of exercise in the elderly, there continues to be much to learn regarding the right exercise prescriptions for individuals with varying fitness levels. The dose-response relationship of each type of exercise training in different subgroups of the elderly needs to be ascertained. Determining what is a clinically significant improvement versus a statistically significant change is needed. To do this, future research is needed to clarify the relationships between exercise, physical performance, and disability.

Research is also needed on the cost-effectiveness of exercise programs in older adults, particularly for institutionalized elderly. Training programs for impaired elderly are costly because they are staff intensive and involve significant time to implement. Are the benefits worth the costs of the programs? Are there other ways to implement exercise interventions in terms of type of staff involved or type of intervention that may be more cost-effective? Could exercise intervention programs for the healthy elderly be developed that are community-based rather than individually or group-based? What would the costs and benefits be to such an approach?

Perhaps the greatest challenge for the future will be how to motivate habitually sedentary older adults to participate in physical activity or exercise training programs. Researchers should incorporate behavioral change theories such as the Transtheoretical Model, social cognitive theory, or theory of planned action (Dishman, 1994), into their exercise programs to determine the most effective strategies for inducing and maintaining exercise behavior in the elderly.

REFERENCES

Adams, G. M., & de Vries, H. A. (1973). Physiological effects of an exercise training regimen upon women aged 52 to 79. *Journal of Gerontology, 28*(1), 50–55.

Ades, P. A., Ballor, D. L., Ashikaga, T., Utton, J., & Nair, K. S. (1996). Weight training improves walking endurance in healthy elderly persons. *Annals of Internal Medicine, 124*(6), 568–572.

Agre, J. C., Pierce, L. E., Raab, D. M., McAdams, M., & Smith, E. L. (1988). Light resistance and stretching exercise in elderly women: Effect on strength. *Archives of Physical Medicine and Rehabilitation, 69*(4), 273–276.

American College of Sports Medicine (1995a). ACSM Position stand on osteoporosis and exercise. *Medicine and Science in Sports and Exercise, 27*(4), I–vii.

American College of Sports Medicine (1995b). ACSM Position Statement: The recommended quantity and quality of exercise for developing and maintaining cardiorespiratory and muscular fitness in healthy adults. *Medicine and Science in Sports and Exercise, 22*, 265–274.

American Heart Association (1995). Exercise standards: A statement for healthcare professionals from the American Heart Association. *Circulation, 91*(2), 580–615.

Amundsen, L. R., DeVahl, J. M., & Ellingham, C. T. (1989). Evaluation of a group exercise program for elderly women. *Physical Therapy, 69*(6), 475–483.

Aniansson, A., & Gustafsson, E. (1981). Physical training in elderly men with special reference to quadriceps muscle strength and morphology. *Clinical Physiology, 1*, 87–98.

Aniansson, A., Sperling, L., Rundgren, A., & Lehnberg, E. (1983). Muscle function in 75-year-old men and women. A longitudinal study. *Scandinavian Journal of Rehabilitation Medicine, Suppl 9*, 92–102.

Astrand, I. (1960). Aerobic capacity in men and women with special reference to age. *Acta Physiological Scandinavia (Suppl 49), 169*, 1–92.

Astrand, I., Astrand, P. O., Hallback, J., & Kilbom, A. (1973). Reduction in maximum oxygen uptake with age. *Journal of Applied Physiology, 35*(5), 649–654.

Badenhop, D. T., Cleary, P. A., Schaal, S. F., Fox, E. L., & Bartels, R. L. (1983). Physiological adjustments to higher-or-lower intensity exercise in elders. *Medicine and Science in Sports and Exercise, 15*(6), 496–502.

Bassett, C., McClamrock, E., & Schmelzer, M. (1982). A 10-week exercise program for senior citizens. *Geriatric Nursing, 3*(2), 103–105.

Blumenthal, J. A., Emery, C. F., Madden, D. J., George, L. K., Coleman, R. E. Riddle, M. W., McKee, B. C., Reasoner, J., & Williams, R. S. (1989). Cardiovascular and behavioral effects of aerobic exercise training in healthy older men and women. *Journal of Gerontology: Medical Sciences, 44*(5), M147–M157.

Brown, M., Birge, S. J., & Kohrt, W. M. (1997). Hormone replacement therapy does not augment gains in muscle strength or fat-free mass in response to weight-bearing exercise. *Journal of Gerontology: Biological Sciences, 52A*(3), B166–B170.

Brown, M., & Holloszy, J. O. (1991). Effects of a low intensity exercise program on selected physical performance characteristics of 60- to 71-year olds. *Aging, 3*(2), 129–139.

Brown, M., & Holloszy, J. O. (1993). Effects of walking, jogging, and cycling on strength, flexibility, speed and balance in 60- to 72-year olds. *Aging Clinical and Experimental Research, 5*(6), 427–434.

Buccola, V. A., & Stone, W. J. (1975). Effects of jogging and cycling programs on physiological and personality variables in aged men. *Research Quarterly, 46*(2), 134–139.

Buchner, D. M., Cress, M. E., de Lateur, B. J., Esselman, P. C., Margherita, A. J., Price, R., & Wagner, E. H. (1997). The effect of strength and endurance training on gait, balance, fall risk, and health service use in community-living older adults. *Journal of Gerontology: Medical Sciences, 52A*(4), M218–M224.

Campbell, J. A., Robertson, M. C., Gardner, M. M., Norton, R. N., Tilyard, M. W., & Buchner, D. M. (1997). Randomised controlled trial of a general practice programme of home based exercise to prevent falls in elderly women. *British Medical Journal, 315*(7115), 1065–1069.

Chandler, J. M., & Hadley, E. C. (1996). Exercise to improve physiologic and functional performance in old age. *Clinics in Geriatric Medicine, 12*(4), 761–784.

Charette, S. L., McEvoy, L., Dyka, G., Snow-Harter, C., Guido, D., Wiswell, R. A., & Marcus, R. (1991). Muscle hypertrophy response to resistance training in older women. *Journal of Applied Physiology, 70*(5), 1912–1916.

Connelly, D. M., & Vandervoort, A. A. (1995). Improvement in knee extensor strength of institutionalized elderly women after exercise with ankle weights. *Physiotherapy Canada, 47*(1), 15–23.

Corbin, C. B., & Lindsey, R. (1997). *Concepts in physical education with laboratories* (8th ed.). Dubuque, IA: Times Mirror Higher Education Group.

Crilly, R. G., Willems, D. A., Trenholm, K. J., Hayes, K. C., & Delaquerriere-Richardson, L. F. O. (1989). Effect of exercise on postural sway in the elderly. *Gerontology, 35*(2–3), 137–143.

Cunningham, D. A., Rechnitzer, P. A., Howard, J. H., & Donner, A. P. (1987). Exercise training of men at retirement: A clinical trial. *Journal of Gerontology, 42*(1), 17–23.

de Vries, H. A. (1970). Physiological effects of an exercise training regimen upon men aged 52 to 88. *Journal of Gerontology, 25*(4), 325–336.

de Vries, H. A. (1971). Exercise intensity threshold for improvement of cardiovascular-respiratory function in older men. *Geriatrics, 26*(4), 94–101.

Dishman, R. K. (Ed.). (1994). *Advances in exercise adherence.* Champaign, IL: Human Kinetics.

Elward, K., & Larson, E. B. (1992). Benefits of exercise for older adults. *Clinics in Geriatric Medicine, 8*(1), 35–50.

Era, P. (1988). Posture control in the elderly. *International Journal of Technology and Aging, 1,* 166–179.

Ettinger, W. H., Burns, R., Messier, S. P., Applegate, W., Rejeski, W. J., Morgan, T., Shumaker, S., Berry, M. J., O'Toole, M., Monu, J., & Craven, T. (1997). A randomized trial comparing aerobic exercise and resistance exercise with a health education program in older adults with knee osteoarthritis: The fitness arthritis and seniors trial (FAST). *Journal of the American Medical Association, 277*(1), 25–31.

Fiatarone, M. A., Marks, E. C., Ryan, N. D., Meredith, C. N., Lipsitz, L. A., & Evans, W. J. (1990). High-intensity strength training in nonagenarians: effects on skeletal muscle. *Journal of the American Medical Association, 263*(25), 3029–3034.

Fiatarone, M. A., O'Neill, E. F., Ryan, N. D., Clements, K. M., Solares, G. R., Nelson, M. E., Roberts, S. B., Kehayias, J.J., Lipsitz, L. A., & Evans, W. J. (1994). Exercise training and nutritional supplementation for physical frailty in very elderly people. *New England Journal of Medicine, 330*(25), 1769–1775.

Fisher, N. M., Pendergast, D. R., & Calkins, E. (1991). Muscle rehabilitation in impaired elderly nursing home residents. *Archives of Physical Medicine and Rehabilitation, 72*(3), 181–185.

Foster, V. L., Hume, J. E., Byrnes, W. C., Dickinson, A. L., & Chatfield, S. J. (1989). Endurance training for elderly women: Moderate vs low intensity. *Journal of Gerontology: Medical Sciences, 44*(6), M184–188.

Frontera, W. R., Meredith, C. N., O'Reilly, K. P., Knuttgen, H. G., & Evans, W. J., (1988). Strength conditioning in older men: skeletal muscle hypertrophy and improved functioning. *Journal of Applied Physiology, 64*(3), 1038–1044.

Frontera, W. R., Meredith, C. N., O'Reilly, K. P., Knuttgen, H. G., & Evans, W. J. (1990). Strength training and determinants of V0₂max in older men. *Journal of Applied Physiology, 68*(1), 329–333.

Grimby, G., Aniansson, A., Hedberg, M., Henning, G. B., Grangard, U., & Kvist, H. (1992). Training can improve strength and endurance in 78–84 year old men. *Journal of Applied Physiology, 73*(6), 2517–2523.

Hagberg, J. M., Graves, J. E., Limacher, M., Woods, D. R., Leggett, S. H., Cononie, C., Leggett, S., Gruber, J., & Pollock, M. (1989). Cardiovascular responses of 70- to 79-yr-old men and women to exercise training. *Journal of Applied Physiology, 66*(6), 2589–2594.

Hamdorf, P. A., Withers, R. T., Penhall, R. K., & Haslan, M. V. (1992). Physical training effects on the fitness and habitual activity patterns of elderly women. *Archives of Physical Medicine and Rehabilitation, 71*(7), 603–608.

Hamdorf, P. A., Withers, R. T., Penhall, R. K., & Plummer, J. L. (1993). A follow-up study on the effects of training on the fitness and habitual activity patterns of 60- to 70-year-old women. *Archives of Physical Medicine and Rehabilitation, 74*(5), 473–477.

Hanson, C. S., Agostinucci, J., Dasler, P. J., & Creel, G. (1992). The effect of short term, light resistive exercise on well elders. *Physical and Occupational Therapy in Geriatrics, 10*(3), 73–81.

Harada, N., Chiu, V., Fowler, E., Lee, M., & Reuben, D. B. (1995). Physical therapy to improve functioning of older people in residential care facilities. *Physical Therapy, 75*(9), 830–838.

Hartard, M., Haber, P., Illieva, D., Preisinger, E., Seidl, G., & Huber, J. (1996). Systemic strength training as a model of therapeutic intervention. *American Journal of Physical Medical and Rehabilitation, 75*(1), 21–28.

Hornbrook, M. C., Stevens, V. J., Wingfield, D. J., Hollis, J. F., Greenlick, M. R., & Ory, M. G. (1994). Preventing falls among community-dwelling older persons: Results from a randomized trial. *Gerontologist, 34*(1), 16–23.

Hu, M. H., & Woollacott, M. J. (1994a). Multisensory training of standing balance in older adults. I. Postural stability and one-leg stance balance. *Journal of Gerontology: Medicial Sciences, 49*(2), M52–M61.

Hu, M. H., & Woollacott, M. J. (1994b). Multisensory training of standing balance in older adults: II. Kinematic and electromyographic postural responses. *Journal of Gerontology: Medical Sciences, 49*(2), M62–M71.

Hunter, G. R., Treuth, M. S., Weinsier, R. L., Kekes-Szabo, T., Kell, S. H., Roth, D. L., & Nicholson, C. (1995). The effects of strength conditioning on older women's ability to perform daily tasks. *Journal of the American Geriatrics Society, 43*(7), 756–760.

Jette, A. M., Harris, B. A., Sleeper, L., Lachman, M., Heislein, D., Giorgetti, M., & Levenson, C. (1996). A home-based exercise program for nondisabled older adults. *Journal of the American Geriatrics Society,* 44(6), 644–649.

Johansson, G., & Jarnlo, G. B. (1991). Balance training in 70-year-old women. *Physiotherapy Theory and Practice, 7,* 121–125.

Judge, J. O. (1997). Resistance training. In J. C. Masdeu, L. Sudarsky, & L. Wolfson (Eds.), *Gait disorders of aging: Falls and therapeutic strategies* (pp. 381–394). Philadelphia: Lippincott-Raven.

Judge, J. O., Lindsey, C., Underwood, M., & Winsemius, D. (1993a). Balance improvements in older women: Effects of exercise training. *Physical Therapy,* 73(4), 254–265.

Judge, J. O., Underwood, M., & Genosa, T. (1993b). Exercise to improve gait velocity. *Archives of Physical Medicine and Rehabilitation,* 74(4), 400–406.

Judge, J. O., Whipple, R., & Wolfson, L. (1994). Effects of resistive and balance exercises on isokinetic strength in older persons. *Journal of the American Geriatrics Society,* 42(9), 937–946.

King, A. C., Haskell, W. L., Taylor, C. B., Kraemer, H. C., & DeBusk, R. F. (1991). Group- vs home-based exercise training in healthy older men and women: A community-based clinical trial. *Journal of the American Medical Association,* 266(11), 1535–1542.

Koroknay, V. J., Werner, P., Cohen-Mansfield, J., & Braun, (1995). Maintaining ambulation in the frail nursing home resident: A nursing administered walking program. *Journal of Gerontological Nursing,* 21(11), 18–24.

Larsson, L., Grimby, G., & Karlsson, J. (1979). Muscle strength and speed of movement in relation to age and muscle morphology. *Journal of Applied Physiology,* 46(3), 451–456.

Lichtenstein, M. J., Shields, S. L., Shiavi, R. G., & Burger, C. (1989). Exercise and balance in aged women: A pilot controlled clinical trial. *Archives of Physical Medicine and Rehabilitation,* 70(2), 138–143.

Lord, S. R., & Castell, S. (1994). Physical activity program for older persons: Effect on balance, strength, neuromuscular control, and reaction time. *Archives of Physical Medicine and Rehabilitation,* 75(6), 648–652.

Lord, S. R., Ward, J. A., & Williams, P. (1996). Exercise effect on dynamic stability in older women. *Archives of Physical Medicine and Rehabilitation,* 77(3), 232–236.

Lord, S. R., Ward, J. A., Williams, P., & Strudwick, M. (1995). The effect of a 12-month exercise trial on balance, strength, and falls in older women: A randomized controlled trial. *Journal of the American Geriatrics Society,* 43(11), 1198–1206.

MacRae, P. G., Asplund, L. A., Schnelle, J. F., Ouslander, J. G., Abrahams, A., & Morris, C. (1996). A walking program for nursing home residents:

Effects on walk endurance, physical activity, mobility, and quality of life. *Journal of the American Geriatrics Society, 44*(2), 175–180.

McCartney, N., Hicks, A. L., Martin, J., & Webber, C. E. (1995). Long-term resistance training in the elderly: Effects on dynamic strength, exercise capacity, muscle, and bone. *Journal of Gerontology: Biological Sciences, 50A*(2), B97–B104.

McCartney, N., Hicks, A., Martin, J., & Webber, C. E. (1996). A longitudinal trial of weight training in the elderly: Continued improvements in year 2. *Journal of Gerontology: Biological Sciences, 51A*(6), B425–B433.

McMurdo, M. E. T., & Johnstone, R. (1995). A randomized controlled trial of a home exercise program for elderly people with poor mobility. *Age and Aging, 24*(5), 425–428.

McMurdo, M. E. T., & Rennie, L. (1993). A controlled trial of exercise by residents of old people homes. *Age and Aging, 22*(1), 11–15.

Means, K. M., Rodell, D. E., O'Sullivan, P. S., & Cranford, L. A. (1996). Rehabilitation of elderly fallers: Pilot study of a low to moderate intensity exercise program. *Archives of Physical Medicine and Rehabilitation, 77*(10), 1030–1036.

Mills, E. (1994). The effect of low intensity aerobic exercise on muscle strength, flexibility, and balance among sedentary elderly. *Nursing Research, 43,* 207–211.

Morey, M. C., Cowper, P. A., Feussner, J. R., DiPasquale, R. C., Crowley, G. M., Kitzman, D. W., & Sullivan, R. J. (1989). Evaluation of a supervised exercise program in a geriatric population. *Journal of the American Geriatrics Society, 37*(4), 348–354.

Morey, M. C., Cowper, P. A., Feussner, J. R., DiPasquale, R. C., Crowley, G. M., & Sullivan, R. J. (1991). Two-year trends in physical performance following supervised exercise among community-dwelling older veterans. *Journal of the American Geriatrics Society, 39*(10), 549–554.

Mulrow, C. D., Gerety, M. B., Kanten, D., DeNino, L. A., & Cornell, J. E. (1994). A randomized trial of physical rehabilitation for very frail nursing home residents. *Journal of the American Medical Association, 271*(7), 519–524.

Naso, F., Carner, E., Blankfort-Doyle, W., Coughey, K. (1990). Endurance training in the elderly nursing home patient. *Archives of Physical Medicine and Rehabilitation, 71*(3), 241–243.

Nichols, J. F., Omizo, D. K., Peterson, K. K., & Nelson, K. P. (1993). Efficacy of heavy-resistance training for active women over sixty. Muscle strength, body composition, and program adherence. *Journal of the American Geriatrics Society, 41*(3), 205–210.

Okumiya, K., Matsubayashi, K., Wada, T., Kimura, S., Doi, Y., & Ozawa,

T. (1996). Effects of exercise on neurobehavioral function in community-dwelling older people more than 75 years of age. *Journal of the American Geriatrics Society, 44*(5), 569–572.

Panton, L. B., Graves, J. E., Pollock, M. L., Hagberg, J. M., & Chen, W. (1990). Effect of aerobic and resistance training on fractionated reaction time and speed of movement. *Journal of Gerontology: Medical Sciences, 45*(1), M26–M31.

Pate, R. R., Pratt, M., Blair, S. N., Haskell, W. L., Macera, C. A., Bourchard, C., Buchner, D., Ettinger, W., Heath, G. W., & King, A. C. (1995). Physical activity and public health: A recommendation from the Centers for Disease Control and Prevention and the American College of Sports Medicine. *Journal of the American Medical Association, 273*(5), 402–407.

Posner, J. D., Gorman, K.M., Gitlin, L. N., Sands, L. P., Kleban, M., Windsor, L., & Shaw, C. (1990). Effects of exercise training in the elderly on the occurrence and time to onset of cardiovascular diagnoses. *Journal of the American Geriatrics Society, 38*(3), 205–210.

Posner, J. D., Gorman, K. M., Windsor-Landsberg, L., Larsen, J., Bleiman, M., Shaw, C., Rosenberg, B., & Knebl, J. (1992). Low to moderate intensity endurance training in healthy older adults: Physiological responses after four months. *Journal of the American Geriatrics Society, 40*(1), 1–7.

Raab, D. M., Agre, J. C., McAdam, M., & Smith, E. L. (1988). Light resistance and stretching exercise in elderly women: Effect upon flexibility. *Archives of Physical and Medical Rehabilitation, 69*(4), 268–272.

Rall, L. C., Meydani, S. N., Kehayias, J. J., Dawson-Hughes, B., & Roubenoff, R. (1996). The effect of progressive resistance training in rheumatoid arthritis. *Arthritis and Rheumatism, 39*(3), 415–426.

Reinsch, S., MacRae, P., Lachenbruch, P. A., & Tobis, J. S. (1992). Attempts to prevent falls and injury: A prospective study. *Gerontologist, 32*(4), 450–456.

Rikli, R., & Edwards, D. J. (1991). Effects of a three year exercise program on motor function and cognitive processing speed in older women. *Research Quarterly in Exercise and Sports, 62*(1), 61–67.

Roberts, B. L. (1989). Effects of walking on balance among elders. *Nursing Research, 38*(3), 180–182.

Rooks, D. S., Kiel, D. O., Parsons, C., & Hayes, W. C. (1997). Self-paced resistance training and walking exercise in community-dwelling older adults. *Journal of Gerontology: Medical Sciences, 52*(3), M161–M168.

Sauvage, L. R., Myklebust, B. M., Crow-Pan, J., Novak, S., Millington, P., Hoffman, M. D., Hartz, A. J., Rudman, D. (1992). A clinical trial of strengthening and aerobic exercise to improve gait and balance in elderly male nursing home residents. *American Journal of Physical Medicine and Rehabilitation, 71*(6), 333–342.

Schaller, K. (1996). Tai chih: An exercise option for older adults. *Journal of Gerontological Nursing, 22*(10), 12–17.

Schnelle, J. F., MacRae, P. G., Giacobassi, K., MacRae, H. S. H., Simmons, S. F., & Ouslander, J. G. (1996). Exercise with physically restrained nursing home patients. *Journal of the American Geriatrics Society, 44*(5), 507–512.

Seals, D. R., Hagberg, J. M., Hurley, B. F., Ehsani A. A., & Holloszy, J. O. (1984). Effects of endurance training on glucose tolerance and plasma lipid levels in older men and women. *Journal of the American Medical Association, 252*(5), 645–649.

Sidney, H., & Shephard, R. J. (1978). Frequency and intensity of exercise training for elderly subjects. *Medicine, Science, and Sport Exercise, 10*(2), 125–131.

Simmons, V., & Hanson, P. D. (1996). Effectiveness of water exercise on postural mobility in the well elderly: An experimental study on balance enhancement. *Journal of Gerontology: Medical Sciences, 51*(5), M233–M238.

Singh, N. A., Clements, K. M., & Fiatarone, M. A. (1997). A randomized controlled trial of progressive resistance training in depressed elders. *Journal of Gerontology: Medical Sciences, 52A*(1), M27–M35.

Sipila, S., & Suominen, H. (1995). Effects of strength and endurance training on thigh and leg muscle mass and composition in elderly women. *Journal of Applied Physiology, 78*(1), 334–340.

Skelton, D. A., & McLaughlin, A. W. (1996). Training functional ability in old age. *Physiotherapy, 82*(3), 159–167.

Skelton, D. A., Young, A., Greig, C. A., & Malbut, K. E. (1995). Effects of resistance training on strength, power, and selected functional abilities of women aged 75 years and over. *Journal of the American Geriatrics Society, 43*(10), 1081–1087.

Stamford, B. A. (1972). Physiological effects of training upon institutionalized geriatric men. *Journal of Gerontology, 27,* 451–455.

Stanford, E. P., Hawkinson, W., Monge, R., & Dowd, D. (1972). Survey of gerontologists opinions on White House Conference on Aging issues on education and training. *Gerontologist, 12*(1), 79–84.

Stevenson, J. S., & Topp, R. (1990). Effects of moderate and low intensity long-term exercise by older adults. *Research in Nursing and Health, 13*(4), 209–218.

Taunton, J. E., Rhodes, E. C., Wolski, L. A., Donelly, M., Warren, J., Elliot, J., McFarlance, L., Leslie, J., Mitchell, J., & Lauridsen, B. (1996). Effect of land-based and water-based fitness programs on the cardiovascular fitness, strength and flexibility of women aged 65–75 years. *Gerontology, 42*(4), 204–210.

Thomas, S. G., Cunningham, D. A., Thompson, J., & Rechnitzer, P. A. (1985). Exercise training and "ventilation threshold" in elderly. *Journal of Applied Physiology, 59*(5), 1472–1476.

Thompson, R. F., Crist, D. M., Marsh, M. M., & Rosenthal, M. (1988). Effects of physical exercise for elderly patients with physical impairments. *Journal of the American Geriatric Society, 36*(2), 130–135.

Tinetti, M. E., Baker, D. I., McAvay, G., Claus, E. B., Garrett, P., Gottschalk, M., Koch, M. L., Trainor, K., & Horwitz, R. I. (1994). A multifactorial intervention to reduce the risk of falling among elderly people living in the community. *New England Journal of Medicine, 331*, 821–827.

Topp, R., Mikesky, A., Dayhoff, N. E., Holt, W. (1996). Effect of resistance training on strength, postural control, and gait velocity among older adults. *Clinical Nursing Research, 5*(4), 407–427.

Topp, R., Mikesky, A., Wigglesworth, J., Holt, W., & Edwards, J. E. (1993). The effect of a 12-week dynamic resistance strength training program on gait velocity and balance of older adults. *Gerontologist, 33*(4), 501–506.

U.S. Department of Health and Human Services (1996). *Physical activity and health: A report of the Surgeon General.* Atlanta, GA: U.S. Department of Health and Human Services, Centers for Disease Control and Prevention, National Center for Chronic Disease Prevention and Health Promotion.

Vitello, M. V., Wilkinson, C. W., Merriam, G. R., Moe, K. E., Prinz, P. N., Ralph, D. D., Colasurdo, E. A., & Schwartz, R.S. (1997). Successful 6-month endurance training does not alter insulin-like growth factor-I in healthy older men and women. *Journal of Gerontology: Medical Sciences, 52A*(3), M149–M154.

Warren, B. J., Nieman, D. C., Dotson, R. G., Adkins, C. H., O'Donnell, K. A., Haddock, B. L., & Butterworth, D. E. (1993). Cardiorespiratory responses to exercise training in septuagenarian women. *International Journal of Sports Medicine, 14*(2), 60–65.

Weiner, D. K., Bongiorni, D. R., Studenski, S. A., Duncan, P. W. & Kochersberger, G. G. (1993). Does functional reach improve with rehabilitation? *Archives of Physical Medicine and Rehabilitiation 74*(8), 796–800.

Whipple, R. H. (1997). Improving balance in older adults: Identifying the significant training stimuli. In J. C. Masdeu, L. Sudarsky, & L. Wolfson (Eds.), *Gait disorders of aging: Falls and therapeutic strategies* (pp. 355–380). Philadelphia: Lippincott-Raven.

Wolf, S., Barnhart, H. X. , Kutner, N. G., McNeely, E., Googlen, C., Xu, T., & the Atlantic FICSIT Group. (1996). Reducing frailty and falls in older persons: An investigation of Tai Chi and computerized balance training. *Journal of the American Geriatrics Society, 44*(5), 489–497.

Wolfson, L., Whipple, R., Derby, C., Judge, J., King, M., Amerman, P., Schmidt, J., & Smyers, D. (1996). Balance and strength training in older adults: Intervention gains and Tai Chi maintenance. *Journal of the American Geriatrics Society, 44*(5), 498–506.

CHAPTER 2

Nutrition

Ronni Chernoff

Nutrition is a key factor in growth, development, the maintenance of health, the recovery from acute illness, and the management of chronic disease. Throughout the life cycle, nutrition is essential to vitality and health. Building muscle strength, developing antibodies to potential invading microorganisms, maintaining immune function, preserving cellular integrity, healing wounds, and experiencing a general sense of well-being and an active lifestyle are all dependent on maintaining nutritional health.

Health promotion and disease prevention strategies are designed to improve health status, contribute to lifelong vitality, and minimize the impact of episodic illnesses. Nutrition has a role in health promotion, disease prevention, and disease treatment throughout the life span (Fishman, 1996; Perry, 1994; Rosenberg, 1994; Wynder & Andres, 1994). In health promotion, there are three levels of intervention, primary, secondary, and tertiary, each with its unique objectives.

Primary Prevention

In nutrition, primary prevention is a strategy that should be instituted early in life. Primary health promotion should focus on establishing healthy habits early in life (McGinnis, 1988). Over past decades, the relationship between nutrition, diet, and disease has been elucidated more fully. Heart disease, certain cancers, obesity, diabetes, hypertension leading to stroke, and anemias, for example, are chronic conditions that are nutrition-related. The nutritional factors that are associated with health risk take years to emerge and be identified. However, nutritional risk factors can be minimized early in life through learned eating behaviors. Teaching young people healthy eating habits through early nutrition education and by example is an important goal in primary prevention.

Health promotion strategies should include 1) educating people on healthier eating behaviors; 2) assisting people to identify risk-related dietary factors and possible genetic predispositions; and 3) promoting sound nutrition information and dispelling nutrition myths (McCabe & Dorey, 1999). Educating a general public of basically healthy people on ways to improve the nutritional value of their dietary intake requires a positive message. There is more success in giving advice on what kinds of foods to eat rather than on which foods not to eat.

There are many tools available to use in nutrition education for a healthy population. Among them are the USDA Food Guide Pyramid (1992) (Figure 2.1), population-specific adaptations by various campaigns of The American Dietetic Association (American Dietetic Association, 1996–1997), the Recommended Dietary Allowances (National Research Council, 1989), and Dietary Reference Intakes (Monson, 1996), and the Dietary Guidelines for Americans (U.S. Department of Agriculture and Health and Human Services, 2000). These are designed as general guidelines that will meet the needs of the vast majority of the American population.

Identifying risk factors for nutrition-related problems relies on the skills of a registered dietitian who can conduct a dietary analysis, identify potential deficiencies or excesses, and help to correct them. Genetic predisposition to the development of diseases or conditions that can be managed with nutrition intervention is the purview of physicians or other health professionals who are trained to look for family history of disease.

Health promotion messages should be based on sound science and should be clear, simple, and easy for people to understand. It is important for messages to be focused and targeted carefully to the population at risk. At the same time, health promotion messages should serve to dispel food and nutrition myths. Sometimes messages become oversimplified and the public hears only part of the information. One example is that the message to reduce dietary fat has become translated through the production and availability of low fat or fat-free foods; people eat reduced fat foods as though

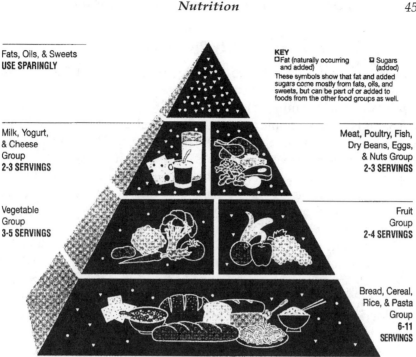

Fats, Oils, & Sweets
USE SPARINGLY

KEY
☐Fat (naturally occurring and added)   ☒ Sugars (added)
These symbols show that fat and added sugars come mostly from fats, oils, and sweets, but can be part of or added to foods from the other food groups as well.

Milk, Yogurt, & Cheese Group
2-3 SERVINGS

Meat, Poultry, Fish, Dry Beans, Eggs, & Nuts Group
2-3 SERVINGS

Vegetable Group
3-5 SERVINGS

Fruit Group
2-4 SERVINGS

Bread, Cereal, Rice, & Pasta Group
6-11 SERVINGS

SOURCE: U.S. Department of Agriculture/U.S. Department of Health and Human Services

Figure 2.1 USDA food guide pyramid.

they are calorie-free. The recommendation for decreasing the total amount of fat in the usual American diet has several objectives: reducing the risk for heart disease, decreasing the risk for certain cancers, and lowering the incidence of obesity. Because of the aggressive marketing of many products that have been reformulated to reduce the total fat, the public believes that these products can be consumed in unlimited amounts. The incidence of obesity, which was expected to decrease with the widespread availability of lower fat food products, in fact, has increased (Berg, 1994). A more comprehensive health message needs to be devised so that this unexpected consequence can be reversed.

For all of these reasons, primary prevention really ought to be targeted to children and young adults so that scientifically sound nutrition information can be the basis for healthy eating behaviors. Young people who are at risk for many nutrition-related chronic conditions can incorporate modifications in their diets at an early age and reap the greatest benefits in their health.

Secondary Prevention

Conditions that are related to nutritional risk factors take years to develop. For adults, exposure to these risk factors occurs over years and can be mitigated if diet is altered early in adulthood (McGinnis, 1988). For older adults, dietary changes may prove difficult and, in some instances, may not be desirable. In fact, some modifications may contribute to subclinical nutritional deficiencies by limiting intake of certain food groups. For example, if individuals are concerned about their cholesterol and eliminate all meat and eggs from their diet, a vitamin B_{12} deficiency may result that may not be detected for some time.

For older adults, other secondary prevention strategies, including assessments of food security, access to shopping, cooking resources, and feeding skills, need to be part of a health promotion program (McCabe & Dorey, 1999). The prevention strategies for elderly people should include early, regular screening and access to needed resources. One example of a screening tool for nutrition risk is the DETERMINE Your Nutritional Health Checklist (1991) (Figure 2.2, pp. 48–49) developed by the Nutrition Screening Initiative, a partnership of The American Dietetic Association, The American Academy of Family Physicians, and the National Council on Aging. This instrument only evaluates risk factors for malnutrition as an awareness tool for people who work with older adults; it is not a tool to assess malnutrition or nutritional deficiency.

The Nutrition Screening Initiative developed more comprehensive assessment tools to actually identify nutritional problems that may exist (Nutrition Screening Initiative, 1991, 1993, 1997). There are two assessments, Level 1 and Level 2, that incorporate more measures that can lead to an actual diagnosis of nutritional deficiency (Nutrition Screening Initiative, 1991). Usually the nutritional deficiencies that are identified are reversible and leave no long-term effects. The nutritional problems that may be detected include vitamin deficiencies, under and over calorie malnutrition, protein undernutrition, and other conditions.

Nutritional problems are often factors in the development of chronic conditions. Frequently nutritional problems are corrected through the treatment for underlying disease pathologies. Sometimes nutritional problems are related to oral health status. In the management of chronic conditions, an evaluation of the condition of the mouth, oral mucosa, tongue, and teeth might be useful and help to identify underlying etiologies for nutritional deficiencies (Martin, 1999; Nutrition Screening Initiative, 1993).

Disease prevention strategies are different for older adults than younger adults for many of the already mentioned reasons. Risk factors for chronic conditions change with age; different risk factors become more predictive in older adults than they are in younger adults. Public health awareness messages need to represent these changes so that appropriate screening tools can be used or developed that are more relevant for this unique population.

Tertiary Prevention

Prevention strategies should have different outcome expectations for older adults. Tertiary prevention may include the use of medical nutrition therapy as an integral part of disease treatment or amelioration. Nutrition interventions should contribute to improving the patients' condition, maintaining health status, rehabilitating chronic conditions, and restoring function when possible (McCabe & Dorey, 1999; McGinnis, 1988).

Medical nutrition therapy may include nutrition counseling for dietary modification, dietary supplements and meal replacement formulas, enteral feeding by tube, or parenteral nutrition therapy.

Health Promotion in Older Adults

One of the challenges in health promotion activities is to prove that the intervention has the desired effect. It is difficult to demonstrate that changing dietary habits in the early years of life prevents the development of a chronic health condition 30 to 40 years later. There is no way to predict who would have developed the condition without the early intervention, therefore, supporting health promotion efforts in nutrition is difficult. However, among the causes of death in adults over the age of 65 (Table 2.1), many of them are linked to nutrition as an etiologic factor or a therapeutic intervention.

There are many factors to consider and assess in order to effectively develop health promotion strategies for older adults. These are listed in Table 2.2.

Dietary Guidelines/Nutrient Recommendations

Dietary guidelines and suggested nutrient intake levels are vague in counsel for the elderly. Dietary guidelines are not age-specific

The Warning Signs of poor nutritional health are often overlooked. Use this checklist to find out if you or someone you know is at nutritional risk.

Read the statements below. Circle the number in the yes column for those that apply to you or someone you know. For each yes answer, score the number in the box. Total your nutritional score.

DETERMINE YOUR NUTRITIONAL HEALTH

	YES
I have an illness or condition that made me change the kind and/or amount of food I eat.	2
I eat fewer than 2 meals per day.	3
I eat few fruits or vegetables, or milk products.	2
I have 3 or more drinks of beer, liquor or wine almost every day.	2
I have tooth or mouth problems that make it hard for me to eat.	2
I don't always have enough money to buy the food I need.	4
I eat alone most of the time.	1
I take 3 or more different prescribed or over-the-counter drugs a day.	1
Without wanting to, I have lost or gained 10 pounds in the last 6 months.	2
I am not always physically able to shop, cook and/or feed myself.	2
TOTAL	

Total Your Nutritional Score. If it's —

0-2   **Good!** Recheck your nutritional score in 6 months.

3-5   **You are at moderate nutritional risk.** See what can be done to improve your eating habits and lifestyle. Your office on aging, senior nutrition program, senior citizens center or health department can help. Recheck your nutritional score in 3 months.

6 or more   **You are at high nutritional risk.** Bring this checklist the next time you see your doctor, dietitian or other qualified health or social service professional. Talk with them about any problems you may have. Ask for help to improve your nutritional health.

These materials developed and distributed by the Nutrition Screening Initiative, a project of:

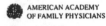 AMERICAN ACADEMY OF FAMILY PHYSICIANS

 THE AMERICAN DIETETIC ASSOCIATION

NATIONAL COUNCIL ON THE AGING, INC.

Remember that warning signs suggest risk, but do not represent diagnosis of any condition. Turn the page to learn more about the Warning Signs of poor nutritional health.

Figure 2.2   DETERMINE your nutritional health checklist.

The Nutrition Checklist is based on the Warning Signs described below. Use the word DETERMINE to remind you of the Warning Signs.

Disease

Any disease, illness or chronic condition which causes you to change the way you eat, or makes it hard for you to eat, puts your nutritional health at risk. Four out of five adults have chronic diseases that are affected by diet. Confusion or memory loss that keeps getting worse is estimated to affect one out of five or more of older adults. This can make it hard to remember what, when or if you've eaten. Feeling sad or depressed, which happens to about one in eight older adults, can cause big changes in appetite, digestion, energy level, weight and well-being.

Eating poorly

Eating too little and eating too much both lead to poor health. Eating the same foods day after day or not eating fruit, vegetables, and milk products daily will also cause poor nutritional health. One in five adults skip meals daily. Only 13% of adults eat the minimum amount of fruit and vegetables needed. One in four older adults drink too much alcohol. Many health problems become worse if you drink more than one or two alcoholic beverages per day.

Tooth loss/ mouth pain

A healthy mouth, teeth and gums are needed to eat. Missing, loose or rotten teeth or dentures which don't fit well or cause mouth sores make it hard to eat.

Economic hardship

As many as 40% of older Americans have incomes of less than $6,000 per year. Having less -- or choosing to spend less -- than $25-30 per week for food makes it very hard to get the foods you need to stay healthy.

Reduced social contact

One-third of all older people live alone. Being with people daily has a positive effect on morale, well-being and eating.

Multiple medicines

Many older Americans must take medicines for health problems. Almost half of older Americans take multiple medicines daily. Growing old may change the way we respond to drugs. The more medicines you take, the greater the chance for side effects such as increased or decreased appetite, change in taste, constipation, weakness, drowsiness, diarrhea, nausea, and others. Vitamins or minerals when taken in large doses act like drugs and can cause harm. Alert your doctor to everything you take.

Involuntary weight loss/gain

Losing or gaining a lot of weight when you are not trying to do so is an important warning sign that must not be ignored. Being overweight or underweight also increases your chance of poor health.

Needs assistance in self care

Although most older people are able to eat, one of every five have trouble walking, shopping, buying and cooking food, especially as they get older.

Elder years above age 80

Most older people lead full and productive lives. But as age increases, risk of frailty and health problems increase. Checking your nutritional health regularly makes good sense.

 The Nutrition Screening Initiative, 1010 Wisconsin Avenue, NW, Suite 800, Washington, DC 20007
The Nutrition Screening Initiative is funded in part by a grant from Ross Laboratories, a division of Abbott Laboratories

Figure 2.2 *Continued*

TABLE 2.1   Common Causes of Death in Older Persons

Heart disease of various types
Atherosclerosis
Malignancies
Cerebrovascular disease and stroke
Chronic pulmonary disease
Diabetes
Infectious processes

and are very general for the public at large. The Recommended Dietary Allowances cluster all adults over age 50 in the same category. Although there has been strong urging by members of the scientific community to stratify dietary recommendations for older adults, it does not seem likely that this will happen. There are some modifications in specific nutrients between adults under and over age 50, including calcium, iron, vitamin B_{12}, vitamin A, and vitamin D (Russell, 1997).

Socioeconomic Factors

Socioeconomic factors can have a significant impact on the maintenance or restoration of nutritional health. One of the risk factors for malnutrition is the lack of funds to purchase a variety of foods in adequate amounts to meet the individual's nutrient requirements. People who have limited financial resources may purchase food products that are filling but that are nutritionally sparse. They may also have to make difficult choices regarding how they will spend their money; sometimes the choices include utility bills, medication, housing costs, or food.

Living situations for many older adults may be dictated by their financial situation. Whether they are residing in their own home or apartment, in a congregate setting, with grown children and their families, in group homes, in a boarding home, or in an institution, housing and access to food preparation facilities may impact on food preparation ability. It is known that individuals who live with others, whether a spouse, family members, or friends; who participate in senior meals programs (Neyman, Zidenberg-Cherr, & McDonald, 1996); and those who receive home-delivered meals (Adams, 1997) generally eat better than those who live alone. This

TABLE 2.2   Factors to Assess Before Developing Health Promotion Strategies for Older Adults

---

Dietary guidelines/nutrient recommendations
Socioeconomic factors
Trends in the food supply
Eating patterns
Nutritional status
Use of dietary supplements
Physical activity
Smoking habits
Alcohol abuse
Medications
Food safety
Health fraud

---

is particularly true when they have suffered the loss of a spouse. Cooking becomes too much trouble.

Another component of socioeconomic impact is access to transportation. The ability to get to the store is a factor in the foods consumed. If grocery shopping can only be accomplished intermittently, it is less likely that fresh fruits and vegetables, fresh meat, poultry, and eggs, and fresh dairy products will be consumed. Frozen, canned, or dried goods may be used more frequently. These foods are generally higher in salt and fat than are fresh items.

Trends in the Food Supply

The food supply in the United States has changed over the years. Foods are manufactured for convenience. They are supplemented and fortified with nutrients that are naturally present, and some that are not. They are packaged to be easy to store and fast to prepare or reheat. It is difficult to know what is actually eaten because most food consumption studies are actually based on purchasing data. There is no adjustment for spoilage or plate waste.

Eating Patterns

Eating patterns can only be assessed by collecting dietary intake data. This requires individual interviews and is expensive and time-consuming and not necessarily accurate. It is important to determine how frequently and what is being consumed by older adults who may be at nutritional risk.

Nutritional Status

Nutritional status is sometimes difficult to determine in older adults due to the lack of appropriate standards against which to measure nutrition parameters (Mitchell & Chernoff, 1999). Many of the assessment tools include measures that are affected by physiologic changes associated with age and with disease. Under the best circumstances, assessment of nutritional status is an estimate; for older adults a wide latitude must be allowed to accommodate other conditions that interact with nutritional status. Nutritional assessment should be evaluated within the context of other assessments of the individual.

Use of Dietary Supplements

Dietary supplements, including liquid snacks, vitamin and mineral preparations, herbal, and non-nutritive compounds are used frequently. Some of these products are harmful, some are inconsequential, and some are actually useful. The benefit of some supplements may be obscure; supplements may be abused to the point of toxicity; and they may be expensive. It is important that a history of supplement use be included in the nutrition history of an older adult because these products may interfere with prescription medications, may contribute to nutritional problems, and may be the etiology of unexplained symptoms.

Physical Activity

Exercise is an important dimension of nutritional status and has an effect of many of the parameters that are used to evaluate nutritional status. Exercise is a significant factor in maintaining muscle mass and strength, reducing bone loss, reducing the risk of falls and fractures, managing blood pressure, altering blood lipid profiles, and managing energy balance (Evans & Cyr-Campbell, 1997). Exercise throughout the life cycle contributes to vitality during each of the phases of life.

Smoking/Alcohol Abuse

Smoking and alcohol abuse are risk factors for poor health and poor nutrition habits. Smokers may have problems with specific nutrients, vitamin C being a prime example, due to the interactions between the inhaled and absorbed components of cigarettes and some of the water soluble vitamins. Alcoholics generally have poor diets and frequently have water soluble vitamin deficiencies, especially thiamine.

Use of Medications

A medication profile should be part of any health evaluation but particularly among older adults. The potential effects of drug-drug or drug-nutrient interactions cannot be underestimated in their impact on well-being (Blumberg & Couris, 1999). Examples include the interaction between phenyotin and hepatic enzymes which may induce folic acid deficiency or the effect of lithium which causes an abnormal unpleasant taste sensation (Blumberg & Couris, 1999).

Food Safety

Food safety is an increasingly important problem. Food-borne illnesses can lead to serious gastrointestinal problems for all people of all ages. Gastrointestinal problems can contribute to serious dehydration and nutritional losses, in addition to fluid and electrolyte imbalances, and deleterious consequences as serious as death may result (American Dietetic Association, 1997).

Health Fraud

Older adults are frequently a target for health fraud. The elderly are sometimes susceptible to extravagant claims associated with recapturing youthful skin, changing graying hair, and regaining youthful exuberance. Many products promoted to elderly people profess to possess magical charms, and all too often have no therapeutic or palliative value at all.

Health Recommendations

Health and nutrition recommendations can have a beneficial effect on the quality of life, health, and the functional status of older adults. There are important considerations that should be reviewed when counseling individuals to modify their eating habits. An evaluation of the potential positive benefits has to be made before alterations in the habits of many years are suggested. Lifestyle changes that have a noticeable and positive effect are those that are most easily complied with.

An evaluation of risk factors, and a realization of changes that occur with age in both risk factors and treatment benefits, should be part of a health promotion program. Nutrition as a health promotion tactic should begin early in life since the nutrition-related chronic conditions take many years to develop and many years to have any health benefit.

REFERENCES

Adams, T. (1997). The effect of home-delivered meals on length of hospitalization for elderly patients (Masters' thesis). Little Rock: College of Health Related Professions, University of Arkansas for Medical Sciences.

Berg, J. (1994). America gains weight: NHANES III finds 33.4% of US adults overweight. *Healthy Weight Journal 8*(6), 107–109.

Blumberg, J. B., & Couris, R. (1999). Pharmacology, nutrition, and the elderly: Interactions and Implications. In Chernoff, R. (Ed.), *Geriatric nutrition: The health professional's handbook* (2nd ed.). Gaithersburg: Aspen Publishers.

DETERMINE Your Nutritional Health (1991). The Nutrition Screening Initiative: Washington, DC.

Evans, W. J., & Cyr-Campbell, D. (1997). Nutrition, exercise, and healthy aging. *Journal of the American Dietetic Association 97*(6), 632–638.

Fishman, P. (1996). Healthy People 2000: What progress toward better nutrition? *Geriatrics 51*(4), 38–42.

Food Guide Pyramid for Children (1996). Nutrition and Health Campaign for Children. Chicago: The American Dietetic Association.

Food Guide Pyramid for Older Adults (1997). Nutrition and Health for Older Americans, a campaign of The American Dietetic Association. Chicago: The American Dietetic Association.

Food Guide Pyramid: A guide to daily food choices (1992). Home and Garden Bulletin No. 252. Washington: U.S. Department of Agriculture, Human Nutrition Information Service.

Martin, W. E. (1999). Oral health in the elderly. In R. Chernoff (Ed.), *Geriatric nutrition: The health professional's handbook* (2nd ed.). Gaithersburg: Aspen Publishers.

McCabe, B. J., & Dorey, J. L. (1999). Health promotion and disease prevention in the elderly. In R. Chernoff (Ed.), *Geriatric nutrition: The health professional's handbook* (2nd ed.). Gaithersburg: Aspen Publishers.

McGinnis, J. M. (1988). Year 2000 health objectives for the nation. In *Surgeon General's Workshop on Health Promotion and Aging* (pp. 20–25). Washington, D.C.: U.S. Department of Health and Human Services.

Mitchell, C. O., & Chernoff, R. (1991). Nutritional assessment of the elderly. In R. Chernoff (Ed.), *Geriatric nutrition: The health professionals handbook* (2nd ed.). Gaithersburg: Aspen Publishers.

Monson, E. (1996). New Dietary Reference Intakes proposed to replace the Recommended Dietary Allowances. *Journal of the American Dietetic Association 96*(2), 54–755.

Neyman, M. R., Zidenberg-Cherr, S., & McDonald, R. B. (1996). Effect of participation in congregate-site meal programs on nutritional status of the healthy elderly. *Journal of the American Dietetic Association 96*(5), 475–483.

Nutrition and your health: Dietary guidelines for Americans (1990). Home and Garden Bulletin No. 232 (3rd ed.). Washington: U.S. Departments of Agriculture and Health and Human Services.

Nutrition intervention manual for professionals caring for older Americans (1991). Nutrition Screening Initiative: Washington, DC.

Nutrition screening manual for professionals caring for older Americans (1993). Nutrition Screening Initiative: Washington, DC.

Perry, D. (1994). The links of aging research to disease prevention. *Nutrition Reviews 52*(8), II S48.

Position of the American Dietetic Association: Food and water safety (1997). *Journal of the American Dietetic Association, 97*(2), 184–189.

Recommended Dietary Allowances (1989). Food and Nutrition Board, National Research Council (10th ed.). Washington: National Academy Press.

Rosenberg, I. H. (1994). Keys to a longer, healthier, more vital life. *Nutrition Reviews 52*(8), II S50–S51.

Russell, R. M. (1997). New views on the RDAs for older adults. *Journal of the American Dietetic Association 97*(5), 515–518.

The role of nutrition in chronic disease care: Executive summary (1997). Nutrition Screening Initiative: Washington, DC.

Wynder, E. L., & Andres, R. (1994). Workshop A: Diet and nutrition research as it relates to aging and chronic disease. *Preventive Medicine 23*(5), 549–551.

CHAPTER 3

Arthritis Self-Management

Kate Lorig

Forty years ago it was written, "Whether the nurse likes it or not, teaching is inherent in her profession . . ." (Harmer & Henderson, 1958). Much has happened since that time. Patient education is now seen as a core function of nursing. In addition, we know more about providing more effective forms of education. This is especially important today as we care for more older people with chronic diseases. This paper will present the evolution of one chronic disease patient education program, the Arthritis Self-Management Program (ASMP), also known as the Arthritis Self-Help (ASH) Course. The sections of this chapter include a brief synopsis of a number of ASMP studies. Except where noted, all of these studies have been previously published. The readers are referred to the cited articles for complete details. In Part II of this chapter, the elements of self-management interventions are discussed; and in Part III, some case histories of how the ASMP has been disseminated are offered. Finally, in Part IV, the future self-management directions are discussed.

ASMP STUDIES

In 1977, the Stanford Arthritis Center was funded by National Institutes of Health. One of the studies in the original center was to determine the effectiveness of arthritis patient education. The study was based on three assumptions: 1) Changes in behavior would lead to changes in health status; 2) The behavioral management tasks of people with different types of arthritis are similar;

and 3) Patient education could be offered in community settings using a public health model and lay instructors.

The first of these assumptions was based on the prevailing wisdom of the day that health outcomes of patient education were largely mediated by behaviors. This assumption was based on early patient education studies, which found that patients who took their hypertension medication had lower blood pressure, or that women who used family planning had fewer pregnancies. In these cases, behavior was directly linked to outcome. The second assumption came from patient interviews and a salient belief study based on the work of Miller (1956). These studies identified pain as the key concern of arthritis patients, followed by disability and psychological concerns such as fear and depression (Lorig, Cox, Cuevas, Kraines, & Britton, 1984). Based on these studies, the ASMP became one of the first patient education programs that addressed the expressed needs of the patients.

The third assumption was based on both the situation and pragmatism. The investigator at the time of this study was a public health doctoral student with a 13-year background in public health. Thus, community-based education seemed "logical," especially when there were few model arthritis patient education programs. The use of lay instructors was probably the most innovative part of the original program; however, there were at least two precedents. The Red Cross had long used lay instructors to teach first aid, and Alcoholics Anonymous used lay leaders for its program. Finally, there were very few health professionals with expertise in arthritis, making the use of lay leaders a practical approach.

Subjects for this study and all other studies discussed in this paper were recruited from several San Francisco Bay Area counties using public service announcements, public talks, and word of mouth. All subjects received validated, mailed, self-administered questionnaires. When these were returned, the subjects were randomized to treatment or control status. The treatment subjects immediately took the ASMP, while the controls waited before taking the program. At the end of 4 months, all subjects again received questionnaires and then the controls were offered the ASMP.

The programs were taught in community sites such as senior centers, libraries, health clinics, and churches. Each program was taught by a pair of lay leaders, one or both of whom usually had arthritis. The leaders received 18 hours of training and taught from a detailed protocol (Lorig, 1992). All participants in the ASMP received a copy of *The Arthritis Helpbook*, which was originally written for the program (Lorig & Fries, 2000). They also received an audio relaxation tape (Regan, 1994).

Study One: A Search For Effectiveness
(Lorig, Lubeck, Kraines, Seleznick, & Holman, 1985)

To test the original assumptions, 190 subjects were randomized to attend the ASMP or to wait 4 months before receiving the intervention (Lorig et al., 1985). The ASMP is a 6-week (2 hours/week), lay-led community-based program. The program content includes an overview of types of arthritis, designing an individualized exercise program, practice of cognitive pain management techniques, discussions on use of medications, nutrition, decision making about use of non-traditional therapies, communication skills, patient provider communications, and problem solving. The program came to be based on self-efficacy theory. Treatment subjects, compared to controls, demonstrated significant ($p < .05$) increases in knowledge, the practice of range of motion and strengthening exercise, and the practice of relaxation techniques. Pain was reduced ($p < .05$). There were no changes in disability or depression. The program appeared to be equally effective for patients who had either rheumatoid arthritis or osteoarthritis. Surprisingly, contrary to our first assumption, no significant associations were found between changes in health behaviors (exercise and relaxation) and changes in pain. The highest correlation was .14 between changes in exercise and changes in pain. The correlation between changes in relaxation and pain was .04 (Lorig, Seleznick, Lubeck, Ung, Chastain et al., 1989). These findings suggested that factors other than positive behavior change influenced pain reduction.

Study Two: A Search for Theory (Lenker, Lorig,
& Gallagher, 1984; Lorig et al., 1989; Lorig, Ung,
Chastain, Shoor, & Holman, 1989)

Based on the findings from study one, open-ended interviews were conducted with 50 former participants of the ASMP (Lenker et al., 1984). Half of the subjects were chosen because they had demonstrated an improvement in pain, while the other half because they had no change in pain or worsened pain. Subjects were asked what benefits, if any, had occurred as a result of taking the ASMP and why they thought these occurred. The transcribed interviews were read by three reviewers and themes were identified. Those subjects who spoke of having experienced an improvement in pain attributed this to feelings of increased "control," while those subjects who had not experienced any improvement felt that nothing they did made a difference.

Several theories were examined in an attempt to operationalize "control." In study one, a post-test comparison of health locus of control scores demonstrated no differences between the treatment and control subjects (Lorig et al., 1985; Wallston, Wallston, Kaplan, & Maides, 1976). Health locus of control was thus rejected as an applicable theoretical construct. We also examined Antonovsky's Congruence Theory (Antonovsky, 1980). The Antonovsky Congruence Scale was found to be highly correlated with depression and thus, not having a means of measuring congruence, this theory was rejected (Antonovsky, 1987). We also examined Stress and Coping Theory which was rejected based on the dissertation findings of Regan, who demonstrated that the ASMP had little effect on stress and coping (Lazarus & Folkman, 1984; Regan, 1990).

At the same time that we were pursuing the usefulness of Congruence and Stress and Coping theories, we were exploring the applicability of Self-Efficacy Theory (Bandura, 1977, 1997) by developing and testing arthritis-specific self-efficacy scales (Lorig, Ung, Chastain, Shoor, & Holman, 1989). We found that the ASMP increased subjects' self-efficacy and that post-intervention self-efficacy was correlated with post-intervention pain, disability, and depression (Pearson's r's ranging from .39 to .71) (Lorig, Seleznick, Lubeck, Ung, Chastain, & Holman, 1989). This finding suggested that self-efficacy might be an independent or mediating variable accounting for the changes in health status demonstrated by the participants in the ASMP. Because of these findings, we conducted several additional studies to determine the effects of self-efficacy.

Study Three: Content versus Process
(Lorig & González, 1992)

In a new study to further investigate the effect of self-efficacy on health status, subjects were randomized to one of three new versions of ASMP or to control status (Lorig & González 1992). Like the original ASMP, the three new versions were each 12 hours, offered over 6 weeks in community settings by pairs of trained lay leaders. All three programs used processes designed to enhance self-efficacy. These included skills mastery, modeling, reinterpretation of physiological symptoms, and social persuasion.

In the first intervention, exercise was emphasized, and no cognitive techniques were taught. In the second intervention, cognitive techniques were emphasized and no exercise was taught. In the third intervention, both exercise and cognitive techniques were taught. Participants in all three interventions demonstrated improvements in health behaviors and health status when compared to controls. No differences in outcomes were found among the participants in the three interventions, suggesting that self-efficacy was more important in determining improvement in health status than the individual or combined behaviors taught. Following this study, the ASMP was further revised to strengthen the efficacy-enhancing strategies and to include content emphasizing both endurance exercise and cognitive pain management techniques.

Study Four: Reinforcement Study
(Lorig & Holman, 1989)

One tenet of patient education is that education needs to be reinforced. There are, however, very few studies that examine the effects of reinforcement. To examine reinforcement effects, 589 ASMP subjects, 1 year after beginning the program, were randomized to receive either a bimonthly newsletter, an advanced arthritis self-management program, or no intervention (Lorig & Holman, 1989). Eight months later, 20 months after beginning the original ASMP, all subjects demonstrated 20% improvement in pain, 14% improvement in depression, and 35% reduction in visits to physicians (all $p < .01$). There were, however, no significant differences among the three groups. This study suggests that the reinforcement techniques utilized in this study did not improve upon the results of the ASMP, which appeared to be self-reinforcing.

Study Five: Long Term Outcomes and Cost Effectiveness
(Lorig, Mazonson, & Holman, 1993)

Building on the findings from study four, we examined 401 ASMP subjects four years after they took the program (Lorig et al., 1993).

Data were collected from 80% of the eligible subjects. Compared to baseline, subjects were found to have a 19% reduction in pain, a 17% increase in self-efficacy, a 9% increase in disability, and a 43% decrease in outpatient visits to physicians (all p < .05). Comparison subjects from both national and local data sets suggest that the normal increase in disability for like patients ranged from 10 to 24% a year. Thus, it appears that while the physiological disease progressed, patients taking the ASMP reported less pain and had fewer visits to physicians. If these findings could be replicated in 1% of people in the United States with osteoarthritis and rheumatoid arthritis, the savings in 1990 dollars would be approximately $32 million. In the face of worsening physiological disease, the ASMP appears to improve patients' quality of life and provide cost savings.

Additional Studies

We have examined three additional aspects of the ASMP, the effects of lay leaders versus health professional leaders, the effects of social support, and the effects of a shortened course.

Lay Led versus Health Professional Led Programs (Lorig, Feigenbaum, Regan, Ung, & Holman, 1986)

One hundred ASMP subjects were randomized to programs taught by lay leaders, programs taught by health professionals, or to control status (Lorig et al., 1986). The professionally taught subjects, compared to controls, demonstrated greater changes in knowledge (p < .05) but no changes in behaviors, pain, or disability. Subjects taught by lay leaders, compared to controls, did not demonstrate changes in knowledge, but did demonstrate changes in behaviors and a trend toward less disability (p < .05). This study suggests that the ASMP can be successfully taught by lay leaders and that there is no advantage in having the program taught by health professionals.

Social Support

In an attempt to document the effects of the ASMP compared to a program developed to give social support, subjects were randomized to one of two programs: the ASMP or a social support program without arthritis content. Subjects in each program were blinded to the existence of the other program. This study was never completed because of the very high (more than 50%)

dropout from the social support program. Because the study was terminated before completion, it has never been published. At least two possible conclusions can be drawn: 1) The ASMP is more acceptable to participants than a social support intervention; and 2) Attention only (the Hawthorne Effect) cannot account for the favorable outcomes of the ASMP.

Shorter versus Longer ASMP Versions
(Lorig, González, Laurent, Morgan, & Laris, 1998)

Recently, a 3-week ASMP was developed to test the effectiveness of a shorter program. Subjects were randomized to take either the 3- or 6-week program, both of which were taught by lay leaders. Four months after beginning the programs subjects in the 3-week program, when compared to baseline, made significant changes in self-efficacy ($p < .05$) and no other changes were seen. Participants in the standard ASMP demonstrated significant ($p < .05$) improvements in health behaviors, pain, and self-efficacy. This study suggests that while we do not know the ideal length of an arthritis patient education program, 3 weeks does not appear to be sufficient time to accomplish the same gains as seen in the 6-week ASMP.

PART II: SELF-MANAGEMENT CHARACTERISTICS

When the ASMP originated in 1978, the name "self-management" was used to distinguish the intervention from the then popular "self-help" movement. At that time, "self-help" had come to mean taking care of oneself outside of the traditional health care system; whereas "self-management" was borrowed from the business field. In business the manager makes day-to-day decisions, but also uses consultants (health professionals) as necessary when faced with new problems or changing conditions. As self-management interventions have evolved, they have taken on several characteristics, which separate them from more traditional patient education courses.

Self-Management Interventions Are Based
on the Problems and Concerns of Patients

The development of all self-management interventions start with a study of the target patients' perception of the disease(s) and the disease-related problems. In a monumental qualitative study,

Corbin and Strauss (1988) have identified three major tasks which patients need to perform to successfully manage a chronic condition. First, they must deal with all the disease-related tasks. These include taking medication, special exercise regimes, changes in diet, and in some cases use of special equipment. Second, patients must learn how to continue or adapt their major life roles in the face of illness. These include being a parent, employee, club member, volunteer, and so on. Finally, people with chronic disease must deal with uncertainty about the future. This uncertainty, along with the first two tasks above, often results in frustration, anger, depression, or other negative emotions.

While traditional patient education programs place most of their emphasis on learning disease-related tasks, self-management education places equal emphasis on all three types of tasks. This means that, in comparison to more traditional programs, self-management de-emphasizes disease-related tasks. When these tasks are discussed, it is always in the context of patient problems or concerns. For example, in the ASMP, patients are urged to exercise in order to strengthen muscles and thereby reduce pain. The role of exercise in decreasing depression is also discussed. Participants are not taught specific exercises. Rather, they are urged to identify activities that they would like to do or have difficulty doing, and then taught to choose and carry out appropriate exercises that will help them accomplish the specific activities. Through this process, each participant has a different, personalized, and self-directed exercise regime. Rather than specific exercises, participants are taught how to choose exercises, how to start a program, how to add to the program, and what to do when setbacks occur. They are also taught how to monitor their exercise, and to judge the appropriateness based on the amount of exercise-induced pain. Finally, to help them overcome fear of exercise, they are reassured that "hurt" does not mean "harm" and that they can exercise safely.

Each self-management intervention takes the major concerns of patients and uses them as the framework for the program. For example, from the salient belief needs assessment discussed earlier in Part 1, we learned that the major concern of arthritis patients is pain. Thus, the ASMP frames all its activities on how these will help reduce pain. Throughout the program we refer to a pain cycle that demonstrates to participants how inactivity, depression, and stress all influence pain and how pain can be lessened by breaking this cycle.

Self-Management Interventions
Use a Public Health Model

The use of a public health model means that the programs are aimed at a population. While individuals attend and benefit from the programs, it is hoped that over time proactive disease self-management will become a community norm. To some extent this is happening as the medical community is beginning to use self-management education as a standard treatment, rather than a nice extra. At the same time, arthritis patients are beginning to understand that self-management is their responsibility.

The recruitment of subjects and selection of the class sites also follow a public health model. Participants can self-refer, as have more than 90% of ASMP participants. The programs are advertised through the media, word of mouth, and community organizations, as well as through health care providers. Another aspect of the public health model is that programs are held at community sites not necessarily associated with health, such as senior centers, libraries, churches, and shopping mall meeting rooms. Self-management differs from both the medical model and the traditional public health model in that it emphasizes tertiary prevention rather then the primary prevention emphasized by public health or secondary prevention emphasized by the medical model.

Self-Management Interventions Emphasize
Both Process and Content

Because of the emphasis on process, the amount of content usually taught in a set amount of time must be judiciously balanced in order to leave enough time for the process portion. Thus, the content to be taught must be carefully crafted. This is accomplished by determining and emphasizing the key educational messages. These are based on a combination of professional expertise about the disease and patient perceptions about the disease. For example, professionals give the message that people with arthritis should exercise. Patients often believe that exercise will "wear out their joints." The message used in the ASMP is that exercise is necessary to reduce pain, that one cannot cause permanent damage to the joints by exercising, and that it is actually more dangerous to joints not to exercise than it is to exercise. A second key message is that there is no way not to manage a chronic disease. The only question is the quality of one's management.

There are several criteria for including or excluding content. Content is more likely to be included if it can be generalized. For example, instead of teaching specific ways to solve arthritis-related problems such as opening doors or going up steps, we teach problem solving as a self-management skill. Instead of teaching that patients should be cautious about non-traditional therapies, we teach ASMP participants how to evaluate and decide about all treatments, whether they are traditional or non-traditional.

Content is either excluded or kept brief if it is not directly related to self-management. Thus, we do not teach any disease-related anatomy or physiology, and only 20 minutes out of the 12-hour program are spent discussing different types of arthritis. In the same way, specific medications are not discussed. Rather, we discuss the general effects (good and bad) of medications as a whole, and how to evaluate and decide about whether to start or continue taking a specific medication.

Content is simplified as much as possible. Instead of teaching regimes for "range of motion exercise," "muscle strengthening exercise," and "aerobic exercise," we teach about how to build an integrated, personalized program which includes "stretching and strengthening exercise" and "endurance exercise."

Self-Management Interventions Are Accompanied by Comprehensive Written Material

Because participants often want more content than is taught in the program and also need to have a reference to material that has been taught, each self-management program is accompanied by extensive written material. For the ASMP this is *The Arthritis Helpbook* (Lorig & Fries, 2000) Often, when questions are asked in class, participants are referred to the material in the *Helpbook*. At other times, participants are referred to voluntary agencies or health libraries to find the information and report back to the class. Part of self-management means being responsible for finding and utilizing information.

In early self-management programs, there was some concern about patient literacy and the ability to utilize written materials. It has been our experience that even people with low literacy utilize and benefit from well-written, comprehensive, and relevant materials. It should be noted that most tests for reading levels were developed to place children into reading groups and that adults can often read well above their "reading level" if the material is of interest and well-written. For example, the sentence, "A rheumatologist is a doctor who treats people with arthritis (problems with their joints)" is at the 11th grade reading level. However, it is quite well understood by and interesting to people with arthritis who have a much lower reading level.

In a more recent experience, a monolingual Spanish-speaking population whose mean educational level was 8 years requested that we write a comprehensive book rather than pamphlets with pictures. They felt that this was the only way they could get the information they needed about their disease (González, Nacif de Brey, Lorig, & Fries, 1997).

Self-Management Interventions Emphasize Educational Processes That Enhance Self-Efficacy

Self-efficacy theory states that 1) the strength of belief in one's capability is a good predictor of motivation and behavior; 2) one's self-efficacy beliefs can be enhanced through performance mastery, modeling, reinterpretation of physiological symptoms, and social persuasion; and 3) enhanced self-efficacy leads to improved behaviors, motivation, thinking patterns, and emotional well-being (Bandura, 1997). Based on this definition, self-management processes must systematically be designed to enhance self-efficacy. In the case of the ASMP, skills mastery is accomplished by having all participants make individual action plans each week and then share or provide feedback on their accomplishments in the next session. The purpose of the action plans is two-fold. First, because action plans can be about any behavior, the accomplishment gives participants who often see their lives as being out of control, the confidence that they can plan and accomplish something of importance to them. Second, the action plans allow participants to practice some of the new self-management skills. Modeling is accomplished by having the ASMP taught by lay leaders who are coping with arthritis on a day-by-day basis, as well as through structured interactions among program participants. Finally, the drawings and photographs in *The Arthritis Helpbook* were designed to represent a variety of people of different ages, body types, and ethnic groups (Lorig & Fries, 2000). Reinterpretation of symptoms (physiological states) is accomplished by discussing the multiple causes of each symptom and offering several ways of dealing with each symptom. For example, fatigue is explained as being caused by the disease, lack of exercise, poor nutrition, depression, or medications. Thus, participants can see that there will also be several ways of managing fatigue. To help with symptom reinterpretation, each activity presents information that corrects misconceptions or debunks common arthritis myths, such as "If exercise causes pain, it is bad for you." Finally, social persuasion is accomplished through the group format, where each participant makes and reports on action plans, and is encouraged to call other class members between sessions.

Self-Management Interventions Emphasize Sharing Among Group Members

In a recent study, we asked self-management participants what they valued most about the program (Campbell, Sengupta, Santos, & Lorig, 1995). A word that was frequently used was "sharing." When asked for further clarification, group members talked about the importance of "helping others." There are several process aspects of the ASMP which enhance sharing. First, every time a participant has a problem, other members of the group are asked to offer suggestions. Second, there are three activities during which participants work in pairs to solve problems, to deal with negative emotions, or to make action plans. In each exercise, participants are given a structure within which to help their partner. Finally, as discussed above, sharing is accomplished by having group members call each other between sessions.

It should be noted that in order to facilitate sharing, the role of the group leader is changed. In most patient education programs, the majority of the communication is between the leader and individual class members, with the members asking questions and the leader answering. In self-management programs, the leader facilitates other group members in answering questions, but seldom answers questions directly. Thus, the role of leader changes from one of teacher and expert to one of facilitator.

Self-Management Interventions Utilize a Building Block, or "Sesame Street" Approach to Education

Many traditional patient education programs are taught utilizing "the topic of the week" approach. One week the class is taught exercise, the next week medications, and so on. This approach is especially useful when the programs are taught by teams of health professionals as it allows a different "expert" to lead the class each week.

In self-management programs, like on "Sesame Street," three or four topics are taught each week, and in the following weeks they are built upon, expanded, or alternative approaches are suggested. Thus, different cognitive techniques are taught starting with the easier ones such as progressive muscle relaxation and proceeding to more difficult ones such as visualization and self-talk. Participants are given limited practice in class, but not enough to become proficient. Rather they are told that these are "tastes" and if they want to become proficient in the technique they need to practice at home. They are given a relaxation tape to facilitate this practice. By using this building block approach, participants have an opportunity to try out new skills, discuss problems, make corrections, and build on their skills during the time the program meets. At the same time, they are learning the generic process of acquiring and maintaining new skills or changing existing behaviors.

Self-Management Interventions Utilize Ritual

One definition for ritual is "a procedure that is repeated customarily or automatically" (*Webster's II*, 1984). In self-management programs, each session has the same format as the previous session. The structure is such that each class begins with feedback on the action plans of the previous week, followed by one or two segments of new content, a break, one or two more segments of content, and ends with each participant verbalizing an action plan for the coming week. Individual activities are usually 10–20 minutes in length. This sense of ritual gives structure to the program and also gives the participants security and comfort, as they know what to expect.

Self-Management Programs Emphasize Patient Problem Solving and Decision Making

While this philosophy is often verbalized, it is seldom carried out in traditional patient education programs. The following examples from the ASMP illustrate how to operationalize patient problem solving and decision making.

Participants are told that we will be giving them many techniques for managing their arthritis. We urge them to try as many as they wish and to give new activities at least a 2-week trial before deciding which to adopt. Ultimately, it is up to them if they continue the activity. There are no "should's" or "must's."

Participants can make the weekly action plans around any activity they wish. While the majority of action plans are directly related to the ASMP content such as exercise, other action plans are less related, such as writing letters to friends or following up on a consumer complaint. If self-management is to foster decision making, then participants must make their own decisions.

In most cases, if the participants want refreshments or copies of something in class, they are told to organize this themselves. This approach is used as there is a mixed message if we tell people to manage, and then do everything for them.

Self-Management Interventions Teach Skills for Working With Health Professionals

Participants are taught to report to their health professionals not only the symptoms of their arthritis but also the trend and tempo of their disease. Three people may have the same intensity and type of symptoms, but one is getting better, one is getting worse, and the third is staying the same. Treatment for these three people may be very different. Patients can get the best treatment only if they report the trends and tempo of their disease along with the symptoms.

In addition, participants are taught how to tell their story effectively. Time is a scarce commodity in today's health care delivery systems. Thus, patients must be taught how to best utilize their time with health professionals, including coming prepared to the visit, knowing what they want from the visit, and being able to articulate this succinctly to the health care provider.

Self-Management Interventions Are Different From, but Not a Replacement for Other Levels of Patient Education

The first level of patient education is usually delivered by health care providers. This is "must know" information such as what medications to take and when. This level might be called survival skills education.

The second level of patient education is basic disease management (note this is not self-management). Disease management education teaches the patient the basics for specific diseases such as how to use an inhaler, how to inject insulin, how use a glucose monitor, or how to use portable oxygen.

Self-management is the third level of patient education and focuses on the tasks of living with a chronic condition as outlined by Corbin and Strauss (1988).

The fourth level of patient education is ongoing patient-run support groups. Today, with a few notable exceptions such as Alcoholics Anonymous, most patient support groups are run by health professionals. In many cases, they are not true support groups but rather therapy sessions or lecture series. Patients skilled in self-management should be able to organize and maintain their own support groups with minimal input from health professionals.

Self-Management Interventions Are
Usually Taught by Lay Instructors

Self-management programs can be taught by health professionals or by lay instructors. As discussed in Part I, there does not appear to be any advantage to professionally taught programs and there are some distinct disadvantages. These include the loss of instructor models, although instructors could be limited to health professionals with chronic illness. In addition there are few professionals, relative to the need, with the process-oriented expertise to teach the programs. This problem, however, could be overcome with training. Finally, most health professionals are responsible for direct patient care and do not have time blocks allotted for self-management teaching. This becomes even more problematic when programs are given in sites other than hospitals or clinics and at times outside of regular working hours such as evenings, Saturdays, and Sundays. Finally, professionally led programs tend to be more expensive than lay-led programs. The less expensive lay-led model allows the program to be offered to more people and reach a large enough segment of the population to begin to bring about changes in community norms.

In order to allow lay leaders to teach the program, and to retain quality control, all self-management programs are taught with a detailed protocol which gives minute-to-minute directions for all program content and process (Lorig, 1992).

The above section offers some of the criteria for self-management programs and attempts to distinguish self-management education from more traditional patient education. It should be noted that traditional patient education/self-management education is not a dichotomy but rather a continuum. The above discussion should not be taken as a checklist but rather as a starting point for creating strong community-based, self-management programs.

PART III: DISSEMINATION AND EXTENSION OF THE ARTHRITIS SELF-MANAGEMENT MODEL

The ASMP has been disseminated to many countries including New Zealand, Australia, Canada, South Africa, Great Britain, Scandinavia, and Lithuania. The following is a brief description of some of these implementation efforts.

United States

In 1981, the Arthritis Foundation (AF) of the United States employed a new group vice president for education. One of his first tasks was to visit the government-funded multipurpose arthritis centers and learn about the types of community service and training programs they were testing. During one such visit to the Stanford Arthritis Center, he attended a session of the ASMP given in a senior center. After review of the preliminary data on this program, the AF's national patient and community services committee gave approval for a national pilot test of the program. This was attended by 25 representatives of the AF, including staff or volunteers from 20 chapters, the regional and national office staff, and two arthritis education opinion leaders, namely, the president and past president of the Arthritis Health Professionals Association. The training consisted of how to teach the ASMP, how to train others, and how to administer the program.

Toward the end of the week, a long and heated discussion took place about the program name. The attendees decided to change it to the Arthritis Self-Help (ASH) Course. This name change was largely symbolic as it represented the passing of the program from its originators at Stanford Arthritis Center to the Arthritis Foundation. While the ASH name is used in the United States, and Challenging Arthritis is used in Great Britian, all other countries continue to use ASMP.

The AF trainees returned to their own chapters to give pilot courses, and then to train other leaders. By the end of 1981, 18 chapters had offered 22 courses. Within the next 2 years, an additional 24 chapters (62% of the total number of chapters) had adopted the program. In 1984–86, the AF received an Administration on Aging grant which provided funding for training workshops, an evaluation study of the program, and five regional support staff who assisted the chapters in collaboration with other organizations to disseminate the program more widely. By the end of this grant, virtually all of the chapters were offering the program.

There were several reasons for this rapid dissemination. First, the program had been shown to be effective in a randomized, controlled trial. Although the results were not published until 1985, they were widely known through presentations at national meetings. Second, the program is low cost and easily replicated because of its use of a detailed and standardized protocol. As a result, the program fit into the ongoing AF program framework. Third, the AF was in need of new programs to serve the public. Before 1982, each chapter had done its own programming; there were no national programs. Fourth, the federal funding provided some staff support. Fifth, and possibly most important, the course was well liked by both participants and leaders who formed strong advocate groups at both the local and national levels for its dissemination and continuation.

In 1997, the program continues to be given throughout the United States. It has also spawned two other self-management programs, one for lupus patients and the other for fibromyalgia patients (Arthritis Foundation, 1994, 1997).

Australia

In 1985, the International League for Arthritis and Rheumatism (ILAR) held its annual meeting in Sydney, Australia. The author was invited to present a paper and to give an ASMP training for the Arthritis Foundation of Victoria in Melbourne. The trainees were a mix of health professionals and lay people, most of whom either worked for or were volunteers for the Arthritis Foundation. In addition, there was one very active volunteer from Western Australia who started the program in Perth.

After this initial training, ASMP programs were given almost immediately, and as had happened in the United States, quickly became very popular. An ASMP coordinator was hired by the Victoria AF. Soon the states of South Australia and Queensland asked for training which was provided by the Victoria staff. Somewhat later, training was also held in Tasmania. Thus, within 2 years of the initial training, the course had spread throughout Australia with the exception of the most populous state, New South Wales. Unlike the United States, where programs were geographically clustered around Arthritis Foundation Chapter offices, in Australia, the program was quickly made accessible to very rural areas, some several days drive from the nearest AF office. This was accomplished by systematically training leaders in rural areas.

The rapid dissemination in Australia occurred largely for the same reasons that dissemination occurred in the United States with a few additions. First, unlike the U.S. staff, the program staff in Australia were all health professionals who felt comfortable training and supervising others. They saw the program as a way of quickly reaching more people and also as a way of enhancing their role. In some cases, the states were able to add staff to specifically supervise the ASMP because the state governments provide support for some AF staff. Finally, the staff members in several states were "mates" who met at least once a year at professional meetings and talked often by phone. They had a ready-made natural support system.

The ASMP was not used in the state of New South Wales (NSW) because the staff in Sydney had developed their own course which was taught by health professionals. They saw the ASMP as competing for the same audience. In 1997, New South Wales adopted the ASMP.

Canada

Unlike the countries where dissemination occurred without special funding or plans, a two-tiered dissemination plan was used in Canada. In 1988, the Arthritis Society of British Columbia received a grant from the Seniors Independence Program of Health Canada to implement and evaluate the feasibility and viability of the ASMP. Program implementation involved regional workshops to train leaders who in time would lead the course in their own communities. The workshops were conducted by paid Arthritis Society (AS) program staff with assistance from a trainer at Stanford. As the effort continued, AS staff from Alberta and the Yukon requested that they also be trained. This was accomplished by having British Columbia and Stanford staff co-train the Alberta and Yukon staff. Thus, two things were accomplished simultaneously: the Alberta and Yukon staff were trained and a group of leaders were prepared to give the ASMP throughout the two provinces. When the grant funding had been spent, the Arthritis Society in these provinces provided ongoing funding to continue the program.

Word of the British Columbia success spread across Canada, resulting in requests for training from most of the other provinces. Documenting the successful experiences in British Columbia, Alberta, and the Yukon as a pilot project, the national office of the Arthritis Society obtained funding from the Seniors Independence Program of Health Canada for complete national dissemination. This occurred between 1992 and 1994. When the money was depleted, the demand for continuation was so strong that the national office of the Arthritis Society decided to solicit continuing funding for the ASMP from corporate sponsorship.

This was a departure for the national office of the Arthritis Society, as up to 1994, they had played a very minor role in providing programs or services. Most of their funding and efforts had been focused on arthritis research. Not surprisingly, there was a great deal of debate to determine whether the national office of the Arthritis Society should take on this new role. The objectors felt that the ASMP might deflect monies from arthritis research into service programs. To date, because of outside sponsorship, this does not appear to have happened.

The success of the Canadian dissemination is largely due to a strong national "champion," the Program Director of the British Columbia Arthritis Society. Also important were his efforts to secure independent funding for both the provincial and national programs, and to include research and evaluation activities in the dissemination.

Simultaneously with these activities, the British Columbia Arthritis Society received requests to train First Nations (Native American) community workers as ASMP leaders. This was done at a residential training center as part of the Community Health Workers training program. These workshops achieved only minimal success, as the trainees never saw arthritis education as central to their jobs. Because they were already overwhelmed with other duties, few trainees ever actually offered the program. Two things, however, were gained from this effort. First, the trainers learned a great deal about working with First Nations people and possible ways to adapt the ASMP for use in rural First Nations Communities. Second, word of the effort spread through the First Nations grapevine, which eventually resulted in a request for a province-wide effort to train First Nations people. This was carried out through a series of training workshops. This second effort resulted in lay First Nations people leading the ASMP in 16 communities. The First Nations ASMP training was made available as part of a peer-reviewed research grant obtained from the British Columbia Health Research Foundation. Again, this was supported and coordinated by British Columbia Arthritis Society staff.

The United States, Australia, and Canada are offered as brief case studies of how the ASMP has been disseminated. In 1997, the program is being offered in more than a dozen countries in several languages including English, Spanish, French, Lithuanian, Afrikaans, and Icelandic. In summarizing the growth and expansion of the ASMP over the last 19 years, several factors seem to predict successful dissemination:

1. A strong central dissemination agency which makes dissemination a specific part of its aims and objectives.
2. A program "champion" who becomes the national "guiding light" for the program. While each country had one easily identifiable champion, the more successful countries quickly disseminated this role into regional champions, who were often paid regional staff.
3. Lack of strong opposition from the professional community. While there has been, and continues to be, skepticism about the ASMP among many health professionals, there has been no strong opposition in the countries where dissemination has been most successful.
4. Early and strong involvement of a core of volunteers with arthritis. These volunteers have become the local advocates of the program, bolstering the role of the professional

coordinators. To a large extent, it has been this core of volunteers who have educated the professional community by telling their health care providers about the program.

5. Funding dedicated to the program. In some cases, this has come from governmental sources, in others from foundations and/or industry.

In addition, there are certain attributes of the ASMP itself which have made dissemination attractive and possible:

1. There is a very detailed protocol to be used by leaders teaching the ASMP, as well as program materials and a protocol for training leaders.
2. The ASMP is low cost and low tech. The only equipment needed is a text book for each participant, an easel pad, and charts that are made by the leaders.
3. The program was designed to be taught by lay people. There is no need for the extensive use of scarce and expensive professional time.
4. There are a number of peer-reviewed, published articles on the effectiveness of the ASMP.
5. Finally, but not unimportantly, the program was developed by a prestigious research medical school. In addition, among its earliest supporters were well-respected opinion leaders in the rheumatology community.

IV: THE FUTURE

In recent years, the ASMP model has been adapted for use with Spanish speakers. A randomized trial of 300 Spanish-speaking people with arthritis was recently completed. The Spanish ASMP is a cultural adaptation of the original ASMP. Results from the Spanish ASMP study suggest that this program has similar outcomes to those achieved by the English program (Lorig, 1999b).

The self-management model has also been expanded beyond arthritis. Three new programs have been studied. The Chronic Disease Self-Management Program (CDSMP) places people with different chronic conditions together in the same program (Lorig, Sobel, Stewart, Brown, Bandura et al., 1999a). The CDSMP is currently being disseminated throughout the United States and Australia by several health care organizations. An HIV/AIDS self-management program has been pilot tested and is currently undergoing a full-scale clinical trial at the University of California in San Diego. Finally, we have cooperated with Group Health Cooperative of Puget Sound to develop a self-management program for people with recurrent chronic low back pain. This program has been found to decrease disability and improve attitudes toward self-management (Von Korff, 1998).

CONCLUSION

This chapter has presented four aspects of the 22-year history of the ASMP. In Part I, the research history of the program with a brief overview of the major studies and their conclusions was presented. In Part II, details of the self-management model were discussed with an attempt to differentiate self-management from more traditional patient education courses. In Part III, some examples of dissemination case histories were provided. Finally, in Part IV, a few visions for the future were offered. Self-management for chronic conditions is very much an emerging movement. Over the past 22 years, we have learned much about self-management. At the same time, our health care delivery system has changed. As we enter the 21st century, self-management has a major role to play in helping individuals and the health care system meet the growing challenges of chronic illness. Everyone has a role to play. Health care systems must support self-management programs by providing staffing to coordinate the programs. Health care professionals must support self-management in their daily encounters with patients. Finally, patients must take on the role of proactively managing their disease. It is our hope that in the future all patients with chronic conditions will have access to appropriate self-management programs and that these programs will become a part of standard treatment.

ACKNOWLEDGMENTS

The author would like to acknowledge the several thousand study participants, hundreds of lay-leaders, and the many research

assistants and students who have made this work possible. Special
thanks to Diana Laurent and Virginia González and to our funding sources The National Institute of Arthritis, Musculoskeletal
and Skin Diseases, The National Institute of Nursing Research,
The Agency for Health Care Policy and Research, The California
Tobacco-Related Disease Program, The National Arthritis Foundation
and the Northern California Chapter of the Arthritis Foundation,
and the Robert Wood Johnson Clinical Scholar Program.

REFERENCES

Antonovsky, A. (1980). *Health stress and coping.* San Francisco: Jossey-Bass
    Publishers.
Antonovsky, A. (1987). *Unraveling the mystery of health.* San Francisco:
    Jossey-Bass Publishers.
Arthritis Foundation (1994). *Systemic lupus crythematosus self-help course;
    Leader's manual.* [Manual].
Arthritis Foundation (1997). *Fibromyalgia self-help course: Course leader's
    manual.* [Manual].
Bandura, A. (1977). Self-efficacy toward a unifying theory of behavioral
    change. *Psychology Review, 84*(2), 191–215.
Bandura, A. (1997). *Self-efficacy: The exercise of control.* New York: W.H.
    Freeman and Company.
Campbell, B., Sengupta, S., Santos, C., & Lorig, K. (1995). Balanced
    incomplete block design: Description, case study, and implications
    for practice. *Health Education Quarterly, 22*(2), 201–210.
Corbin, J. & Strauss, A. (1988). *Unending work and care: Managing chronic
    illness at home.* San Francisco: Jossey-Bass Publishers.
González, V. M., Nacif de Brey, V., Lorig, K. R., & Fries, J. F. (1997). *Cómo
    convivir con su artritis: Una guía para una vida activa y saludable [Living
    with arthritis: A guide for an active and healthy life].* Palo Alto: Bull
    Publishing.
Harmer, B., & Henderson, V. (1958). *The Textbook of the principles and prac-
    tice of nursing* (5th ed.). New York: Macmillan Company.
Lazarus, R., & Folkman, S. (1984). *Stress appraisal and coping.* New York:
    Springer Publishing Company.
Lenker, S., Lorig, K., & Gallagher, D. (1984). Reasons for the lack of asso-
    ciation between changes in health behavior and improved health sta-
    tus: An explanatory study. *Patient Education Counsel, 6*(2), 69–72.
Lorig, K. (1992). *Arthritis self-management leader's manual (revised).* Atlanta:
    Arthritis Foundation.

Lorig, K., Cox, T., Cuevas, Y., Kraines, R., & Britton, M. (1984). Converging and diverging beliefs about arthritis: Caucasian patients, Spanish-speaking patients and physicians. *Journal of Rheumatology, 11*(1), 76–79.

Lorig, K., Feigenbaum, P., Regan, C., Ung, E., & Holman, H. (1986). A comparison of lay-taught and professional-taught arthritis self-management courses. *Journal of Rheumatology, 13*(4), 763–767.

Lorig, K., & Fries, J. (2000). *The arthritis helpbook.* Cambridge, MA: Perseus Books.

Lorig, K., & González, V. (1992). The integration of theory with practice: A 12 year case study. *Health Education Quarterly, 19*(3), 355–368.

Lorig, K., González, V. M., Laurent, D. D., Morgan, L., & Laris, B.A. (1998). Arthritis self-management program variations: 3 studies. *Arthritis Care and Research, 11*(6), 448–454.

Lorig, K., González, V. M., Ritter, P. (1999). Community-based Spanish language arthritis education program: A randomized trial. *Medical Care, 37*(9), 957–963.

Lorig, K., & Holman, H. (1989). Long-term outcomes of an arthritis self-management study: Effects of reinforcement efforts. *Social Science and Medicine, 29,* 221–224.

Lorig, K., Lubeck, D., Kraines, R., Seleznick, M., & Holman, H. (1985). Outcomes of self-help education for patients with arthritis. *Arthritis and Rheumatism, 28*(6), 680–685.

Lorig, K., Mazonson, P., & Holman, H. (1993). Evidence suggesting that health education for self-management in patients with chronic arthritis has sustained health benefits while reducing health care costs. *Arthritis and Rheumatism 36*(4), 439–446.

Lorig, K., Seleznick, M., Lubeck, D., Ung, E., Chastain, R., & Holman, H. (1989). The beneficial outcomes of the arthritis self-management course are not adequately explained by behavior change. *Arthritis and Rheumatism, 32*(1), 91–95.

Lorig, K., Ung, E., Chastain, R., Shoor, S., & Holman, H. (1989). Development and evaluation of a scale to measure perceived self-efficacy in people with arthritis. *Arthritis and Rheumatism, 32*(1), 37–44.

Lorig, K., Sobel, D. S., Stewart, A. L., Brown, W.B. Jr., Bandura, A., Ritter, P., González, V. M., Laurent, D. D., & Holman, H. R. (1999a). Evidence suggesting that a chronic disease self-management program can improve health status while reducing hospitalization: A randomized trial. *Medical Care, 37*(1), 5–14.

Lorig, K. González, V., Ritter, P. (1999b). Community-based Spanish language arthritis education program: A randomized trial. *Medical Care, 37,* 957–963.

Miller, G. (1956). The magical number seven, plus or minus two: Some limits on our capacity for processing information. *Psychological Review, 63,* 81–97.

Regan, C. (1994). Time for healing: Relaxation for mind and body. [Audio tape]. Palo Alto: Stanford Patient Education Research Center.

Regan, C. A. (1990). Appraisal and coping in older persons with osteoarthritis. *School of Education.* Standford University.

Von Korff, M., Moore, J.E., Lorig, K., Cherkin, D.C., Saunders, K., González, V., Laurent, D., Rutter, C., & Comite, F. (1998). A randomized trail of a lay-led self-management group intervention for back pain patients in primary care. *Spine, 23*(23), 2608–2615.

Wallston, B., Wallston, K., Kaplan, G., & Maides, S. (1976). Development and validation of the Health Locus of Control (HLC) scale. *Journal of Consulting and Clinical Psychology, 44*(14), 580–585.

Webster's II (1984). Houghton Mifflin Company.

CHAPTER 4

Oral Health

Ronald L. Ettinger

In the recent past, the elderly population comprised a relatively small proportion of the population and the majority of these people were edentulous. These individuals utilized dental care infrequently and then only when previous unmet needs could no longer be ignored (Burt, Ismail, Morrison, & Beltran, 1990; Ettinger, 1971). Now however, there is ample evidence to show that a new group of dental consumers have emerged who are better educated, more politically aware, and more importantly, many of them have some remaining natural teeth. As patients, these people have a wider range of needs and expectations and are demanding a greater variety of services than the previous emphasis on complete dentures (Ettinger & Beck, 1982).

The elderly have been defined as a cohort of people aged 65 years or older. It became clear that a chronological definition of the aging population was not particularly useful in dentistry. Thus we developed a functional definition which categorized the aging population into three groups based upon their ability to seek services (Ettinger & Beck, 1984). The groups are:

a. the functionally independent older adult
b. the frail older adult, and
c. the functionally dependent older adult.

It became apparent that different older adults had different needs and that their functional disabilities affected their ability to accept and/or receive dental treatment. In this chapter some of the specific oral needs and problems and preventive interventions applicable for each group will be identified.

Utilization of Oral Health Services

It can be shown that as a population ages, visits to physicians increase, whereas visits to dentists tend to decrease (Atchison, Mayer-Oakes, Schweitzer, Lubben, DeJong et al., 1993; Ettinger, 1993; Health Care Financing Administration, 1996; National Center for Health Statistics, 1988). These findings can be attributed to an increased risk of chronic systemic diseases as one ages, as well as an increased rate of edentulousness associated with aging. The attitudes of older adults toward the importance of oral health and a lack of availability of third party payment systems for dental services may also be significant factors (Ettinger, 1993). Data from the U.S. National Health Study (United States Department of Health and Human Services, 1987) during 1985–86 indicated that 58.5% of employed adults aged 18 to 64 had visited a dentist within the last 12 months while 54.5% of dentate adults older than age 65 had visited a dentist in the same time period. However, only 13% of edentulous adults over age 65 had such a visit (Figure 4.1). The majority (62.2%), of these edentulous older adults had not utilized the services of a dentist for at least 3 years. Therefore, older persons with some natural teeth were using dental services in a manner similar to employed adults during 1985 and 1986. It seems that the differences in utilization of dental health services which have usually been attributed to aging were not related to age, but rather to the absence of a natural dentition. It also has been shown that the value older adults place on dental care seems to influence utilization more than any other factor, including ability to pay for care (Evashwick, Conrad, & Lee, 1982; Kiyak, 1984).

In the United States, the accepted stereotype has been that most older adults are in need of multiple extractions or are edentulous. As a result, the fabrication of complete dentures has been synonymous with the needs of elderly patients (Burt, 1978; Ettinger, 1993). This common stereotype suggested that as individuals age there was an increasing requirement for dentures and a decreased requirement for all other forms of dental treatment. This stereotype is changing, as the public's attitudes are improving, but health behaviors still need to be modified, for the need for dental care is irrelevant to program planning unless it can be translated into a demand for care.

Over 5 million persons over the age of 65 have limitation with at least one activity of daily living (ADL: bathing, dressing, use of

Length of Time Since Last Dental Visit NIDR – USA – (1985–1986)

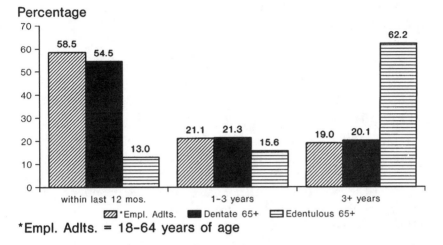

*Empl. Adlts. = 18–64 years of age

Figure 4.1 Bar graph showing the length of time since the last dental visit by dental status for the non-institutionalized population of the United States (1985–86). The employed adults include both dentate and edentulous persons and are compared with dentate and edentulous persons aged 65 and older.

the toilet, feeding, mobility) and one instrumental activity of daily living; (IADL: shopping, use of telephone, housework, handling finance, cooking, taking medications) (Leon & Lai, 1990). Many of these individuals have problems with their ability to clean their teeth. Currently, little is known about the oral health and needs of these community-dwelling frail older adults as they tend to selectively remove themselves from most dental epidemiological studies (Strayer, 1993). These persons seem to only seek care if they are in pain.

For functionally dependent older adults who are institutionalized, even though studies have consistently shown that their oral health is very poor and many individuals are in need of dental care, very few seek dental services (Berkey, Berg, Ettinger, & Meskin, 1991). There is very limited information on persons who are homebound, except that dental care is only sought for them if they are in discomfort or pain (Strayer, 1993). One explanation may be provided by Davis (1981), who stated for disadvantaged groups with folk memories of emergency dental treatment, and confronted with continuing physical and economic barriers to care, the development of preventive styles of dental visiting and treatment make little sense.

Oral Health Problems

Edentulousness (Complete Loss of Teeth)

Tooth loss is the dental equivalent of mortality. It is the end product of oral disease but also reflects the attitudes of patients and providers, availability and accessibility of care, and the teaching philosophies of dental treatment at various times in the past (Weintraub & Burt, 1985). However, it is now accepted that tooth loss is not a consequence of normal aging. The number and percentage of edentulous older adults has declined consistently over the last 30 years. The greatest decline has occurred among those aged 55 to 64 year olds in the time period between 1960 and 1985 (Ainamo, 1983; Marcus, Joshi, Jones, & Morgano, 1996; Meskin, Brown, Brunelle & Warren, 1988; Weintraub & Burt, 1985) (Figure 4.2). The most recent data comes from the 1991 New England Elders Dental Study (NEEDS) (Marcus et al., 1996), which found that 36.7% of persons over age 70 were completely edentulous, which is significantly lower than the 46.3% reported by NIDR in 1985–86 (United States Department of Health & Human Services, 1987).

These changes in edentulousness may be explained by the changing values and attitudes to dentistry of various age cohorts. These attitudes have been influenced by the technological advances in restorative dentistry such as development of effective local anesthesia, the emergence of the high speed handpiece, by fluoridation of water supplies, and by an increasing prosperity of society which includes third party payment of dental care. The attitude of dentists has also changed from one of extraction and replacement with complete dentures, to one of restoration and maintenance of teeth and more recently to prevention and restoration of function and esthetics (Burt, 1978; Ettinger, 1993).

Even though edentulousness is increasing, it has been estimated that the total number of edentulous elderly will remain constant at 9 million a year until the year 2020 (Douglass & Furino, 1990) (Table 4.1). However, edentulousness is still associated more

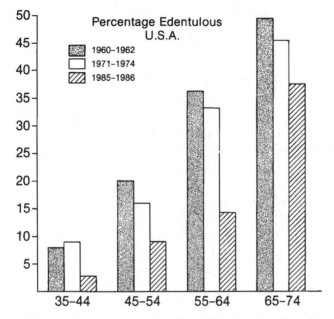

Figure 4.2 Bar graph comparing data from three national studies of edentulousness in various age groups over three decades in the United States.

frequently with lower socioeconomic groups and is strongly influenced by education, place of residence, geographic region, and cultural factors. In the 1991 NEEDS study (Marcus et al., 1996), edentulousness was still found to be negatively related to both education and income levels. The authors go on to say lack of

TABLE 4.1 Edentulous Persons in the USA: Projections

Year	% Edentulous	Population aged 65+ in millions	Edentulous population aged 65+ in millions
1980	35%	27	9
2000	25%	36	9
2020	15%	60	9

Adapted from: Douglass, C. W. and Furino, A. (1990). Balancing dental service requirements and supplies: Epidemiologic and demographic evidence. *J Am Dent Assoc, 121,* 587–592.

education about the importance of oral health, the need for preventive services, and the consequences of neglect appears to contribute a significant barrier to dental health care.

Periodontal Disease (Gum Disease)

Periodontal disease is an infectious disease caused by the colonization of the plaque on the teeth by potentially pathogenic organisms. The daily removal of plaque thus becomes the prime preventive measure to preserve oral health. It was accepted that in older adults periodontal disease was widespread and severe, that the prevalence of caries was low, and that most older adults were in need of multiple extractions or were edentulous. These beliefs were supported by early epidemiologic studies of dental patients which suggested that gingivitis progressed with time to periodontitis and that once periodontitis was established, tooth loss was absolutely inevitable (Page, 1995). However, concepts related to the universality of progressive periodontal disease have changed. For instance, more recent studies (Goodson, Haffajee, Socransky, 1984; Goodson, Tanner, Haffajee, Sornberger, & Socransky, 1982; Haffajee, Socransky, & Goodson, 1983; Haffajee, Socransky, Linde, Kent, Okamoto et al., 1991; Page, 1995) have shown that comparatively few older individuals harbor the majority of tooth sites with progressive periodontal disease. These data came from studying untreated patients with pocketing and it showed that progression at any given site occurred infrequently and usually at a slow rate except in a small group of "susceptible individuals." (Badersten, Nilveus, & Egelberg, 1990; Becker, Berg, & Becker, 1979; Lindhe, Haffajee, & Socransky, 1983). In these "susceptible individuals," the loss of attachment has been found to increase only 20 to 30% during periods varying in length from 1 to 5 years (Goodson, 1992; Jeffcoat & Reddy, 1991; Lang, Joss, Orsanic, Gusberti, & Siegrist, 1986; Vanooteghem, Hutchens, Garrett, Kiger, & Egelberg, 1987; Wennström, Dahlen, Svensson, & Nyman, 1987). Susceptible individuals are those with diagnostic signs and symptoms such as bleeding on probing, probing depths of 6 mms, and the presence of certain periopathogens.

The clinical implication is that we still cannot easily identify the "at risk population" but need to follow all older adults carefully to determine who is at risk. Nevertheless, it appears that mild forms of gingivitis and periodontal pocketing affect almost all of the aging population. A much smaller proportion of elderly population (less than 10%) is at risk for advanced periodontal disease, which has been defined as persons who have at least one tooth which has bone loss greater than one-third of the supporting periodontal tissues (Beck, Koch, & Offenbacher, 1994; Hunt, 1986). These data indicate that the majority of elderly people need scaling and routine periodontal treatment which can be carried out by a dental hygienist or dentist, but only a small minority need complex treatment from a specialist periodontist.

Persons who are functionally dependent because of physical frailty, mental confusion, or dementia are at the highest risk for periodontal disease because of their inability to maintain oral hygiene independently. Prevention of disease for them depends upon caregivers or significant others being trained and motivated to maintain their oral health, otherwise disease will be inevitable (Berkey et al., 1991; Strayer, 1993).

Caries (Decay)

Caries also is a bacterial infection of teeth caused by colonization of the plaque but by different microorganisms which are acidogenic. Caries is influenced by the combination of the virulence of the acidogenic bacteria in the mouth, the acidogenic potential of the pattern of food intake, the ability of the individual to maintain oral hygiene, as well as the inherent resistance of the teeth to demineralization (MacEntee, 1994). The United States, like a number of other industrialized societies, can be characterized by a decreased caries rate in children and an increasing caries rate in the aging population. In fact, it can be shown that the incidence of caries in a population aged 65 and older is greater than in a population of 14 year olds living in a non-fluoridated area (Hand, Hunt, & Beck, 1988; Klein, Bohannan, Bell, Disney, Foch et al., 1985). The studies which have evaluated the aging population have found that untreated caries was most commonly found on the crowns of the teeth (25%) although a substantial number (18%) also had root caries (Heft & Gilbert, 1991) A longitudinal study of caries in older adults has found that over 3 years, caries developed on an average of 2.4 coronal surfaces and 1.1 root surfaces per person per year (Hand et al., 1988) Persons who are functionally frail and are unable to manage oral hygiene independently were more likely than non-institutionalized older adults to be edentulous and to have fewer filled teeth (Slade, Locker, Leake, Price, & Chao, 1990). The increased prevalence of caries in the older population can be attributed to an increase in the number of risk factors which include poor oral hygiene, loss of periodontal attachment exposing more root surfaces, increased use of potentially xerostomic medications, lack of access to dental service, and a lack of understanding or compliance with preventive behaviors.

A summary of the existing data suggests that caries can be found in over 95% of the elderly population. Those at highest risk are persons who are physically frail or mentally confused and the majority of these persons are homebound or institutionalized. A major difficulty for the dentist is the question of whether it is appropriate to simply restore the teeth of older adults without making sure that they get help to manage their diet or their personal oral hygiene. There is good evidence that topical fluoride use can remineralize early carious lesions, and that the use of antimicrobials rinses such as chlorhexidine can reduce the number of acidogenic bacteria. Also, the use of sugar substitutes will reduce the acidogenic environment of the plaque on the teeth (Bowen, Young, & Pearson, 1990; Clark, Morgan, & MacEntee, 1991; Heifetz, 1994; Jensen & Kohout, 1988; Ripa, Leske, Forte, & Varma, 1987). The enduring problem remains, how does one educate the older adult population and especially, how does one educate and motivate the significant others or caregivers of frail and functionally dependent older adults, to perform oral hygiene for them regularly.

Oral Mucosal Lesions

The health and integrity of the oral cavity is dependent on an intact mucosa protecting the tissues beneath it from desiccation, infection and chemical, thermal and mechanical injury. The mucosa must be able to impede ingress of noxious or infectious material, to respond to injury, and to mount an effective inflammatory and immune response to deal with any materials or organisms which may penetrate the barrier (Ettinger, 1994).

The clinical changes which have been often associated with aging are more likely to be related to the expression of oral manifestations of systemic disease (e.g., blood dyscrasias and endocinopathy), poor nutritional status (e.g., vitamin deficiencies, iron, or zinc deficiency), pharmacological side effects and oral infections. Traumatic injuries can also be a factor. The loss of teeth and denture wearing seems to be one of the more common factors associated with changes in the oral mucosa of elderly persons. The changes induced are mucosal inflammatory changes such as diffuse and granular denture stomatitis, hyperplastic lesions, and atrophic changes. A strong relationship has been shown between the inflammatory changes of stomatitis and the presence of *candida albicans*. Dentures which are worn continuously and not kept adequately clean develop a plaque which becomes colonized by a variety of organisms including *candida albicans*. These organisms produce toxins which induce an inflammatory response in the mucosa (diffuse stomatitis), sometimes with an associated hyperplasia (granular denture stomatitis/inflammatory papillary hyperplasia) (Budtz-Jorgensen, 1981; Ettinger, 1975; Iacopino & Wathen, 1992; Jeganathan & Lin, 1992). The prevalence of denture stomatitis in older populations varies greatly but has been shown to affect at least 20% of that population wearing dentures (Axtell, 1976; Hand & Whitehill, 1986; Mikkonen, Nyssonen, Paunio, & Rajala, 1984; Moskona & Kaplan, 1992; Österberg, Öhman, Heyden, & Svanborg, 1985). Angular chelitis is often associated with both the diffuse and granular forms of denture stomatitis. It does not seem as prevalent as denture stomatitis and has been described as having a multifactorial etiology (Cawson, 1963; Ohman, Dahlen, Moller, & Ohman, 1986; Rose, 1968).

The continuous resorption of the residual ridges beneath dentures results in slow change in the fit of the dentures over time. If the oral mucosa is stimulated by low grade chronic irritation, it responds by a hyperplastic reaction (Nordenram & Landt, 1969; Watson & McDonald, 1982). The most common site is the periphery of complete dentures especially in the mandibular arch where support is poor and the rate of resorption is four times greater than the maxilla. Occurrence among older subjects (age 60 and older) has been reported to be higher with an odds ratio of 2.47 (Silverglade & Stablein, 1988; Skinner & Weir, 1987; Weir, Davenport, & Skinner, 1987). If the trauma becomes greater, the tissues will either ulcerate or they may hyperkeratose to form white patches in the mouth (leukoplakia). These areas of ulceration and hyperkeratosis have the potential to undergo malignant transformation. The rate of change, that is period prevalence of malignant transformation for leukoplakia, varies from 4 to 6% with follow-up periods of 3–20 years (Banoczy & Sugar, 1972; Kramer, el-Labban, & Lee, 1978;

Kramer, Lucas, el-Labban, & Lister, 1970; Lind, 1987; Pindborg, Joslt, Renstrup, & Roed-Petersen, 1968; Silverman, Gorsky, & Lozada, 1984; Waldron & Shafer, 1975). However, the transformation of these kinds of denture induced lesions is unknown. In the United States, the estimated incidence for oral cancer for 1997 will be 30,750 new cases and 8,440 deaths from oral cancer. The majority of these persons will be aged 55 to 74 years (Parker, Tong, Bolden, & Wingo, 1997).

Many older persons are likely to have chronic diseases, most of which are age dependent and so the prevalence of drug treatment increases in complexity with advancing years. These medications also may have a direct effect on the oral mucosa by causing hyposalivation or xerostomia, bleeding diseases of the tissues, lichenoid reactions, tissue overgrowth, and hypersenstivity reactions (Baker & Ettinger, 1985, Baker, Levy, & Chrischilles, 1991; Levy, Baker, Semla, & Kohout, 1988; Parker et al., 1997; Seymour, 1988; Sreebny & Schwartz, 1986) (Tables 4.2 and 4.3). Therefore, an annual oral examination of the soft and hard tissues must be incorporated as a routine preventive measure for all elderly persons.

Treatment Need

Dental care for the majority of older adults often has been an ongoing process in which a dental practitioner maintains a heavily restored dentition using conservative, conventional restorative techniques. Preventive therapies have not been a significant part of such a treatment regimen (Douglass & Gammon, 1985; Gordon, 1989; Reinhardt & Douglass, 1989). A key preventive assessment a dentist needs to make is, what level of ability does an older adult patient have to maintain oral hygiene independently, as it influences the level of treatment which is appropriate for that patient. Many older adults have never been taught how to adequately clean their dentition. Even if they have a significant other/caregiver to do it for them, the teeth may not be cleaned. Most caregivers have never been shown how to care for another person's oral health. Older adults often do not understand that the primary function of toothbrushing is to reduce plaque levels in the mouth. Many older adults have not had their mouths professionally cleaned, or if they have, then only infrequently.

It has been shown that in the United States, more than 60% of the population over the age of 65 years have some remaining

TABLE 4.2   Medications with Potential Oral Side Effects

	Non-Institutionalized* N = 3217	Institutionalized** N = 481
Xerostomia	50.9%	73.9%
Abnormal hemostasis	39.1%	39.1%
Lichenoid reactions	28.2%	49.7%
Need to minimize:		
Vasoconstrictor use	19.7%	38.1%
Altered host resistance	7.1%	14.6%
Movement disorders	2.1%	22.2%
Gingival overgrowth	1.0%	5.6%

Modified from:
* Levy, S. M. et al. (1988). Use of medications with dental significance by a non-institutionalized elderly population. *Gerodontics, 4,* 119–125.
** Baker, K. A. et al. (1991). Medications with dental significance: Usage in a nursing home population. *Spec. Care Dent, 11,* 19–25.

natural teeth (Douglass & Gammon, 1985; Gordon, 1989; Reinhardt & Douglass, 1989) (Table 4.4). As long as these individuals remain healthy, few problems occur which cannot be solved. However, what happens when such a patient becomes medically impaired, physically disabled, or cognitively impaired? The planning of their oral care now requires the dentist, the family or caretakers, and the physician to work together with the rest of the health care team to plan prevention and treatment which is in the best interest of the patient (Ettinger, 1990).

The major oral diseases, caries and periodontal disease, can be prevented by daily oral hygiene programs which remove plaque. Therefore, any preventive program must target the education of elderly consumers and their families. When older adults become frail or functionally dependent and are homebound or institutionalized they will need help from other family members or their caretakers in maintaining oral health (Ettinger, 1992).

Nurses and Nurses Aides

Most of the day-to-day care in long-term care (LTC) facilities is provided by nurse's aides. In nursing, there has been no tradition of maintaining oral and dental health care, as there has been with

TABLE 4.3   Medications with Potential Xerostomic Side Effects

	Non-institutionalized* *N = 3217*	*Institutionalized*** *N = 481*
Diuretics: Lasix®, Dyazide®	39.0%	50.7%
Antihypertensive: Inderal®, Catapres®	20.0%	11.0%
Antihistamine/Decongestants:		
Benadryl®, Actifed®, Dimetapp®	5.3%	13.1%
Antidepressants: Elavil®, Tofranil®	3.8%	11.7%
Bronchodilators: Theodur®*, Brethine®	2.9%	3.9%
Gastointestinals: Pro-Banthine®, Librax®	2.8%	4.0%
Antipsychotics: Mellaril®, Throrazine®	1.1%	16.8%

Modified from:
* Levy, S. M. et al. (1988). Use of medications with dental significance by a non-institutionalized elderly population. *Gerodontics, 4,* 119–125.
** Baker, K. A. et al. (1991). Medications with dental significance: Usage in a nursing home population. *Spec. Care Dent, 11,* 19–25.

other personal hygiene and medical needs. Nursing aides working in LTC institutions often are busy because the facility is understaffed and they may not be adequately reimbursed. In many institutions nursing aides are not rewarded or penalized for not helping the residents with their personal oral hygiene (Benson, Maibusch, & Zimmer, 1980; Buckwalter, Eldredge, McLeran, Bitterman, Levin et al., 1986; Hunt, 1987). Consequently, dental care is only sought for residents when they complain of pain. When the majority of the residents were edentulous and had an oral problem, the nursing staff removed their dentures and the residents ate a soft diet. This did not harm the residents physically, but it certainly deprived them of the emotional pleasure of chewing. But, the majority of older individuals now have some natural teeth, so if they have discomfort or pain they need the services of a dentist.

It is clear that oral health as part of the overall care of patients needs to be emphasized. A review of the nursing literature suggests that there is an awareness of the importance of oral health and some authors have encouraged nurses to be sensitive to the

TABLE 4.4   Projections for Number of Persons Number of Teeth and Teeth Per Person

Year	Persons over 65 in millions	No. of teeth in millions	Teeth/person
1990	31.7	369	20.3
2030	64.6	933	25.9
Percent increase	104%	153%	28%

Adapted from Reinhardt, J. W., & Douglass, C. W. (1989). The need for operative dentistry services: Projecting the effects of changing disease patterns. *Opt Dent, 14,* 114–120.

oral problems of their patients. For instance, Ginsberg (1961) stated that patients benefited most from mouth care procedures which were tailored to their individual needs. Gannon and Kadezabek (1980) suggested that even patients with good home oral hygiene habits needed support with brushing and flossing when they become ill. They stated that it was one of the nurse's tasks to motivate patients by reminding them to take care of their mouths, and they believed most patients who could, would do so. A number of authors in the past two decades have reported on oral hygiene techniques that could be used by nurses caring for their patients, but the recommendations lack consistency and appear infrequently in the literature (Bersani & Carl, 1983; Blaney, 1986; Danielson, 1988; Longman & DeWalt, 1986; Meckstroth, 1989; Winkley, Brown, & Stone, 1993). In addition, it has been suggested that the training nurses receive in oral health care, has not been standardized (Gannon & Kadezabek, 1980). Schweiger, Lang, and Schweiger (1980) suggested that the reason nurses do not routinely consider their patient's oral health status is due to a lack of understanding and awareness. In a recent study, Logan, Ettinger, McLeran, and Casko (1991) evaluated the dental knowledge and attitudes of 703 nurses and nurses aides in 129 agencies caring for homebound elderly persons. Over half (54%) did not feel comfortable with their knowledge about oral health. Over 35% missed 10 items out of 60 in a knowledge questionnaire. These items related to the use of dentures, and recognition of oral cancer, as well as knowing the oral side effects of commonly used drugs, such as the xerostomic potential of antidepressants. The results of this study suggest that the particular oral health problems of the homebound and institutionalized should be regularly presented by dentists or hygienists to nursing personnel caring for such individuals.

Physicians

Historically, the health care of older individuals has been coordinated by physicians, and dentistry falls outside of their sphere of direct control (Ettinger, 1992). This circumstance has been perpetuated by the fact that rarely are medical and dental students trained together nor are physicians trained to recognize oral problems or oral lesions. Often medications used by physicians to treat many of the chronic diseases associated with aging have direct oral side effects (Baker & Ettinger, 1985; Baker et al., 1991; Levy et al., 1988) (Table 4.3). When patients complain to their physicians about these side effects, such as dry mouth, their complaints are ignored (Table 4.4). It is possible with the help of a pharmacologist to ask the physician to change the drug, to modify the dose, or if that is not possible, then for the dentist to treat the xerostomia with saliva substitutes and other therapies (Ettinger, 1996). Education of physicians to recognize oral lesions and refer patients to the dentist for joint treatment must become a priority.

Dentists

There have been many financial disincentives for dentists to care for elderly patients because of low levels of reimbursement and a paucity of third party coverage. Further, many older patients require more time to treat and, for many frail or institutionalized patients, care must be carried out in their residential homes with portable equipment which most dentists do not possess and have not been trained to use.

A report by MacEntee, Weiss, Waxler-Morrison, and Morrison (1984) summarized the attitudes of dentists and their reasons for caring, or refusing to care, for residents in long-term care facilities. Only 19% had provided treatment for patients in a LTC. The main reasons for not providing care reported were:

55%   -   Had never been asked
33%   -   Too busy to leave the office
33%   -   No or poor treatment facilities in the LTC

25%	-	Felt inadequately trained
54%	-	Level of financial reimbursement was too low
56%	-	Required encroachment on their leisure time

National surveys in the United States have identified that most U.S. dental schools report that they now have geriatric curricula with some extracurricular experiences (Beck & Ettinger, 1987; Moshman, Warren, Blanford, & Aumack, 1985). In 1985, an assessment was made of the comprehensive program in Iowa which had been in existence for 5 years. The dentists who had clinical geriatric training were more likely to be practicing in larger population centers and more likely to be carrying out comprehensive dental care in long-term care institutions (Ettinger, McLeran, & Jacobsen, 1990).

CONCLUSION

Dental and oral diseases may be the most prevalent and the most preventable conditions affecting older Americans. Preventive intervention is relatively simple; that is, the daily removal of plaque with food debris from the teeth or from dentures by the subject or his/her caretaker. In addition, a yearly examination by a dentist to diagnose soft tissue lesions or potentially malignant changes is a necessity. However, elderly persons and the health care professions have not been socialized to recognize these oral health needs.

REFERENCES

Ainamo, J. (1983). Changes in the frequency of edentulousness and use of removable dentures in the adult population of Finland, 1970–1980. *Community Dentistry and Oral Epidemiology, 11*(2), 122–126.

Atchison, K. A., Mayer-Oakes, S. A., Schweitzer, S. O., Lubben, J. E., De Jong, F. J., & Matthias, R. E. (1993). The relationship between dental utilization and preventive participation among a well-elderly sample. *Journal of Public Health Dentistry, 53*(2), 88–95.

Axell, T. (1976). The prevalence study of oral mucosal lesions in an adult Swedish population. *Odontologisk Revy, 27* (Suppl 36), 1–103.

Badersten, A., Nilveus, R., & Egelberg, J. (1990). Effect of nonsurgical periodontal therapy VII: Bleeding, suppuration and probing depth in sites with probing attachment loss. *Journal of Clinical Periodontology*, *17*(2), 102–107.

Baker, K. A., & Ettinger, R. L. (1985). Intra-oral effects of drugs in elderly persons. *Gerodontics*, *1*(3), 111–116.

Baker, K. A., Levy, S. M., & Chrischilles, E. A. (1991). Medications with dental significance: Usage in a nursing home population. *Special Care in Dentistry*, *11*(1), 19–25.

Banoczy, J., & Sugar, L. (1972). Longitudinal studies in oral leukoplakias. *Journal of Oral Pathology*, *1*(6), 265–272.

Beck, J. D., & Ettinger, R. L. (1987). The development of geriatric curricula in US Dental Schools 1979–1984. *Journal of Dental Education*, *51*(9), 523–527.

Beck, J. D., Koch, G. G., & Offenbacher, S. (1994). Attachment loss trends over 3 years in community-dwelling older adults. *Journal of Periodontology*, *65*(8), 737–743.

Becker, W., Berg, L., & Becker, B. E. (1979). Untreated periodontal disease: A longitudinal study. *Journal of Periodontology*, *50*(5), 234–244.

Benson, C. M., Maibusch, R., & Zimmer, S. E. (1980). Oral health of hospitalized patients, part I, an overview of oral hygiene nursing care. *Dental Hygienist*, *54*(8), 384–386.

Berkey, D. B., Berg, R. G., Ettinger, R. L., & Meskin, L. H. (1991). Research review of oral health status and service use among institutionalized older adults in the United States and Canada. *Special Care in Dentistry*, *11*(4), 131–136.

Bersani, G., & Carl, W. (1983). Oral care for cancer patients. *American Journal of Nursing*, *83*(4), 533–536.

Blaney, G. M. (1986). Mouth care—basic and essential. *Geriatric Nursing*, *7*(5), 242–243.

Bowen, W. H., Young, D. A., & Pearson, S. K. (1990). The effects of sucralose on coronal and root-surface caries. *Journal of Dental Research*, *69*(8), 1485–1487.

Buckwalter, K. C., Eldredge, J. B., McLeran, H., Bitterman, B. J., Levin, B., & Pynn, M. F. (1986). Nursing and dental hygiene for the elderly. *Family and Community Health*, *9*(2), 73–75.

Budtz-Jorgensen, E. (1981). Oral mucosal lesions associated with the wearing of removable dentures. *Journal of Oral Pathology*, *10*(2), 65–80.

Burt, R. A. (1978). Influences for change in the dental health status of populations: An historical perspective. *Journal of Public Health Dentistry*, *38*(4), 272–278.

Burt, B. A., Ismail, A. I., Morrison, E. C., & Beltran, E. D. (1990). Risk factors for tooth loss over a 28-year period. *Journal of Dental Research*, *69*(5), 1126–1130.

Cawson, R. A. (1963). Denture sore mouth and angular cheilitis (Oral Candidiasis in adults). *British Dental Journal*, *115*, 441–449.

Clark, D. C., Morgan, J., & MacEntee, M. I. (1991). Effects of a 1 percent chlorhexidine gel on the cariogenic bacteria in high risk elders. *Special Care in Dentistry, 11*(3), 101–103.

Danielson, K. H. (1988). Oral care and older adults. *Journal of Gerontological Nursing, 14*(11), 6–9.

Davis, P. (1981). Culture, inequality and patterns of dental care in New Zealand. *Social Sciences in Medicine, 15A*(6), 801–805.

Douglass, C. W., & Furino, A. (1990). Balancing dental service requirements and supplies: Epidemologic and demographic evidence. *Journal of the American Dental Association, 121*(6), 587–592.

Douglass, C. W., & Gammon, M. D. (1985). Implications of oral disease trends for the treatment needs of older adults. *Gerodontics, 1*(2), 51–58.

Ettinger, R. L. (1971). An evaluation of the attitudes of a group of elderly edentulous patients to dentists, dentures and dentistry. *Dental Practitioner and Dental Record, 22*(3), 85–91.

Ettinger, R. L. (1975). The etiology of inflammatory papillary hyperplasia. *Journal of Prosthetic Dentistry, 34*, 254–261.

Ettinger, R. L. (1990). Restoring the ageing dentition: repair or replacement. *International Dental Journal, 40*(5), 275–282.

Ettinger, R. L. (1992). Oral care for the homebound and the institutionalized. *Clinics in Geriatric Medicine, 8*(3), 659–672.

Ettinger, R. L. (1993). Cohort differences among aging populations: A challenge for the dental profession. *Special Care in Dentistry, 13*(1), 19–26.

Ettinger, R. L. (1994). Clinical manifestations of oral mucosal aging. In C. A. Squier & M. W. Hill (Eds.), *The Effect of Aging in Oral Mucosa and Skin* (pp. 15–23). Boca Raton: C.R.C. Press.

Ettinger, R. L. (1996). Review: Xerostomia: A symptom which acts like a disease. *Age and Aging, 25*(5), 409–412.

Ettinger, R. L., & Beck, J. D. (1982). The new elderly: What can the dental profession expect? *Special Care in Dentistry, 2*(2), 62–69.

Ettinger, R. L., & Beck, J. D. (1984). Geriatric dental curriculum and the needs of the elderly. *Special Care in Dentistry, 4*(5), 207–213.

Ettinger, R. L., McLeran, H., & Jacobsen, J. (1990). Effect of a geriatric educational experience on graduates' activities and attitudes. *Journal of Dental Education, 54*(5), 273–278.

Evashwick, C., Conrad, D., & Lee, F. (1982). Factors related to utilization of dental services by the elderly. *American Journal of Public Health, 72*(10), 1129–1135.

Gannon, E. L., & Kadezabek, E. (1980). Meticulous mouth care. *Nursing, 10*(3), 70–75.

Ginsberg, M. K. A. (1961). A study of oral hygiene nursing care. *American Journal of Nursing, 61*, 67–69.

Goodson, J. M. (1992). Diagnosis of periodontitis by physical measurement: Interpretation from the episodic disease hypothesis. *Journal of Periodontology, 63*(4 suppl), 373–382.

Goodson, J. M., Haffajee, A. D., & Socransky, S. S. (1984). The relationship between attachment level loss and alveolar bone loss. *Journal of Clinical Periodontology, 11*(5), 384–359.

Goodson, J. M., Tanner, A. C. R., Haffajee, A. D., Sornberger, G. C., & Socransky, S. S. (1982). Patterns of progression and regression of advanced destructive periodontal disease. *Journal of Clinical Periodontology, 9*(6), 472–481.

Gordon, S. R. (1989). Older adults: Demographics and the need for quality care. *Journal of Prosthetic Dentistry, 61*(6), 737–741.

Haffajee, A. D., Socransky, S. S., & Goodson, J. M. (1983). Clinical parameters as predictors of destructive periodontal disease activity. *Journal of Clinical Periodontology, 10*(3), 257–265.

Haffajee, A. D., Socransky, S. S., Lindhe, J., Kent, A. L., Okamoto, H., & Yoneyama, T. (1991). Clinical risk indicators for periodontal attachment loss. *Journal of Clinical Periodontology, 18*(2), 117–125.

Hand, J. S., Hunt, R. J., & Beck, J. D. (1988). Coronal and root caries in older Iowans: 36-month incidence. *Gerodontics, 4*(3), 136–139.

Hand, J. S., & Whitehill, J. M. (1986). The prevalence of oral mucosal lesions in an elderly population. *Journal of the American Dental Association, 112*(1), 73–76.

Health Care Financing Administration, Office of the Actuary from the Office of National Health Statistics (1996).

Heft, M. W., & Gilbert, G. H. (1991). Tooth loss and caries prevalence in older Floridians attending senior activity centers. *Community Dentistry and Oral Epidemiology, 19*(4), 228–232.

Heifetz, S. B. (1994). Fluorides for the elderly. *Journal of the Californian Dental Association, 22*(3), 49–54.

Hunt, M. (1987). The process of translating research findings into nursing practice. *Journal of Advanced Nursing, 12*(1), 101–110.

Hunt, R. J. (1986). Periodontal treatment needs in an elderly population in Iowa. *Gerodontics, 2*(1), 24–27.

Iacopino, A. M., & Wathen, W. F. (1992). Oral candidal infection and denture stomatitis: A comprehensive review. *Journal of the American Dental Association, 123*(1), 46–51.

Jeffcoat, M. K., & Reddy, M. S. (1991). Progression of probing attachment loss in adult periodontitis. *Journal of Periodontology, 62*(3), 185–189.

Jeganathan, S., & Lin, C. C. (1992). Denture stomatitis: A review of the aetiology, diagnosis and management. *Australian Dental Journal, 37*(2), 107–113.

Jensen, M. E., & Kohout, F. (1988). The effect of a fluoridated dentrifice on root and coronal caries in an older adult population. *Journal of the American Dental Association, 117*(1), 829–832.

Kiyak, H. A. (1984). Utilization of dental services by the elderly. *Gerodontology, 3,* 17–25.

Klein, S. P., Bohannan, H. M., Bell, R. M., Disney, J. A., Foch, C. B., & Graves, R. C. (1985). The cost and effectiveness of school-based preventive dental care. *American Journal of Public Health, 75*(4), 382–391.

Kramer, I. R. H., el-Labban, N., & Lee, K. W. (1978). The clinical features and risk of malignant transformation in sublingual keratosis. *British Dental Journal, 144*(6), 171–180.

Kramer, I. R. H., Lucas, R. B., el-Labban, N., & Lister, L. (1970). A computer-aided study on the tissue changes in oral keratoses and lichen planus, and an analysis of case groupings by subjective and objective criteria. *British Journal of Cancer, 24*(3), 407–426.

Lang, N. P., Joss, A., Orsanic, T., Gusberti, F. A., & Siegrist, B. E. (1986). Bleeding on probing. A predictor for progression of periodontal disease? *Journal of Clinical Periodontology, 13*(6), 590–596.

Leon, J., & Lai, R. T. (1990). Functional status of the non-institutionalized elderly: Estimates of ADL and IADL difficulties. *Agency for Health Care Policy and Research* (DHHS Pub No. (PHS) 90-3462). Rockville, MD.

Levy, S. M., Baker, K. A., Semla, T. P., & Kohout, F. J. (1988). Use of medications with dental significance by a non-institutionalized elderly population. *Gerodontics, 4*(3), 119–125.

Lind, P. O. (1987). Malignant transformation in oral leukoplakia. *Scandinavian Journal of Dental Research, 95*(6), 449–455.

Lindhe, J. Haffajee, A. D., & Socransky, S. S. (1983). Progression of periodontal disease in adult subjects in the absence of periodontal therapy. *Journal of Clinical Periodontology, 10*(4), 433–442.

Logan, H. L., Ettinger, R. L., McLeran, H., & Casko, R. (1991). Common misconceptions about oral health in the older adult: Nursing practices. *Special Care in Dentistry, 11*(6), 243–247.

Longman, A. J., & DeWalt, R. M. (1986). A guide for oral assessment. *Geriatric Nursing, 7*(5), 252–253.

MacEntee, M. I. (1994). How severe is the threat of caries to old teeth? *Journal of Prosthetic Dentistry, 71*(5), 473–477.

MacEntee, M. I., Weiss, R., Waxler-Morrison, N. E., & Morrison, B. T. (1984). Factors influencing oral health in long term care facilities. *Community Dentistry and Oral Epidemiology, 15,* 314–316.

Marcus, P. A., Joshi, A., Jones, J. A., & Morgano, S. M. (1996). Complete edentulism and denture use for elders in New England. *Journal of Prosthetic Dentistry, 76*(3), 260–266.

Meckstroth, R. L. (1989). Improving quality and efficiency in oral hygiene. *Journal of Gerontological Nursing, 15*(6), 38–42.

Meskin, L. H., Brown, L. J., Brunelle, J. A., & Warren, G. B. (1988). Patterns of tooth loss and accumulated prosthetic treatment potential in U. S. employed adults and seniors 1985–86. *Gerodontics, 4*(3), 126–135.

Mikkonen, M., Nyssonen, V., Paunio, I., & Rajala, M. (1984). Prevalence of oral mucosal lesions associated with wearing removable dentures in Finnish adults. *Community Dentistry and Oral Epidemiology, 12*(6), 191–194.

Moshman, J., Warren, G., Blanford, D., & Aumack, L. (1985). Geriatric dentistry in the predoctoral curriculum. *Journal of Dental Education, 49*(10), 689–695.

Moskona, D., & Kaplan, I. (1992). Oral lesions in elderly denture wearers. *Clinical Preventive Dentistry, 14*(5), 11–14.

National Center for Health Statistics (1988). *Department of Health and Human Services. Health United States 1987: Utilization of health resources* (PHS Pub No. 88-1232). Bethesda, MD.

Nordenram, A., & Landt, H. (1969). Hyperplasia of the oral tissue in denture cases. *Acta Odontologica Scandinavica, 27*(5), 481–491.

Ohman, S. C., Dahlen, G., Moller, A., & Ohman, A. (1986). Angular cheilitis: A clinical and microbial study. *Journal of Oral Pathology, 15*(4), 213–217.

Österberg, T., Öhman, A., Heyden, G., & Svanborg, A. (1985). The condition of the oral mucosa at age 70: A population study. *Gerodontology, 4*(2), 71–75.

Page, R. C. (1995). Critical issues in periodontal research. Journal of Dental Research, 74(4), 1118–1128.

Parker, S. L., Tong, T., Bolden, S., & Wingo, P. A. (1997). Cancer statistics, 1997. *Cancer Journal for Clinicians, 47*(1), 5–27.

Pindborg, J. J., Joslt, O., Renstrup, G., & Roed-Petersen, B. (1968). Studies in oral leukoplakia: A preliminary report on the period prevalence of malignant transformation in leukoplakia based on a follow-up study of 248 patients. *Journal of the American Dental Association, 76*(4), 767–771.

Reinhardt, J. W., & Douglass, C. W. (1989). The need for operative dentistry services: Projecting the effects of changing disease patterns. *Operative Dentistry, 14*(3), 114–120.

Ripa, L. W., Leske, G. S., Forte, F., & Varma, A. (1987). Effect of a 0.05% neutral NaF mouthrinse on coronal and root caries of adults. *Gerodontology, 6*(4), 131–136.

Rose, J. A. (1968). Aetiology of angular cheilosis (iron metabolism). *British Dental Journal, 125*(2), 67–72.

Schweiger, J. L., Lang, J., & Schweiger, J. W. (1980). Oral assessment: How to do it. *American Journal of Nursing, 80*(4), 654–657.

Seymour, R. A. (1988). Dental pharmacology problems in the elderly. *Dental Update, 15*(9), 375–381.

Silverglade, L. B., & Stablein, M. J. (1988). Diagnostic survey of 9,000 biopsies from three age groups: Under 60 years, 60–69 and over 70. *Gerodontics, 4*(6), 285–288.

Silverman, S., Gorsky, M., & Lozada, F. (1984). Oral leukoplakia and malignant transformation: A follow up study of 257 patients. *Cancer, 53*(3), 563–568.

Skinner, R. L., & Weir, J. C. (1987). Histologic diagnosis of oral lesions in geriatric dental patients: A survey of biopsied lesion. *Gerodontics, 3*(5), 198–200.

Slade, G. D., Locker, D., Leake, J. L., Price, S. A., & Chao, I. (1990). Differences in oral health status between institutionalized and non-institutionalized older adults. *Community Dentistry and Oral Epidemiology, 18*(5), 272–276.

Sreebny, L. M., & Schwartz, S. S. (1986). A reference guide to drugs and dry mouth. *Gerodontology, 5*(2), 75–99.

Strayer, M. S. (1993). Dental health among homebound elderly. *Journal of Public Health Dentistry, 53*(1), 12–16.

United States Department of Health and Human Services (August, 1987). *Oral Health of United States Adults, National Findings* (NIH Publication No. 87-2868). Bethesda, MD.

Vanooteghem, R., Hutchens, L. H., Garrett, S., Kiger, R., & Egelberg, J. (1987). Bleeding on probing and probing depth as indicators of the response to plaque control and root debridement. *Journal of Clinical Periodontology, 14*(4), 226–230.

Waldron, C. A., & Shafer, W. G. (1975). Leukoplakia revisited. A clinico-pathologic study of 3,256 leukoplakias. *Cancer, 36*(4), 1386–1392.

Watson, I. B., & MacDonald, G. D. (1982). Oral mucosa and complete dentures. *Journal of Prosthetic Dentistry, 47*(2), 133–140.

Weintraub, J. B., & Burt, B. A. (1985). Oral health status in the United States: Tooth loss and edentulism. *Journal of Dental Education, 49*(6), 368–376.

Weir, J. C., Davenport, W. D., & Skinner, R. L. (1987). A diagnostic and epidemiologic survey of 15,783 oral lesions. *Journal of the American Dental Association, 115*(3), 439–442.

Wennström, J. L., Dahlen, G., Svensson, J., & Nyman, S. (1987). Actinobacillus actinomycetemcomitans, bacterioides gingivalis and bacteroides intermedius: Predictors of attachment loss. *Oral Microbiology and Immunology, 2*(4), 158–162.

Winkley, G. P., Brown, J. O., & Stone, T. (1993). Interventions to improve oral care: The nursing assistant's role. *Journal of Gerontological Nursing, 19*(11), 47–48.

CHAPTER 5

Smoking Cessation Among Older Clients

Kathleen A. O'Connell

The year is 1945. The movie "To Have and to Have Not," features a young, handsome Humphrey Bogart and an even younger and incredibly beautiful Lauren Bacall. Bacall's first line in this, her first movie scene, is "Anybody got a match?" Bogart's character quickly finds her one, with which she lights a cigarette. The fire of their relationship is fanned by numerous other scenes during which cigarettes are used as unmistakable, yet, morally acceptable, symbols of sexual encounters. Small wonder that so many took up smoking. There were no warnings on cigarettes then, and some advertisements said that doctors smoked them and found them quite satisfying. The young men and women who adored this movie and these actors in 1945 are now in their 60s and 70s. They adopted smoking like they adopted many other fads. However, unlike other fads, smoking stayed with them. Now we know that it is an addiction, but it is not only that. It is a habit, a friend, a symbol, and a reminder of one's youth and sexuality. And though all older smokers now know that smoking kills, they did not know that then. Despite all the warnings, many still want to smoke.

The purpose of this chapter is to discuss issues in smoking and smoking cessation that are relevant to older smokers. Suggested interventions for the older smoker will be discussed. Then, a theoretical basis for understanding smoking, the attraction of cigarettes despite the health risks, and the difficulty of smoking cessation will be presented.

Many of the findings reported in this chapter are based on the work of Barbara Rimer and C. Tracy Orleans, who together with several colleagues have carried out most of the research that is available on older smokers (Rimer & Orleans, 1993; Rimer, Orleans, Fleisher, Cristinzio, Resch, Telepchak, & Keintz, 1994; Rimer, Orleans, Keintz, Cristinzio, & Fleisher, 1990). Rimer and Orleans (1993) stated that in the United States about 28% of those over age 50 smoke and this rate is comparable to the prevalence in the entire adult population. They also pointed out, however, that among certain subgroups of the older population, smoking rates are higher. Forty percent of Hispanic males aged 55 to 74 smoke; and 46% of African American men aged 55 to 74 smoke. The prevalence of smoking declines with age; rates for smokers between the ages of 65 to 74 vary from around 10% to 25% depending on the study, and rates after age 75 range from 6% to 15% (Colsher, Wallace, Pomrehn, LaCroix, Cornoni-Huntley et al., 1990; Rimer & Orleans, 1993). The decline in rates happens for two reasons. First, as cohorts age, the smokers are the ones who are more likely to die (Maxwell & Hirdes, 1993). Secondly, even when this effect is controlled, smoking cessation increases with increasing age (Rimer & Orleans, 1993; USDHHS, 1990).

Smoking is a significant risk factor in six of the 14 major causes of death among those over age 60 and a complicating factor for three others (USDHHS, 1990). Cancer, cardiovascular disease, cerebrovascular disease, and respiratory disease are strongly influenced by smoking. In addition to being a mortality risk factor, smoking is associated with complications of illness including duodenal ulcers, hypertension, and diabetes (Rimer & Orleans, 1993). In addition, smoking can alter the effects of pharmacological agents, causing smokers to have to take higher doses of some drugs. Some of the drugs affected are listed in Table 5.1. For instance, smoking decreases serum levels of theophylline (Talseth, Boye, Kongerud, & Bredesen, 1981). Health care providers should be alert to the special problems of smokers whose drug therapies may be subtherapeutic because of smoking. In addition, when clients quit smoking, their drug dosages may need to be altered.

Rimer and her colleagues (Rimer, Orleans, Keintz, Cristinzio, & Fleisher, 1990) showed that older smokers were less likely than nonsmokers to engage in preventive health behavior such as regular physical examinations, pap smears, blood pressure checks,

TABLE 5.1   The Effects of Smoking on Medications[1]

Drug	Effect of smoking
Antidepressants, trycyclic	Plasma levels lower in smokers
Benzodiazepines	Increases metabolism of drug
Caffeine	Increases metabolism of drug
Cimetidine	Decreases efficacy
Cyanocobalamin (B_{12})	Lower levels in smokers
Estrone, Estradiol	Increases metabolism of drug
Flecainide (Tambocor)	Increases metabolism of drug
Heparin	Increases metabolism of drug
Nefedipine	Decreases efficacy
Pentazocine HCl (Talwin)	Increases metabolism of drug
Phenothiazines	Decreases efficacy
Phenylbutazone (Butazolidin)	Increases metabolism of drug
Propoxyphene HCL (Darvon)	Decreases efficacy
Propranolol HCL (Inderal)	Decreases therapeutic effect
Theophylline	Increases metabolism of drug

[1] Based on Bennett & Plum (1996) and Lipman (1985).

and mammograms. It may be that smokers are avoiding opportunities to find out about the health effects of smoking, but in so doing they are also avoiding the chance for early detection of other diseases, even ones that may not be related to smoking.

SMOKING AND QUALITY OF LIFE AMONG ELDERS

Although mortality is one endpoint for smoking research, it is, after all, an inescapable one for smokers and nonsmokers alike. Quality of life indicators have become important outcome variables in research. Interventions that add a few years to life, but that result in poor quality of life are of questionable value. Studies of the relationship of smoking to quality of life in later years are, therefore, important. It could be that although smokers do not live as long as nonsmokers, the quality of their lives may be better. Studies have not shown this to be the case, however. Among those over 65, smoking is significantly related to higher risk of poorer self-rated health (Colsher et al. 1990; Maxwell & Hirdes, 1993;

Rimer et al., 1990), respiratory problems (Maxwell & Hirdes, 1993), including trouble breathing and frequent coughing (Rimer et al., 1990), trouble walking 400 meters without resting among men, increased central nervous system and gastrointestinal medication use among females, and increased analgesic use among males (Maxwell & Hirdes, 1993). Furthermore, among females over 65, smoking was significantly related to higher risk of dissatisfaction with family and friends, low life satisfaction, and low happiness (Maxwell & Hirdes, 1993). Among males over 65, smoking was significantly related to high life stress (Maxwell & Hirdes, 1993). These associations were independent of the effects of marital status, education, income, and age.

Such findings contradict the notion that smoking has positive effects on quality of life among elders. Maxwell and Hirdes (1993) stated that these results suggest two possible patterns: (1) smoking leads to negative quality of life outcomes for elderly individuals ; or (2) elderly individuals who have a low quality of life are more likely to continue to smoke. Both interpretations are probably accurate, and could describe elements of a vicious cycle among elderly smokers.

WHO QUITS SMOKING AFTER AGE 65?

Salive, Cornoni-Huntley, LaCroix, Ostfeld, Wallace et al. (1992) analyzed data bases of over 10,000 persons over the age of 65. Their analyses focused on measures taken from current and former smokers at the beginning of the study, and 3 and 6 years later. The results of the study showed that smoking cessation increases with age; there was a lower rate of smoking at each follow-up. Smoking cessation at the 3-year follow-up was associated with older age. Compared to persons in the 65- to 69-year-old group, persons over 85 were 3.5 times more likely to be nonsmokers, and people between the ages of 75 and 84 were 1.9 times more likely to be non-smokers. Smoking cessation at the 3-year follow-up was also associated with smoking fewer cigarettes per day, and fewer years of smoking. The relationship of cessation to the occurrence of medical problems depended on the recency of the problems. Smokers who had a history of myocardial infarction, stroke, cancer, or intermittent claudication at the beginning of the study were less likely to have quit 3 years later. However, smokers who had sustained a myocardial infarction, stroke, or a diagnosis of cancer in the 3 years since the start of the study were more likely to quit smoking. Thus, it appears that if smokers are going to respond to a major health event by quitting smoking, they will quit smoking within a short time of diagnosis. Smokers who do not quit shortly after the onset of a major health event are less likely to quit later. It should also be noted that the diagnoses related to cessation are usually those that are experienced as having a sudden onset rather than those with a slow onset. Thus, myocardial infarctions, strokes, and the diagnosis of cancer are experienced as discrete and sudden events, and often lead to immediate cessation. But diagnoses like congestive heart failure and emphysema, which are usually gradual in onset, do not appear to have the motivational impact on smokers that sudden events precipitate.

Kviz, Clark, Crittenden, Warnecke, and Freels (1995) compared three age groups, 18–29 years, 30–40 years, and 50 and older, and found no age differences in the likelihood of making a cessation attempt or of success in smoking cessation during a 3-month period. For all age groups, trying to quit during the year prior to the study was a significant predictor of trying to quit during the 3-month study period.

Older smokers may have more difficulty quitting than younger smokers. One reason is that older smokers are more addicted to nicotine. In a study of members of the American Association of Retired Persons (AARP) (Rimer et al., 1990), 66% of smokers reported smoking within 30 minutes of waking, an indicator of dependence, and they had smoked an average of 46 years. Also, older smokers may have more difficulty quitting for social and psychological reasons. The AARP study revealed that current smokers in the elderly age groups are more likely to live with smokers or have smokers in their social network than are nonsmokers in this group. Their self-efficacy for quitting is low because most have failed at quit attempts. As many as 77% of smokers over 65 have tried to quit before (Rimer & Orleans, 1993). Furthermore, older smokers may have reduced motivation to quit because they believe that it is too late. Optimists among this group may believe that they have beaten the odds and will not get a smoking-related disease, while pessimists may believe that the damage is already done. Often the smoking-related symptoms that occur among the elderly are attributed to aging rather than to smoking.

Older smokers have a variety of concerns about quitting. One study (Rimer et al., 1990) indicated that 68% of older smokers were concerned about the cravings they would feel if they quit smoking and more than half were concerned about being irritable and tense. Forty-seven percent were concerned about weight gain, a concern shared by younger smokers, and 42% were concerned with handling boredom after they quit. Impressive links have been found between depression and smoking (Glassman, Helzer, Covey, Cottler, Stetner et al., 1990). Smokers in general are likely to be more depressed than nonsmokers; and smokers who quit often get depressed. These links may be especially important for older smokers, because depression is prevalent among elderly individuals (Carstensen, 1988).

BENEFITS OF SMOKING CESSATION AMONG OLDER SMOKERS

The 1990 Surgeon General's Report on the health benefits of smoking cessation (USDHHS, 1990) pointed out that the benefits of quitting smoking extend to older age groups. Quitting has been shown to extend both "years of life and years of active life" (Rimer, Orleans, Fleisher, Cristinzio, Resch et al., 1994). Smoking cessation yields benefits for those who already have a smoking-related disease. Cessation markedly reduces risk of recurrence of myocardial infarctions among those with coronary heart disease. Cessation helps in peripheral occlusive disease. In addition, cessation improves the clinical course of those with duodenal ulcers, reduces the risk of developing another primary cancer among those who have already developed cancer, and reduces the risk of respiratory infections. Rogers, Meyer, Judd, and Mortel (1985) also showed that quitting smoking improved cerebral perfusion among elderly chronic smokers.

INTERVENTIONS FOR SMOKING

O'Connell (O'Connell, 1992; O'Connell & Koerin, 1999) has described a generic nursing intervention for outpatient settings. Outpatient settings appear to be an excellent means for reaching many smokers.

Rimer et al. (1990) showed that nearly 75% of smokers in a study of AARP members reported at least one health care visit a year. Older adults visit the physician an average of 6.3 times per year (Rimer & Orleans, 1993). However, only about 40% of smokers reported receiving medical advice to quit smoking (Rimer et al., 1990).

The generic nursing intervention suggested by O'Connell (O'Connell, 1992; O'Connell & Koerin, 1999) is similar to the guidelines for smoking cessation developed by the Agency for Health Care Policy Research (AHCPR) (USDHHS, 1996). The steps for the recommended intervention can be summarized by four key words: Ask, Advise, Assist, and Arrange. Systematic efforts should be made by outpatient facilities to identify the smokers in their practices. This may require additions to health care records so that smoking status is frequently assessed. Health care records in outpatient services for elderly patients should be structured so that current smokers are easily identified. The AHCPR panel found that identification practices have been shown to remind health care providers to ask patients about their smoking status and increase the probability that smokers will be advised to quit smoking (USDHHS, 1996).

Current smokers must be given clear advice to quit smoking. Although the research reviewed by the AHCPR panel was not specific to older smokers, there is strong evidence that advice from a health care provider significantly increases rates of smoking cessation (USDHHS, 1996). Given the findings that older smokers are particularly influenced by health events, the health care provider should tell the client about the relationship, if any, of smoking to the client's current health problems or concerns. Clients who are not ready to quit should be given a pamphlet about the benefits of quitting. Materials relevant to the benefits to older smokers may be particularly useful (Rimer et al., 1994). Exploring the clients' prior experience with cessation attempts may help to elucidate some of the barriers preventing another attempt at quitting. Clients who have been thinking about quitting should be assisted in doing so. Helping such clients set a definite quit date is one way to assist in their efforts. Recommending or prescribing pharmacological aids to smoking cessation may also be in order. Nicotine replacement therapy has been shown to double success rates in smoking cessation (USDHHS, 1996). Such therapies include nicotine gum, transdermal nicotine, nicotine nasal spray, and nicotine inhalers.

Non-nicotine aids to quitting smoking are also becoming available. Bupropion hydrochloride, which had been marketed as an antidepressant, appears to have significant benefit for smoking cessation when therapy is started at least a week prior to the quit day (Ferry, Robins, Scarlati, Masterson, Abbey et al., 1992; Hurt, Glover, Sachs, Dale, & Schroeder, 1996). Although the mechanism of action is not clear, the success of this preparation may be related to its effects on the neurochemicals dopamine and norepinephrine.

Other ways to assist clients include providing written materials that recommend standard activities for quitting, such as getting rid of all cigarettes and smoking paraphernalia, staying away from environments where smoking often occurs, and planning coping strategies to use when the urge strikes. Our recent research (O'Connell & Koerin, 1999) has shown that smokers who are trying to quit employ a variety of coping strategies. Table 5.2 lists the ones used most often by a sample of 35 subjects who used tape recorders to record their coping strategies immediately after they had coped with urges to smoke. This study also indicated that smokers require fewer coping strategies during the second week of cessation than they do in the first week. However, the results also showed that an average of three coping strategies was needed during each urge episode and this number did not change over the first 10 days of cessation. Thus, smokers who are trying to quit should be encouraged to practice a variety of strategies and to employ more than one of them when coping with smoking urges.

The final step of the AHCPR guidelines is to arrange follow-up. It is necessary to continue to demonstrate interest and concern about the client's smoking status at subsequent visits. Nothing could be more discouraging than to struggle to quit smoking in response to the advice of a health care provider and have your cessation attempt overlooked at the next visit. Follow-up is necessary to reinforce those who are succeeding and to encourage those who have relapsed or who have not yet made an attempt. The health care provider may believe that follow-up on those who continue to smoke is a waste of time. However, it is clear that smokers may need to hear the message repeatedly before they are ready to quit. A health care provider's silence about smoking during a follow-up health care visit may be misinterpreted by the smoker as

TABLE 5.2   Most Frequently Used Coping Responses

Behavioral distraction (e.g., knitting, working harder)
Breathing exercises (e.g., taking deep breaths)
Food or drink
Self-encouraging thoughts
Distracting thoughts
Oral non-ingestion activities (e.g., chewing on toothpicks)
Thinking about the negative effects of smoking
Stimulus control (e.g., avoiding usual smoking situations)
Informal exercise (e.g., walking down the hall)

an indication that quitting is no longer necessary. Of course, nagging the smoker to quit is also probably counter-productive.

The smoking intervention outlined here is generic for smokers of any age. Rimer and her team (Rimer et al., 1994) did focus groups with older smokers and ex-smokers and found several factors that may enhance success rates among older smokers. First, medical and potential medical problems are critical motivating factors for older smokers whose experience with such problems is likely to be more direct than that of younger smokers. Older adults prefer materials that picture at least some older people. Self-help programs are preferred to group programs by older smokers. Clear evidence that smoking is affecting their own health, and assurance of the benefits of quitting are factors that are especially important to those who are considering cessation. Kviz, Crittenden, Clark, Madura, and Warnecke (1994) showed that buddy support was helpful with older smokers, especially in the 50–59 age group. Morgan, Noll, Orleans, Rimer, Amfoh et al. (1996) also suggested that contacts with health care providers that give an older smoker "a clean bill of health" may be regarded as permission to continue smoking.

Rimer et al. (1994) also showed that older smokers rated a self-help manual specifically designed for the older smoker more highly than a generic guide, and read significantly more of the specially designed guide than the generic guide. Morgan et al., (1996) showed that a physician-delivered intervention using the specifically designed guide and two follow-up counseling phone calls yielded 6-month quit rates of 15.4% among smokers aged 50 to 74 compared to quit rate of 8.2% in a usual care group.

WHAT KINDS OF QUIT RATES
CAN BE EXPECTED?

In an era of outcomes-based care, the meaning of the success rates of interventions needs to be understood. The success rates of the interventions described above are relatively low, about 8 to 10% are abstinent, when assessed 6 to 12 months from the quit date. The findings that quit rates are doubled by specially designed self-help manuals or by nicotine replacement therapy means that success rates rise to 15 to 20% and occasionally to 30%. Thus, with even the best interventions yielding long-term failure rates of 70%, the obvious question becomes "Is it worth it?" Numerous experts answer a resounding "Yes" to this question. From a public health perspective, lowering the smoking rates by as little as 10% reaps huge benefits in years of lives saved and money spent on smoking-related diseases. Clearly, however, we have a lot more to learn about smoking cessation.

THEORIES OF SMOKING
CESSATION AND RELAPSE

Smoking is a relatively simple behavior with complex effects. An individual who has smoked a pack per day for 40 years has smoked 290,000 cigarettes. Not all of these cigarettes were smoked for the same reason. Some were used to meet the demands of nicotine addiction. By allowing the smoker to titrate nicotine blood levels to acceptable ranges, these cigarettes forestalled, foreshortened, or eliminated withdrawal symptoms. Such cigarettes include those smoked in the early morning, and those smoked after relatively long periods of abstinence. But addiction does not explain all smoking. Until recently, one could smoke practically any place and any time. Thus, smoking co-occurred with a wide variety of common behaviors, including talking on the phone, driving, drinking coffee, working, and waiting. The timing of many of these cigarettes was related to one's daily habits and unrelated to the need to titrate nicotine. But addiction and habit do not explain all smoking. Some smoking constituted instrumental behavior to alter internal states, especially negative affect ones. Smoking can be used to increase arousal, to decrease arousal, and perhaps to manipulate certain brain chemicals related to affect. But addiction, habit, and negative affect manipulation still do not account for all of the variance. Some cigarettes are used to enhance pleasant situations. Years, sometimes decades, after cessation, former smokers report being tempted to smoke after a meal, with a drink, and in celebratory or sexual situations. The extent to which people smoke for reasons of addiction, habit, negative affect reduction, and pleasure enhancement varies among smokers. In addition, the strength of the reasons probably changes over time, with addictive reasons providing little motivation early in a smoking career, but growing more important as years pass.

Many theories have been used to explain smoking behavior, smoking cessation, and relapse. These include the Health Belief Model (Becker, 1974), the Stages of Change Model (Prochaska, DiClemente, & Norcross, 1992), learning theory, and addiction models (USDHHS, 1988). The Health Belief Model and the Stages of Change address variables important in the decision to quit smoking, but deal less effectively with the actual process of quitting. Addiction theories account for the addictive elements of smoking behavior, such as withdrawal symptoms, but do not explain other reasons for smoking. The behavioral theories, which focused on conditioning, account well for instances of habitual and automatic smoking. But none of these theories adequately addresses the instrumental reasons for smoking. And none account for the paradoxical thinking and irrational behavior that are important components of smoking and relapse. For many smokers, having a cigarette, especially during a quit attempt represents what philosophers have termed akratic behavior, or behavior that is carried out despite the individual's firm commitment not to do so (O'Connell, 1996).

Reversal theory accounts for the instrumental reasons for smoking and suggests alternative methods smokers can use to meet the emotional needs that smoking met. Moreover, reversal theory suggests that certain states of mind experienced by all normal individuals are more likely to engender akratic behavior than other states of mind (O'Connell, 1996). By understanding these states of mind, methods for helping smokers avoid relapses during a quit attempt can be developed.

Although a thorough description of the theory is beyond the scope of this chapter, a brief description of parts of the theory that are especially relevant to smoking cessation is given below. Reversal theory is a general theory postulated by British psychologist Michael Apter (Apter, 1982, 1989) that holds that personality is inherently inconsistent. This inconsistency is not chaotic, however. Instead, individuals reverse back and forth between opposing states of mind, termed metamotivational states. One's interpretation of experience and indeed one's motivations to do certain things like refrain from smoking differ, and can be opposite to each other, in opposing metamotivational states. Apter has posited four pairs of metamotivational states: they are telic (serious-minded)/paratelic (playful), negativistic/conformist, mastery/sympathy and autic (self-centered)/alloic (other-centered). With respect to any one of these pairs, the states are mutually exclusive. Thus, one cannot be telic and paratelic at the same time. However, the pairs combine to engender 16 different state-combinations. For example, the combination of telic, conformist, mastery, and autic states is associated with being serious-minded, wanting to follow rules, and being concerned about, and getting satisfaction from, being in control. On the other hand, the combination of paratelic, negativistic, sympathy, and autic states is associated with being playful, wanting to break rules, and feeling that you are in need of nurturance. One's motivation to quit smoking is likely to be vastly different in these two state combinations.

Reversal theory posits that our personalities are constantly changing in important ways. These changes are undoubtedly adaptive for the human organism and for society, but may become problematic during a smoking cessation attempt. Telic states are necessary for goal accomplishments, but it is also necessary to be playful sometimes. Paratelic states are associated with sexual behavior, creativity, and humor. Mastery states are associated with asserting one's power and being independent, qualities especially important to Western cultures. Sympathy states are associated with being cooperative, nurturant of oneself and of others, and caring, qualities that undoubtedly strengthen social bonds. However, our research with groups of adults over the age of 18 has shown that paratelic and sympathy states are related to lapses during highly tempting situations (O'Connell, Cook, Gerkovich, Potocky, & Swan, 1990; O'Connell, Gerkovich, & Cook, 1995). Although this research has not been carried out specifically with older clients, we have no reason to believe that our results would be different with this age group.

Smoking probably occurs in all states and all combinations of states. But the reason for smoking at least some cigarettes, especially those that are instrumental for meeting emotional needs, may differ depending on state. For instance, there is some evidence to indicate that smokers smoke to increase arousal in the paratelic state and to decrease arousal in the telic state (Cook, Gerkovich, Hoffman, McClernon, Cohen et al., 1995). Reversal theory provides a framework for understanding the situations in which smoking is instrumental in meeting emotional needs. It delineates several different types of negative affect and suggests that different types of coping strategies would be effective in different states. For instance, boredom is a negative affect associated with the paratelic (playful and arousal seeking state) state. Performing a relaxation strategy to cope with the urge to smoke when one is bored is likely to be ineffective. In addition to providing a framework for understanding urge situations and appropriate coping strategies, reversal theory also suggests that the commitment to quit smoking and to use coping strategies is often incompatible with some metamotivational states. The present-orientation and sensation seeking that characterize the paratelic state make the long-term benefits of smoking cessation appear irrelevant to one's current situation. Feelings of deprivation and needs for nurturance that characterize some types of sympathy states tend to make the discomforts of smoking cessation appear to be an unnecessary affliction for one whose major focus at that moment is the need for comfort. Thus, the deliberate and rational decisions that are made in telic and mastery states often founder in paratelic or sympathy states.

It might appear, then, that the way to quit smoking is to remain in telic and mastery states. However, reversal theory posits that reversals to paratelic and sympathy states are necessary, inevitable, and involuntary for psychologically normal individuals. Does reversal theory therefore imply that smoking cessation is impossible? No, but the theory does suggest why cessation is so difficult. Success in smoking cessation demands two critical components: First, ex-smokers must find different methods or strategies to meet all the needs that smoking once met, and second, ex-smokers must be motivated to use these methods instead of smoking in all the states they experience. For example, the smoker must come to believe, that smoking after a wonderful meal with good friends and fine wine will, in fact, ruin your good time. It's an idea that's hard to sell oneself, especially when you grew up watching Bogie and Bacall in those unforgettable movies.

CONCLUSION

This chapter has summarized the research on older smokers. Smoking is an important risk factor for chronic diseases among older clients. Despite higher rates of addiction in older smokers as compared to younger smokers, increasing age is related to higher cessation rates. Cessation, in turn, is related to better quality of life and decreased morbidity and mortality among elderly individuals. However, smoking cessation is a difficult undertaking for elderly clients. Many are discouraged by previous failures. Although few interventions have been directed at elderly smokers specifically, the AHCPR guideline for smoking cessation (USDHHS, 1996) presents research-based recommendations for interventions that are appropriate for elderly clients. Reversal theory provides a framework for understanding the difficulty with quitting smoking and for suggesting ways to cope with urges to smoke in specific situations. Older smokers started smoking before the deleterious consequences were known. The movies of the 1940s associated smoking with glamour and youth. In more recent years, science has associated smoking with addiction and disease. Health care providers are challenged to help older smokers overcome old associations and new realities in order to enjoy maximal vitality in later life.

REFERENCES

Apter, M. J. (1982). *The experience of motivation: The theory of psychological reversals.* London: Academic Press.

Apter, M. J. (1989). *Reversal theory: Motivation, emotion, and personality.* London: Routledge.

Becker, M. H. (Ed.) (1974). The health belief model and personal health behavior. *Health Education Monographs, 2,* 324–473.

Bennett, J. C. & Plum, F. (1996). *Cecil textbook of medicine* (20th ed., vol. 1). Philadelphia: W.B. Saunders.

Carstensen, L. L. (1988). The emerging field of behavioral gerontology. *Behavior Therapy, 19,* 159–181.

Colsher, P. L., Wallace, R. B., Pomrehn, P. R., LaCroix, A. Z., Cornoni-Huntley, J., Blazer, D., Scherr, P. A., Berkman, L., & Hennekens, C. H. (1990). Demographic and health characteristics of elderly smokers: Results from epidemiologic studies of the elderly. *American Journal of Preventive Medicine, 6*(2), 61–70.

Cook, M. R., Gerkovich, M. M., Hoffman, S. J., McClernon, F. J., Cohen, H. D., Oakleaf, K. L., & O'Connell, K. A. (1995). Smoking and EEG power spectra: Effects of differences in arousal seeking. *International Journal of Psychophysiology, 19*(3), 247–256.

Ferry, L. H., Robbins, A. S. Scarlati, P. D., Masterson, A., Abbey, D. E., & Burchette, R. J. (1992). Enhancement of smoking cessation using the antidepressant bupropion hydrochloride (Abstract). *Circulation, 86,* 671.

Glassman, A. H., Helzer, J. E., Covey, L. S., Cottler, L. B., Stetner, F., Tipp, J. E., & Johnson, J. (1990). Smoking, smoking cessation, and major depression. *Journal of the American Medical Association, 264*(12), 1546–1549.

Hurt, R. D., Glover, E. D., Sachs, D. P. L., Dale, L. C., & Schroeder, D. R. (1996). Bupropion for smoking cessation: A double-blind, placebo-controlled dose response trial (Abstract). *Journal of Addictive Diseases, 15,* 137.

Kviz, F. J., Clark, M. A., Crittenden, K. S., Warnecke, R. B., & Freels, S., (1995). Age and smoking cessation behaviors. *Preventive Medicine, 24*(3), 297–307.

Kviz, F. J., Crittenden, K. S., Clark, M. A., Madura, K. J., & Warnecke, R. B. (1994). Buddy support among older smokers in a smoking cessation program. *Journal of Aging and Health, 6,* 229–254.

Lipman, A. G. (1985). How smoking interferes with drug therapy. *Modern Medicine, 53*(8), August, 1985, pp. 141–142.

Maxwell, C. J., & Hirdes, J. P. (1993). The prevalence of smoking and implications for quality of life among the community-based elderly. *American Journal of Preventive Medicine, 9*(6), 338–345.

Morgan, G. D., Noll, E. L., Orleans, C. T., Rimer, B. K., Amfoh, K., & Bonney, G. (1996). Reaching midlife and older smokers: Tailored interventions for routine medical care. *Preventive Medicine, 25*(3), 346–354.

O'Connell, K. A. (1992). Smoking cessation. In J. McCloskey & G. Bulechek (Eds.), *Nursing interventions: Treatments for nursing diagnoses* (2nd. ed., pp. 472–481). Philadelphia: W.B. Saunders.

O'Connell, K. A. (1996). Akrasia, health behavior, relapse, and reversal theory. *Nursing Outlook, 44*(2), 94–98.

O'Connell, K. A., Cook, M. R., Gerkovich, M. M., Potocky, M., & Swan, G. E. (1990). Reversal theory and smoking: A state-based approach to ex-smokers highly tempting situations. *Journal of Consulting and Clinical Psychology, 58*(4), 489–94.

O'Connell, K. A., Gerkovich, M. M., & Cook, M. R. (1995). Reversal theory's mastery and sympathy states in smoking cessation. *Image: Journal of Nursing Scholarship, 27*(4), 311–316.

O'Connell, K. A., Gerkovich, M. M., Cook, M. R., Shiffman, S., Hickcox, M., & Kakolewski, K. E. (1998). Coping in real time: Using ecological momentary assessment techniques to assess coping with the urge to smoke. *Research in Nursing and Health, 21*(6), 487–497.

O'Connell, K. A., & Koerin, C. A. (1999). Smoking cessation assistance. In J. McCloskey & G. Bulechek (Eds.), *Nursing interventions: Effective nursing treatments* (3rd ed., pp. 438–450). Philadelphia: W.B. Saunders.

Prochaska, J. O., DiClemente, C. C., & Norcross, J. C. (1992). In search of how people change: Applications to the addictive behaviors. *American Psychologist, 47*(9), 1102–1114.

Rimer, B. K., & Orleans, C. T. (1993). Older smokers. In C.T. Orleans & J. Slade (Eds.), *Nicotine addiction: Principles and management* (pp. 385–395). New York: Oxford University Press.

Rimer, B. K., Orleans, C. T., Fleisher, L., Cristinzio, S., Resch, N., Telepchak, J., & Keintz, M. K. (1994). Does tailoring matter? Impact of a tailored guide on ratings and short-term smoking-related outcomes for older smokers. *Health Education Research, 9*(1), 69–84.

Rimer, B. K., Orleans, C. T., Keintz, M. K., Cristinzio, S., & Fleisher, L. (1990). The older smoker: Status, challenges and opportunities for interventions. *Chest, 97*(3), 547–553.

Rogers, R. L., Meyer, J. S., Judd, B. W., & Mortel, K. F. (1985). Abstention from cigarette smoking improves cerebral perfusion among elderly chronic smokers. *Journal of the American Medical Association, 253*(20), 2970–2974.

Salive, M. E., Cornoni-Huntley, J., LaCroix, A. Z., Ostfeld, A. M., Wallace, R. B., & Hennekens, C. H. (1992). Predictors of smoking cessation and relapse in older adults. *American Journal of Public Health, 82*(11), 1268–1271.

Talseth, T., Boye, N. P., Kongerud, J., & Bredesen, J. E. (1981). Aging, cigarette smoking and oral theophylline requirement. *European Journal of Clinical Pharmacology, 21*(1), 33–37.

United States Department of Health and Human Services (1988). The health consequences of smoking: Nicotine addiction. A report of the Surgeon General. United States Department of Health and Human Services, Public Health Service, Centers for Disease Control, Center for Health Promotion and Education, Office on Smoking and Health, DHHS Publication No. (CDC) 88–8406.

United States Department of Health and Human Services. (1990). The health benefits of smoking cessation: A report of the Surgeon General. United States Department of Health and Human Services, Public

Health Service, Centers for Disease Control, Center for Chronic Disease Prevention and Health Promotion, Office on Smoking and Health, DHHS Publication No. (CDC) 90–8416.

United States Department of Health and Human Services (1996). Smoking cessation: Clinical practice guideline, No. 18. Washington D.C.: USD-HHS Public Health Service, Agency for Health Care Policy and Research. DHHS Publication No. (AHCPR) 96–0692.

CHAPTER 6

Reducing Falls Among Older Adults Residing in the Community

Dorothy I. Baker

Falls are a serious public health problem because of the frequency with which they occur and the associated human suffering measured in terms of morbidity, mortality, and health care utilization. Nearly a third of community-dwelling persons over age 65 in the United States fall each year (Tinetti, Speechley, & Ginter, 1988), and half those experience recurrent events (Nevitt, Cummings, Kidd, & Black, 1989). The mean incidence of falls among nursing home residents is even higher, having been estimated at 1.5 falls per bed per year (Rubenstein, Josephson, & Robbins, 1994). It has been estimated that among those 70 years and older 14% fall in the first month after hospital discharge; the incidence is 20% among those ill enough to require referral for home care (Mahoney, Sager, Cross Dunham, & Johnson, 1994).

Most falls (60%) result in a minor scrape or bruise (Nevitt, Cummings, & Hudes, 1991), however 5% of falls result in a fracture commonly of the hip, pelvis, humorous, or wrist (Nevitt et al., 1989; Tinetti et al., 1988). In addition to the primary fall-related physical injury, other sequella include secondary injury due to an inability to arise after a fall (Tinetti, Liu, & Claus, 1993), psychological trauma and activity limitation due to fear of falling (Tinetti et al., 1988; Tinetti, Richman, & Powell, 1990), and functional decline, increasing the likelihood of needing long-term care (Kellogg International Work Group on the Prevention of Falls by the Elderly, 1987; Sattin, Lambert Huber, DeVito, Rodriguez, Ros et al., 1990).

Compared to children, older adults are ten times more likely to be hospitalized and eight times more likely to die as a result of falling (Runge, 1993).

In the United States in 1991, greater than half of the injury and poisoning-related hospital admissions among those over 65 years of age were due to fractures, most commonly (57%) fractured hips (Hall & Owings, 1994). Falls accounted for the largest percentage (20.5%) of injury-related visits to the emergency department in 1995 (Stussman, 1997) and are the leading cause of injury-related mortality, ranking as the sixth leading cause of death among older adults (National Safety Council, 1988). In 1994, fractures accounted for 3.8% of the Medicare acute care discharges (Health Care Finance Review, 1997). The average 1994 Medicare payment for fracture-related hospital, nursing home, and home care episode was $15,500 (Health Care Finance Review, 1997). In 1995, a major insurer report-ed that falls, again, made up the largest number of claims against the nursing homes they insured, with fall-related claims compris-ing seven of the top 10 reasons for filing law suits. The average cost per fall-related settlement ranged from $7,500 for falls by vis-itors in the nursing homes to $39,000 for patient falls in the bath-rooms (Nursing Home Update, 1995).

Data such as these prompted the National Institute on Aging and the (then) National Center for Nursing Research to collaborate in sponsoring a coordinated set of clinical trials designed to reduce the biomedical, behavioral, and environmental risk factors for falling among the elderly (Ory, Schechtman, Miller, Hadley, Fiatarone et al., 1993). Eight sites in the United States were funded to undertake these investigations beginning in April 1990. This paper summa-rizes the results of one of these clinical trials, Yale Frailty and Injury: Cooperative Studies of Intervention Trials (Yale FICSIT).

METHODS

The design and methods used in Yale FICSIT have been described in detail (Koch, Gottschalk, Baker, Palumbo, & Tinetti, 1994; Tinetti, Baker, Garrett, Gottschalk, Koch et al., 1993) and are summarized here. Yale FICSIT was a randomized, controlled clinical trial com-paring the effectiveness of usual health care and social visits (UC) to a multifactorial, targeted risk factor abatement intervention (TI) designed to decrease falls among at-risk community living older adults. A matched block design was used: 16 physicians from the participating health maintenance organization (HMO) were divided into four groups based upon their number of geriatric patients and the average number of medications prescribed during outpatient visits. Two physicians from each quadrant were then randomly assigned to either the TI or UC group. Patients were randomly selected until approximately 20 participants were enrolled from each physician's practice. Participants were 301 members of a HMO who gave consent, were at least 70 years of age, had a score of at least 20 on the Folstein Mini Mental State examination (Folstein, Folstein, & McHugh, 1975), not engaged in active sports, not terminally ill, not enrolled in another aging study, ambulatory at least in their own homes, and who had at least one of the following fall risk factors: orthostatic hypotension, use of > 3 targeted medications, use of sedative hypnotics, upper or lower extremity strength or range of motion impairments, and gait, balance, or transfer dysfunctions.

Screening and enrollment for all subjects was accomplished via an introductory letter and screening telephone call followed by baseline assessments provided in participants' homes by a nurse practitioner (NP) and a physical therapist (PT). Randomization was revealed after the baseline assessment was complete. After the baseline assessments, the number of targeted risk factors were identified for each subject. This information was used to estimate the number of visits to UC and TI subjects and to develop the intervention strategy with those in the TI group. The intervention consisted of 3 months of home visits by the NP and PT followed by three monthly follow-up contacts. Participants in the UC group received an equivalent number of home visits during which structured life reviews were conducted by social work students.

Previous studies have shown a strong association between the number of impairments possessed by an individual and the risk of falling (Tinetti et al., 1988). Based on this research it was hypothesized that the incidence of falls could be lowered by reducing as many fall risk factors as possible. The targeted intervention was thus unique in two ways, it was: 1) multifactorial focusing on eight risk factors known to be associated with falling, and 2) targeted so that each participant received interventions only for the risk factors personally exhibited. The interventions were standardized and prioritized to insure that all TI participants with a risk factor received the same intervention. The interventions were: Medication adjustments made in consultation with the primary physician; environmental modifications; education regarding risk factors and unsafe behaviors; gait and transfer training; and graduated exercises to improve balance, gait and transfers. Participants were taught to do the exercises by the PT and were asked to perform them for 15 minutes twice daily.

To actively engage TI participants in the study and improve their adherence to the recommended interventions, study staff contracted with each individual regarding which interventions they wished to undertake. Adherence to recommended exercises and to environmental and behavioral changes were measured by participants' self-report recorded weekly. The primary outcome of falls, defined as unintentionally coming to rest on the ground, floor or other lower level (Buchner, Hornbrook, Kutner, Tinetti, Ory et al., 1993), were measured by self-report using a special fall calendar completed daily and mailed monthly to the research office by all participants in both groups. A calendar that indicated a fall, was illegible, or arrived late, precipitated a follow-up telephone interview. The intermediate outcomes of physical performance abilities were measured 4 months after enrollment during a home visit conducted by a PT. All outcomes were measured by assessors blinded to group assignment.

As has been described fully elsewhere (Rizzo, Baker, McAvay, & Tinetti, 1996), costs of the intervention were determined based on documentation completed by the NP and PT of the time, supplies, and equipment necessary to screen, assess, and treat participants. One year of health care utilization costs for each subject were ascertained using: 1) bill files from the HMO for outpatient visits; 2) bill files from two area hospitals for emergency room and inpatient admissions; 3) Yale FICSIT monthly telephone interviews to track the number of nursing home days; and 4) bill files from the two home health care agencies that were the preferred providers for the HMO, to quantify the type and amount of home care utilization.

RESULTS

The complete analyses and results of Yale FICSIT are reported elsewhere and summarized here (Rizzo et al., 1996; Tinetti, Baker,

McAvay, Claus, Garrett et al., 1994; Tinetti, McAvay, & Claus, 1996). The 301 participants were predominantly white females (69%) with an average age of 78. 31% had post high school education. Participants had an average of 3.72 (S.D. 1.7) targeted fall risk factors identified on the baseline assessments. Randomization was successful in distributing risk factors equitably between the two groups except that the TI group was slightly better educated and had a lower proportion of impairments of lower extremity strength at baseline, relative to those in the UC group. The fall rates were compared, during 12 months of follow-up, between UC and those who received our targeted risk reduction interventions (TI). During the 1 year of follow-up, 35% of the TI versus 47% of the UC participants fell (P = 0.04). The fall risk reduction, adjusted for age, gender, history of previous falls, and number of risk factors, was 0.69 (95% confidence interval, 0.52 to 0.90) for the TI group as compared to the UC group. Although the numbers were too small for statistical testing, a trend in the same direction was observed with respect to falls requiring medical care (25 versus 36) or resulting in serious injury (13 versus 18), both of which were lower in the TI relative to those in the UC group.

Analyses comparing the percent of participants who had a risk factor at baseline and at the 4-month outcome assessment revealed lower proportions among the TI participants relative to the UC participants for: use of > 3 prescription medications (P = 0.009); balance or bed to chair transfer impairment (P = 0.0001); impairment in bathing or toileting transfer skills (P = 0.05); and gait impairment (P = 0.07) (Tinetti et al., 1994). Analyses of continuously distributed measures revealed an improvement in TI relative to UC participants in postural blood pressure (p = .003), timed balance score (p = .09), and gait-step length (.03) (Tinetti et al., 1996). There were no significant differences found between groups with respect to range of motion and strength of upper and lower extremities or use of sedative hypnotics.

Participants' responses to the interventions were carefully monitored throughout the study. There were no significant between group differences with respect to the number of participants who died or were hospitalized; however, the TI participants had fewer hospitalizations and used fewer hospital days. There were no reports of serious intervention-related injuries. Ten subjects in the TI group reported transient musculoskeletal symptoms that were probably related to preexisting conditions and the exercise program. Each of these events was self-limited. Eighty-five percent of the TI participants reported performing over half of the prescribed exercises.

To fully assess the merits of the fall risk reduction strategy, cost considerations were weighed against falls prevented. These included costs associated with delivering the intervention and potential costs savings in the form of reduced use of hospital, outpatient, nursing home, and home care services. We tracked utilization costs for all participants for 1 year following their entry into the study and found that TI participants had mean total costs of care, including the average of $907 to deliver the intervention, totaling $8,310 versus $10,439 in the UC group. The TI appears to be especially cost effective for persons at high risk of falling. Among the group with 4+ fall risk factors the mean total costs, again including $907 of intervention costs, were $10,500 for the TI group versus $14,200 for the UC group (Rizzo et al., 1996). By reducing the fall risk factors among intervention participants we not only decreased the rate of falling but *likely* decreased the incidence of other geriatric syndromes associated with health care utilization.

CONCLUSION

These analyses suggest that the Yale FICSIT interventions are feasible, safe, effective, and cost effective in reducing a significant public health problem. They are feasible and safe, as 85% of TI subjects reported adhering to 72% of the recommended exercises and there were no reports of serious intervention-related injuries. The multifactorial, targeted intervention was effective in reducing falls by 30% among TI relative to UC participants, and there was a trend toward fewer injurious falls among TI group. The $907 average cost of delivering the intervention was offset by lower utilization of health services in the 12 months of follow-up among the TI participants, relative to those who received UC. The intervention appears to be particularly cost effective when targeted to those elderly people who have 4+ of the fall risk factors.

We are now engaged in several projects designed to foster implementation of this home-based multiple risk factor abatement strategy among more frail older adults who are living in the community. Among them is Project Independence, funded by an anonymous donor to Gaylord Rehabilitation Hospital in Wallingford, Connecticut. The project targets health care providers and consumers in two Connecticut towns for fall prevention. Nurse practitioners, home care nurses, physical therapists, home health aides, pharmacists, physicians, and older adults themselves are completing fall assessments and implementing risk reduction interventions. The goal is to test the feasibility of translating our research protocols into clinical protocols that are practical and cost effective to implement in community-based clinical practice and effective in changing clinician and consumer behavior patterns to reduce falls.

REFERENCES

Buchner, D. M., Hornbrook, M. C., Kutner, N. G., Tinetti, M. E., Ory, M. G., Mulrow, C. D., Schechtman, K. B., Gerety, M. B., Fiatarone, M. A. Wolf, S. L., Rossiter, J., Arfken, C., Kanten, K., Lipsitz, L. A., Sattin, R. W., DeNino, L. A., & The FICSIT Group. (1993). Development of the common data base for the FICSIT trials. *Journal American Geriatric Society, 41*(3), 297–308.

Folstein, M. F., Folstein, S. E., & McHugh, P. R. (1975). Mini-mental state: A practical method for grading the cognitive state of patients for the clinician. *Journal of Psychiatric Research, 12*(3), 189–198.

Hall, M. J., & Owings, M. F. (1994). Hospitalizations for injury and poisoning in the United States, 1991. Advance data from vital and health statistics; no. 252. Hyattsville, MD: National Center for Health Statistics.

Health Care Financing Review (1997). Medicare and Medicaid Statistical Suppl, (1996). USDHHS, HCFA, ORD. 7500 Security Boulevard, C-3-11-07, Baltimore, Maryland 1244–1850.

Kellogg International Work Group on the Prevention of Falls by the Elderly (1987). The prevention of falls in later life. *Danish Medical Bulletin, 34*(Suppl. 4), 1–24.

Koch, M., Gottschalk, M., Baker, D. I., Palumbo, S., & Tinetti, M. E. (1994). An impairment and disability assessment and treatment protocol for community-living elderly persons. *Physical Therapy, 74*(4), 286–294.

Mahoney, J., Sager, M., Cross Dunham, N., & Johnson, J. (1994). Risk of falls after hospital discharge. *Journal of American Geriatric Society, 42*(3), 269–274.

National Safety Council (1988). *Accident facts.* Chicago; National Safety Council.

Nevitt, M. C., Cummings, S. R., & Hudes, E. S. (1991). Risk factors for injurious falls: A prospective study. *Journal of Gerontology, 46*(5) M164–170.

Nevitt, M. C., Cummings, S. R., Kidd, S., & Black, D. (1989). Risk factors for recurrent nonsyncopal falls. *Journal of American Medical Association, 261*(18) 2663–2668.

Nursing Home Update (1995). St. Paul's Fire and Marine Insurance Company 1995 Annual Report to Policyholders. Medical Services 385 Washington Street, St. Paul Minnesota 55102.

Ory, M. G., Schechtman, K. B., Miller, J. P., Hadley, E. C., Fiatarone, M. A., Province, M. A., Arfken, C. L., Morgan, D., Weiss, S., Kaplan, M., & The FICSIT Group (1993). Frailty and injuries in later life: The FIC-SIT trials. *Journal of American Geriatric Society,41*(3), 283–296.

Rizzo, J., Baker, D. I., McAvay, G., & Tinetti, M. E. (1996). Cost effectiveness of a multifactorial targeted prevention program for falls among community elderly persons. *Medical Care, 34*(9), 954–969.

Rubenstein, L. Z., Josephson, K. R., & Robbins, A. S. (1994). Falls in nursing homes. *Annuals of Internal Medicine, 121*(6), 442–451.

Runge, J. W. (1993). The cost of injury. *Emergency Medicine Clinics of North America, 11*(1), 241–253.

Sattin, R. W., Lambert Huber, D. A., DeVito, C. A., Rodriguez, J. G., Ros, A., Bacchelli, S., Stevens, J. A., & Waxweiler, R. J. (1990). The incidence of fall injury events among the elderly in a defined population. *American Journal of Epidemiology, 131*(6), 1028–1037.

Stussman, B. J. (1997). National hospital ambulatory medical care survey: 1995 emergency department summary. Advance data from vital and health statistics; no. 285. Hyattsville, Maryland: National Center for Health Statistics.

Tinetti, M. E., Baker, D. I., Garrett, P. A., Gottschalk, M., Koch, M. L., & Horwitz, R. I. (1993). Yale FICSIT: Risk factor abatement strategy for fall prevention. *Journal of American Geriatric Society, 41*(3), 315–320.

Tinetti, M. E., Baker, D. I., McAvay, G., Claus, E., Garrett, P., Gottschalk, M., Koch, M. L., Trainor, K., & Horwitz, R. (1994). A multifactorial intervention to reduce the risk of falling among elderly people living in the community. *New England Journal of Medicine, 331*(13), 821–873.

Tinetti, M. E., Liu, W. L., & Claus, E. B. (1993). Predictors and prognosis of inability to get up after falls among elderly persons. *Journal of American Medical Association, 269*(1), 65–70.

Tinetti, M. E., McAvay, G., & Claus, E. (1996). Does multiple risk factor reduction explain the reduction in fall rate in the Yale FICSIT trial? *American Journal of Epidemiology, 144*(4), 389–399.

Tinetti, M.E., Richman, D., & Powell, L. (1990). Falls efficacy as a measure of fear of falling. *Journal of Gerontology, 45*(6), 239–243.

Tinetti, M. E., Speechley, M., & Ginter, S. F. (1988). Risk factors for falls among elderly persons living in the community. *New England Journal of Medicine, 319*(26), 1701–1707.

CHAPTER 7

Urinary Continence: Prevention Focused Research

Mary H. Palmer

The purpose of this chapter is to discuss an updated continence promotion model and recent research efforts to prevent or reverse urinary incontinence. Barriers to the development and implementation of prevention focused interventions directed at the older adult population will also be discussed and recommendations for nursing research and practice will be made.

Urinary incontinence is not a disease but a symptom (International Continence Society, 1990). It occurs in men and women alike, at all stages of life and under many different conditions. Over 13 million adult Americans have bladder control problems. Approximately 15 to 35% of community-dwelling older adults and 50% of nursing home residents are incontinent (U.S. Department of Health and Human Services, 1996). See Table 7.1.

In 1996, the Agency for Health Care Policy and Research estimated the annual costs of urinary incontinence as more than $15 billion. More recently it was reported that the 1995 direct and indirect costs of incontinence in adults over 65 years was $27.9 billion (Newman, 1997). See Figure 7.1.

Because of its prevalence and costs, urinary incontinence is a significant public health issue. Yet, the natural history of urinary incontinence is not completely understood. There is little understanding about the intrinsic factors at the cellular, organ, and functional levels that place an individual at-risk for the development of the condition. What is known, however, is that urine will empty from the bladder when the intravesical pressure (ie., pressure

TABLE 7.1 Prevalence of Urinary Incontinence

Study	Population sample	Definition of incontinence	Prevalence
Setting: Acute care			
Sullivan & Lindsay (1984)[1]	N = 315 (pts 65+ yrs) admitted over a 6 week period	Any inappropriate loss of urine, regardless of amount or frequency. Included use of external catheter. Excluded indwelling catheter	19%
Sier, Ouslander, & Orzeck (1987)[2]	N = 363 (pts 65+ yrs) admitted over a 14-week period	One or more episodes of incontinence documented on Incontinence Monitoring Record while hospitalized	Age (years): 65–74 = 24% 75+ = 48%
MA Medical Society (1991)[3]	N = 41.4 million hospital discharge records (Medicare A)	First mention of incontinence in discharge records	Women: 16.6* Men: 10.1* * per 10,000 population
Setting: Long-term care			
Ouslander, Kane, & Abrass (1982)[4]	N = 842 (pts 65+ yrs) from seven nursing homes	Any uncontrolled leakage of urine, regardless of amount or frequency	50%
Ouslander & Fowler (1985)[5]	N = 7853, all VA patients in 90 nursing home facilities	Any uncontrolled leakage of urine, regardless of amount or frequency	41%

TABLE 7.1 (Continued)

Study	Population sample	Definition of incontinence	Prevalence
Hing and Sekscenski (1986)[6]	N = 1.4 million (pts 55+ yrs)	Difficulty controlling bladder	10.7% bladder only; 32.5% bladder and bowel
Palmer, German, & Ouslander (1991)[7]	N = 430 (pts 60+ yrs) newly admitted nursing home residents	Incontinent during the day	39% at 2 weeks after admission 41% 1 year after admission
Setting: Community			
Diokno, Brock, Brown, & Herzog (1986)[8]	N = 1955 (adults 60+ yrs)	Any uncontrolled urine loss in the prior 12 months without regard to severity	30% average (18.9% males, 37.7% females)
Harris (1986)[9]	N = 5637 (adults 65+ yrs) who answered questions regarding urinary problems on the National Health Interview Survey	Includes those with any difficulty controlling urination as well as those with catheters	9%
Mohide, Pringle, Robertson, & Chambers (1988)[10]	N = 2801 (avg. age 74 yrs) patients of four (4) home care programs	Involuntary urine loss in association with strong desire to void, physical exertion; no apparent sensation of need to void if irregular toileting occurred	22%

TABLE 7.1 Prevalence of Urinary Incontinence (Continued)

Study	Population sample	Definition of incontinence	Prevalence
Wetle, Scherr, Branch, Resnick, Harris, Evans, & Taylor (1995)[11]	N = 3809 (study participants 65+ yrs)	"Difficulty holding urine until they can get to a toilet"	28%

Adapted: Palmer, M. (1993). Urinary incontinence. In V. Carrieri-Kohlman, A. Lindsay, & C. West (Eds.). *Pathophysiological phenomena in nursing. Human response to illness.* W. B. Saunders: Philadelphia. Permission granted.

[1] Sullivan, D., & Lindsay, R. (1984). Urinary incontinence in the geriatric population of an acute care hospital. *Journal of the American Geriatrics Society, 31*(11), 694–697.

[2] Sier, H., Ouslander, J., & Orzeck, S. (1987). Urinary incontinence among geriatric patients in an acute-care hospital. *Journal of the American Medical Association, 257*(31), 1767–1771.

[3] Massachusetts Medical Society (1991). Urinary incontinence among hospitalized persons aged 65 years and older—United States, 1984–1987. *Morbidity and Mortality Weekly Reports, 40,* 433–436.

[4] Ouslander, J., Kane, R., & Abrass, I. (1982). Urinary incontinence in elderly nursing home patients. *Journal of the American Medical Association, 248*(10), 1194–1198.

[5] Ouslander, J., & Fowler, E. (1985). Management of urinary incontinence in Veterans Administration nursing homes. *Journal of the American Geriatrics Society, 33*(1), 33–40.

[6] Hing, E., & Sekscenski, E. (1986). Use of health care-nursing home care. NCHS Analytical and Epidemiological Series 3, No. 25, 71–75.

[7] Palmer, M., German, P., & Ouslander, J. (1991). Risk factors for urinary incontinence one year after nursing home admission. *Research in Nursing and Health, 14,* 405–412.

[8] Diokno, A., Brock, B., Brown, M., & Herzog, R. (1986). Prevalence of urinary incontinence and other urological symptoms in the noninstitutionalized elderly. *Journal of Urology, 136*(5), 1022–1025.

[9] Harris, T. (1986). Aging in the eighties. Prevalence and impact of urinary problems in individuals age 65 years and over. Washington DC, NCHS Advance Data.

[10] Mohide, E. A., Pringle, D., Robertson, D., & Chambers, L. (1988). Prevalence of urinary incontinence in patients receiving home care services. *CMAJ, 139,* 953–956.

[11] Wetle, T., Scherr, P., Branch, L., Resnick, N., Harris, T., Evans, D., & Taylor, J. (1995). Difficulty with holding urine among older persons in a geographically defined community: prevalence and correlates. *Journal of the American Geriatrics Society, 43,* 349–355.

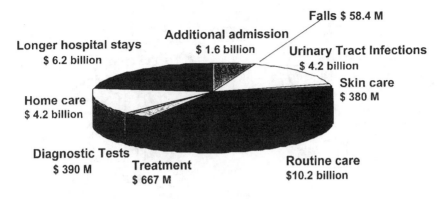

Falls $ 58.4 M

Additional admission
$ 1.6 billion

Longer hospital stays
$ 6.2 billion

Urinary Tract Infections
$ 4.2 billion

Skin care
$ 380 M

Home care
$ 4.2 billion

Diagnostic Tests
$ 390 M

Treatment
$ 667 M

Routine care
$10.2 billion

Total costs of $ 27.9 billion (T.W.Hu, 1997)

Figure 7.1 Costs of urinary incontinence to older people (65+) in the United States (permission granted).
Source: Newman, D. (1997). Guest editorial: How much society pays for urinary incontinence. *Ostomy/Wound Management*, 43(1), 18–25.

within the bladder) exceeds intraurethral pressure. Urinary incontinence, then, is essentially a problem of emptying or storing urine, or a combination of both. See Figure 7.2.

In continent individuals, emptying occurs at the discretion of the central nervous system leading to voluntary emptying of the bladder, or micturition. This complex physiologic process of interactions between genitourinary organs and neural control is also shaped by societal norms. The timing and location of micturition in Western society is rigidly shaped. Children at very early ages learn that control over bowel and bladder is a skill that is highly rewarded and which provides entree to adult society. By age 5 years, children are expected to be continent. Despite all the emphasis and energy expended on achieving continence in early childhood, little research or clinical interests have been focused on the maintenance of this function over the lifespan. Until the past 2 decades, urinary incontinence was rarely mentioned in medical and nursing textbooks and care of incontinent individuals received little attention in nursing curricula (Moore & Paul, 1997; Morishita, Uman, & Pierson, 1994).

Insufficient knowledge among the lay population about normal developmental stages, such as pregnancy and aging, may lead people to erroneously believe that urinary incontinence is a

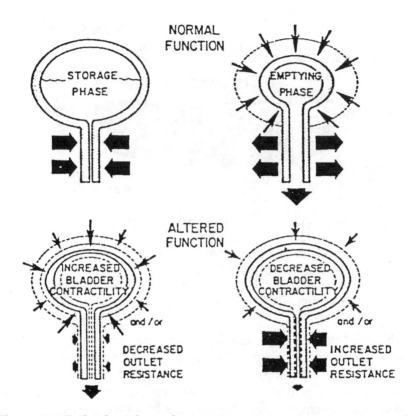

Figure 7.2   Pathophysiology of urinary incontinence (permission granted).
Source: Wyman, J. (1991). Incontinence and related problems. In Chenitz, W.
C., Stone, J. T., & Salisburg, S. A., *Clinical gerontological nursing: A guide to
advanced practice* (pp. 181–201). Philadelphia: W. B. Saunders.

normal part of these changes. Urinary incontinence may result in a
psychological response of shame or embarrassment, leading affected
individuals to hide the condition from others and attempt to deal
with it as best they can. In any discussion about interventions to prevent incontinence, it must be acknowledged that factors outside the
genitourinary organs and nervous system, such as knowledge level
and psychological response, play a role, albeit a poorly understood
one, in the development and presence of urinary incontinence.

Until recently, consumers paid little attention to the prevention
of urinary incontinence. In a provocative paper written in 1979,
Isaacs stated: "Dear old ladies do not carry round collecting boxes
for the incontinent, and it is of little use reminding them that they

are the future victims of this disorder" (p. 157). Past societal attitudes including the stigma associated with incontinence, lack of
acknowledgement that urinary incontinence is a worthy area of
scientific investigation, and the inadequacy of the medical model
to address urinary incontinence in adults, have been barriers to the
development of prevention-focused interventions. For too long
health care providers had thought of urinary incontinence as a
management and containment issue. There had been a sense of
futility among health care providers and society in general that
incontinence will inevitably occur in old age. The fact is that urinary incontinence is occurring at all ages and its prevention has
not been adequately addressed by health care providers.

Health care provider and public awareness and attitudes, however, are changing. Since 1992, over 5 million copies of the *Agency
for Health Care Policy and Research Clinical Practice Guideline Urinary
Incontinence in Adults: Acute and Chronic Management* have been disseminated. The guideline addresses public education and prevention as areas in need of research. Dr. Nancy Watson conducted a
study about the use and implementation in clinical practice of the
guideline in nursing homes (Agency for Health Care Policy and
Research, 1997). In the popular lay publication, *People*, a recent article discussed the stresses of caregiving for an older parent (Berman,
1997). With one in four families in the United States providing
some kind of caregiving for an older relative, a health promotion
approach to urinary continence is needed. The impact of incontinence can be devastating. Berman noted, "Many people reach their
limit when the parent becomes incontinent" (p. 84). This issue of
caregiver burden poses the challenge to researchers to determine if
urinary incontinence can be prevented and its onset delayed.

Siu, Beers, and Morgenstern (1993) hypothesized that 50,000
cases of moderate to severe urinary incontinence in women could
be reduced annually through the use of behavioral interventions.
Before an intervention can be applied, however, the problem must
be reported to or identified by the health care provider. Researchers
have found that older adults often do not report urinary incontinence to their health care provider, even when the older adult per-
ceives it as a problem (Burgio, Ives, Locher, Arena, & Kuller, 1994).
Therefore, the health care provider cannot depend upon self-report
but must actively solicit information about bladder control problems.
If behavioral interventions are indicated from the assessment and

diagnostic procedures, patient education is necessary to maintain the protocol and evaluate the outcomes.

Interventions, however, must be developed in context with consumer needs. A recent survey reported that 62% of the respondents were unsatisfied with treatment outcomes (National Association for Continence, 1996). Therefore, both the consumer and the provider of an intervention must make clear their respective expectations of the intervention's outcomes.

CONCEPTUAL MODEL FOR CONTINENCE PROMOTION

The model in Figure 7.3 makes the assumption that urinary incontinence is a public health problem with multiple etiological factors (Palmer, 1994). Environment plays a role both in etiology and with interventions. Using this approach, interventions, therefore, can be classified as primary, secondary, and tertiary prevention. There is also an assumption that prevalence (i.e., number of people with incontinence) and incidence (i.e., number of people who develop incontinence) can be reduced through the strategies outlined.

Outcomes have also been identified with each level of intervention. These outcomes were developed due to the inadequacy of the dichotomous outcome: continent versus incontinent. The terms social, independent, and dependent continence were devised by Dr. David Fonda, an Australian physician, who was aware that dependency on help from others is often a factor in the maintenance of continence in older adults (Fonda, 1990). The term partial continence was created because this is a realistic outcome for many older adults. That is, through various interventions incontinent episodes may be reduced, but the person will not become totally dry (Palmer, 1996).

Independent continence is the appropriate outcome for already continent individuals who can handle their eliminative needs without the physical intervention of another person. Primary prevention strategies are focused on this group whereas dependent continence refers to the outcome for individuals who remain totally dry solely through the efforts of a caregiver. It may be that secondary prevention strategies are so successful that an incontinent person becomes totally dry through the efforts of the caregiver.

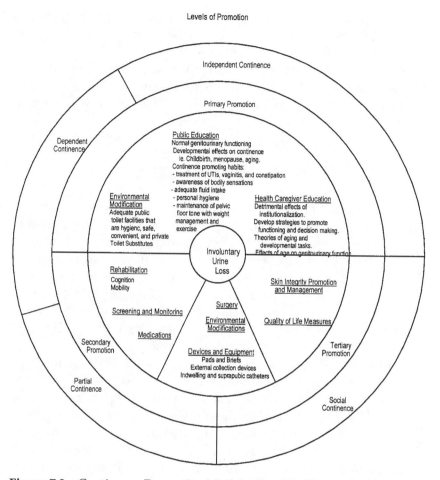

Figure 7.3 Continence Promotion Model—Levels of Promotion (Adapted from Palmer, M. (1991)). Urinary Incontinence. *Nursing Clinics of North America*, 25(4), 919–934. Figure 1. (In public domain, written while employed by The National Institutes of Health).

Primary prevention interventions would then be appropriate to help maintain urinary continence.

Partial continence indicates an improvement in dryness and maintenance of that improvement, but total continence is not achieved. An individual for whom partial continence is an appropriate outcome is one who has some ability to delay voiding until the appropriate time to toilet. Behavioral interventions (ie., prompted voiding) with absorbent products as adjunct therapy is one example of secondary strategies for achieving partial continence.

Social continence is an appropriate outcome for individuals who are unable to attain control over bladder function and who would not benefit from rehabilitative strategies such as prompted voiding or bladder training. The purpose of social continence interventions is to retain urine on the body by means of pads, briefs, external urine collection devices, and so on, while maintaining skin integrity and controlling odor.

PRIMARY PREVENTION

The overall goal of primary prevention strategies is to prevent urinary incontinence from occurring in continent individuals, mainly by removing causes of incontinence. Primary prevention strategies are directed at reducing incidence, that is new cases of incontinence. See Figure 7.4 for the difference between incidence and prevalence. Little primary prevention research on urinary continence has been conducted. This model identifies three major areas for primary prevention strategies: environmental modification, public education, and health caregiver education.

To prevent the development of urinary incontinence development, it is necessary to understand its causes and pathophysiology. Urinary incontinence has been classified into two patterns—established or transient. Established incontinence is a pattern that has persisted over time. It is further classified into types, for example, stress, urge, overflow. Urinary incontinence that occurs as a result of inadequate access to toilet facilities and deficits other than genitourinary deficits (ie., dementia, mobility impairment) is considered functional incontinence. Urinary incontinence that has an abrupt onset and resolves once an underlying pathology or condition resolves is considered transient incontinence. See Table 7.2 for examples of each pattern of urinary incontinence.

Epidemiological research has led to the identification of some risk factors for urinary incontinence. Researchers must use these findings as a basis for the development of interventions designed to prevent the initial occurrence of incontinence. The incidence of urinary incontinence has been difficult to determine because of the necessary longitudinal design of studies. One study investigated the changes in continence status in newly admitted residents over their first year of admission in eight nursing homes (Palmer, German,

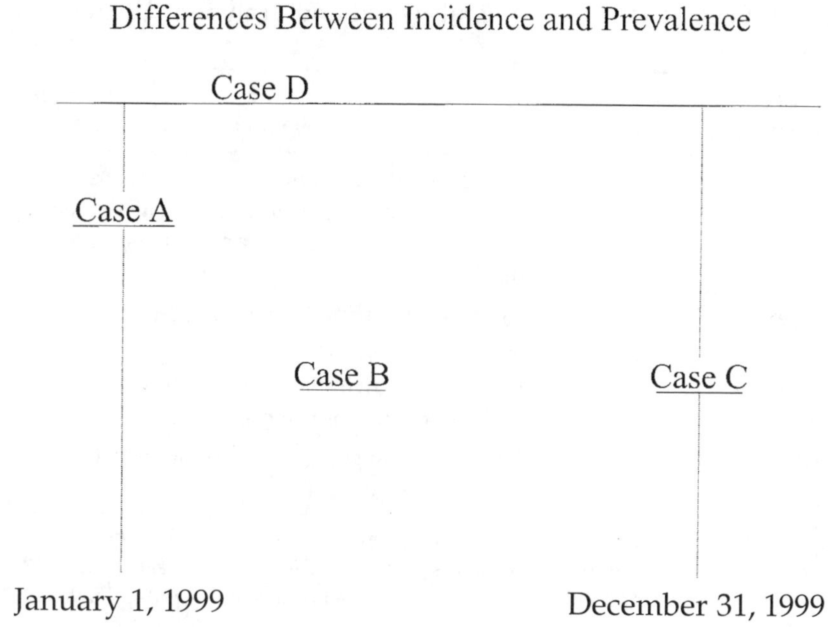

Differences Between Incidence and Prevalence

Case D

Case A

Case B   Case C

January 1, 1999   December 31, 1999

Figure 7.4 Case B and Case C are considered incident cases because they developed during the observation period of January 1, 1999 to December 31, 1999. In calculating incidence, the denominator is the number of people who do not have the disease or condition, but who are at risk for developing it. The numerator are the cases that developed during the specified time frame. Cases A, B, C, and D are prevalent cases because all were present during the observation period.

& Ouslander, 1991). It found that of the remaining residents who had been admitted continent, 27% (30/112) were incontinent at the year's end. Risk factors included male gender, cognitive impairment, and mobility impairment. Prevention focused interventions addressing the needs of people with these risk factors still need development and empirical testing.

Changes in continence status were also explored in a group of 100 older adults who underwent surgical repair of a hip fracture (Palmer, Myers, & Fedenko, 1997). Of the 76 patients who had been continent pre-operatively, 24 became incontinent post-operatively (32%). Two factors were statistically significant: gender and presence of cognitive impairment. Men developed incontinence at a

TABLE 7.2   Examples of Established and Transient Urinary Incontinence

Types of established urinary incontinence	Symptoms
Stress	Urine loss coincident with an increase in intra-abdominal pressure in the absence of detrusor contraction on an overdistended bladder
Urge	Involuntary urine loss associated with a strong desire to void
Overflow	Involuntary urine loss associated with overdistension of the bladder
Functional	Urine loss caused by factors outside the lower urinary tract

Source: U. S. Department of Health and Human Services. (1996). *Clinical Practice Guideline Urinary Incontinence in Adults: Acute and Chronic Management No. 2 1996 Update.* Agency for Health Care Policy and Research, AHCPR Pub. No. 96-0682. Rockville, MD.

higher rate than women (48% versus 24%) and cognitively impaired individuals developed incontinence at a higher rate than cognitively intact (56% versus 25%). In the presence of cognitive impairment, however, the risk of incontinence is similar between men and women. See Figure 7.5.

It may be that different underlying mechanisms are at work for men, the cognitively impaired, and the general population which puts each group at-risk for developing urinary incontinence. Meanwhile, individualized interventions need to be developed and used. While these interventions are being tested, research investigating the underlying mechanisms leading to the development of incontinence needs to be conducted. Some questions for research include:

1. Is incidence due to a change in voiding stance for men?
2. Is there urinary retention due to the combination of the presence of benign prostatic hypertrophy, use of anti-cholinergic medications, the volume of peri-operative fluid infusion, and post-operative voiding stance?

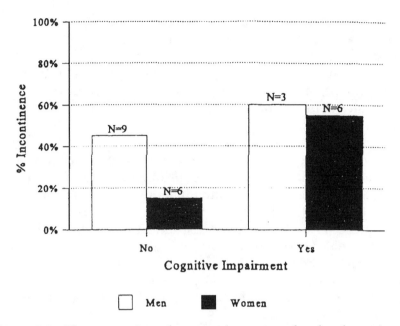

Figure 7.5   The proportion of men and women who develop urinary incontinence by cognitive status (permission granted).
Source: Palmec, M., Myers, A., & Fedenko, K. (1997). Urinary continence changes after hip fracture repair. *Clinical Nursing Research, 6*(1), 8–24.

3. What role does post-operative pain play in the development of incontinence?
4. Are toileting opportunities available to men and women post-operatively?
5. Is teaching self-toileting to capable individuals an option to prevent incontinence?
6. Are external urinary collection devices feasible for women to use post-operatively?

Environmental modification is an injury control technique in the public health model. The aim is to make the performance of a desired behavior easy for people. Therefore, timely access to toilets or toilet substitutes where people can relieve themselves in a socially appropriate manner is one strategy. Maintenance of an impaired older adult's continence can be difficult for informal caregivers. Flaherty, Miller, and Coe (1992) reported that family members or friends who acted as caregivers of dependent continent elderly people found that maintaining urinary function was a burden because of the magnitude of the caregiving effort. Understanding the needs of the caregiver and those of the vulnerable adult can often be the first step in the development and testing of interventions, such as modifying the environment or using toilet substitutes at night, for example, female urinals and external collection devices.

Public education is another important component of primary prevention strategies. Many older adults believe incontinence is inevitable with old age (Mitteness, 1990). Therefore, effective educational strategies to help individuals to understand how their bodies work and to clarify misconceptions are needed. Moore and Saltmarche (1993) developed an instrument to determine the needs of individuals for information about incontinence and its management that can be used when planning educational programs and research. User friendly, culturally diverse, and multi-media educational strategies need to be developed (U. S. Department of Health and Human Services, 1996).

Health caregiver education, especially for direct caregivers, is needed. There are differences in level of knowledge among nursing staff. Therefore, continuing education curricula addressing aging changes, identification of risk factors, and causes of transient incontinence is needed in all health care delivery settings. Access to education resources on the Internet is becoming more readily available. With the momentum for evidence-based practice, the need for dissemination of state-of-the-art clinical interventions is even more pressing.

SECONDARY PREVENTION

The goal of secondary prevention interventions is to prevent incontinence from becoming worse. The majority of efforts by continence researchers have been spent on secondary prevention strategies. The overall goal has been reducing prevalence of incontinence.

A recently reported study using Minimum Data Set (MDS) data from nursing homes found that potentially reversible causes of incontinence (see Table 7.3) can be easily identified and potentially modified. The authors suggest that these modifications could

TABLE 7.3   Transient or Reversible Incontinence Associated With:

- Urinary tract infection
- Delirium
- Immobility
- Congestive heart failure
- Diabetes mellitus
- Fecal impaction
- Lack of toilet access
- Depression
- Recent stroke
- Medications

result in the reduction in the prevalence of incontinence in nursing homes (Brandeis, Baumann, Hossain, Morris, & Resnick, 1997).

Brown, Seeley, Fong, Black, Ensrud et al. (1996) conducted a large study investigating osteoporotic fractures (N = 7949) in postmenopausal women. They found that age, hysterectomy, use of estrogen, obesity, poor overall health, and several medical conditions were associated with urinary incontinence. Research is needed to determine if prevalence can be reduced when behaviors associated with some of these factors, such as the use of estrogen and obesity, are modified.

In the long-term care setting where mobility and cognitive impairments are predominant, behavioral interventions such as prompted voiding and patterned urge response toileting (PURT) have been found effective in reducing incontinent episodes (Engel, Burgio, McCormick, Hawkins, Scheve et al., 1990; Colling, Ouslander, Hadley, Eisch, & Campbell, 1992). Prompted voiding and patterned urge response toileting are toileting assistance interventions. Prompted voiding involves three major steps. The first step consists of monitoring the person on a regular basis by both physically checking and asking if wet or dry. The person is then prompted to use the toilet, and finally the person receives praise for either being dry or using the toilet. Patterned urge response toileting involves a toileting schedule based on the individuals' voiding pattern. Both interventions require staff adherence to the toileting schedules to achieve optimal results.

Jirovec and Wells (1990) found that mobility level was the best predictor of a nursing home resident's bladder control. Therefore, improving mobility status may have a positive impact on continence. In the community setting, pelvic muscle exercises have been found effective in women with stress and urge incontinence and in some men post-prostatectomy (U. S. Department of Health and Human Services, 1996).

Because of the labor intensity of behavioral interventions, there also have been studies conducted related to the costs of different behavioral interventions, especially in the nursing home setting. For example, Schnelle, Keeler, Hays, Simmons, Ouslander et al. (1995) found that prompted voiding added $4.31 to each patient's daily care costs. They also noted that families preferred behavioral interventions over other alternatives, for example, private rooms.

In addition to the labor-intensive nature of behavioral interventions, current reimbursement mechanisms regulatory oversight, and staffing levels in nursing homes make careful assessment of incontinent residents essential. Identification of expected outcomes, for example, dependent continence or partial continence should occur prior to the intervention with periodic evaluation of the success of the intervention. These questions must be asked: What are the staff's, affected adult's, and family's expectations of the intervention? What will be the measure of success?

Educational interventions geared to affected adults have also been used. Newman, Wallace, Blackwood, and Spencer (1996) reported on an educational program that used elder peer educators to teach healthy bladder habits (ie., monitoring of voiding, bowel management, and use of absorbent products). The participants reported that they had greater bladder control after the program.

TERTIARY PREVENTION

Tertiary prevention strategies are used when reversing the condition is not a viable option. It should be noted that the employment of surgery, devices, and equipment may be either secondary or tertiary strategies depending on the expected outcome. If surgery is expected to improve dryness, such as with collagen injections, then it is a secondary intervention. If however, surgery is used to divert urine, as with an ileal conduit, to preserve skin integrity and to prevent infection, then surgery is a tertiary prevention strategy.

The goals of tertiary strategies, such as topical barriers to protect the skin are to prevent further complication and to preserve the quality of life.

Although there is a wide array of products and devices to contain incontinence, more research is required to determine physical and psychosocial effects of these products. Comparisons between reusable and disposable products are also needed. External urine collection devices for women, especially those who are unable to abduct their legs, should be made readily available.

IMPLICATIONS TO RESEARCH AND CLINICAL CARE

Prevention-focused interventions require sophisticated clinical and research skills. A multidisciplinary approach is needed to address all the aspects of the promotion of continence in older adults. Continent individuals need to be viewed as potentially incontinent people, just as incontinent individuals should be viewed as potentially continent, and interventions to protect vulnerable or at-risk individuals need to be identified and implemented.

Societal issues, such as the decline model of aging and the stigma of urinary incontinence, must be confronted head on with a multimedia educational approach. The needs and preferences, however, of older adults and caregivers must be incorporated into these activities. The lack of participation in health promotion activities has been noted in older adults with lower income and less community involvement than those who did participate in these activities (Wagner, Grothaus, Hecht, & LaCroix, 1991). Therefore, special efforts must be made to recruit individuals with these characteristics who would most likely benefit from educational and other forms of primary prevention activities.

The development of prevention-focused interventions has been slow. Historically, most interventions have focused on managing or containing urine loss. Acting on existing information while continually updating knowledge, nurses and other health care providers can achieve the paradigm shift regarding urinary continence that is sorely needed. The shift will be towards the goal of making continence an attainable and lifelong attribute.

```

144      Health Promotion and Disease Prevention

## REFERENCES

Agency of Health Care Policy and Research (1997, August). Publication No. AHCPR Pub. No. 97-0054. [On-line]. Available: http:\\www. ahcpr.gov\research\longtrm2.htm#head8.
Berman, C. (1997, August 25). Taking care. *People, 48,* pp. 83–86.
Brandeis, G., Baumann, M., Hossain, M., Morris, J., & Resnick, N. (1997). The prevalence of potentially remediable urinary incontinence in frail older people: A study using the Minimum Data Set. *Journal of the American Geriatrics Society, 45*(2), 179–184.
Brown, J., Seeley, D., Fong, J., Black, D., Ensrud, K., & Grady, D. (1996). Urinary incontinence in older women: Who is at risk? *Obstetrics & Gynecology, 87*(5 pt 1), 715–721.
Burgio, K. Ives, D. Locher, J., Arena, V., & Kuller, L. (1994). Treatment seeking for urinary incontinence in older adults. *Journal of the American Geriatrics Society, 42*(2), 208–212.
Colling, J., Ouslander, J., Hadley, B., Eisch, J., & Campbell, E. (1992). The effects of patterned urge response toileting (PURT) on urinary incontinence among nursing home residents. *Journal of the American Geriatrics Society, 40*(2), 135–141.
Engel, B., Burgio, L., McCormick, K., Hawkins, A, Scheve, A., & Leahy, E. (1990). Behavioral treatment of incontinence in the long-term care setting. *Journal of the American Geriatrics Society, 38*(3), 361–363.
Flaherty, J., Miller, D., & Coe, R. (1992). Impact on caregivers of supporting urinary function in noninstitutionalized, chronically ill seniors. *Gerontologist, 32*(4), 541–545.
Fonda, D. (1990). Improving management of urinary incontinence in geriatric centres and nursing homes. Victoria Geriatrician Peer Review Group, *Australian Clinical Review (Sydney), 10*(2), 66–71.
International Continence Society (1990). The standardization of terminology of lower urinary tract function. *British Journal of Obstetrics and Gynecology,* (Suppl. 6), 1–16.
Isaacs, B. (1979). Water, water everywhere . . . it's time we stopped to think. *Royal Society Health Journal, 99*(4), 155–157.
Jirovec, M., & Wells, T. (1990). Urinary incontinence in nursing home residents with dementia: The mobility-cognition paradigm. *Applied Nursing Research, 3*(3), 112–117.
Mitteness, L. S. (1990). Knowledge and beliefs about urinary incontinence in adulthood and old age. *Journal of the American Geriatrics Society, 38*(3), 374–378.
Moore, K., & Paul, P. (1997). A historical review of selected nursing and medical literature on urinary incontinence between 1850 and 1976. *Journal of Wound, Ostomy and Continence Nursing, 24*(2), 106–122.
```

Moore, T., & Saltmarche, A. (1993). Developing and testing an instrument to assess the information needs of persons with urinary incontinence. *Perspectives, 17*(1), 2–6.

Morishita, L., Uman, G., & Pierson, C. (1994). Education on adult urinary incontinence in nursing school curricula: Can it be done in two hours? *Nursing Outlook, 42*(3), 123–129.

National Association For Continence (1996). NAFC Consumer Focus '96: A Survey of Community-dwelling Incontinent People. Spartansburg, SC: National Association For Continence.

Newman, D. (1997). How much society pays for urinary incontinence. *Ostomy/Wound Management, 43*(1), 18–25.

Newman, D., Wallace, J. Blackwood, N., & Spencer, C. (1996). Promoting healthy bladder habits for seniors. *Ostomy/Wound Management, 42*(10), 18–28.

Palmer, M. (1994). A health-promotion perspective of urinary continence. *Nursing Outlook, 42*(4), 163–169.

Palmer, M. (1996). A new framework for urinary continence outcomes in long-term care. *Urologic Nursing, 16*(4), 146–151.

Palmer, M., German, P., & Ouslander, J. (1991). Risk factors for urinary incontinence one year after nursing home admission. *Research in Nursing & Health, 14,* 405–412.

Palmer, M., Myers, A., & Fedenko, K. (1997). Urinary continence changes after hip-fracture repair. *Clinical Nursing Research, 6*(1), 8–24.

Schnelle, J., Keeler, E., Hays, R., Simmons, S., Ouslander, J., & Siu, A. (1995). A cost and value analysis of two interventions with incontinent nursing home residents. *Journal of the American Geriatrics Society, 43*(10), 1112–1117.

Siu, A., Beers, M., & Morgenstern, H. (1993). The geriatric "medical and public health" imperative revisited. *Journal of the American Geriatrics Society, 41*(1), 78–84.

U. S. Department of Health and Human Services (1996). Urinary incontinence in adults: Acute and chronic management. Clinical practice guideline. Number 2. 1996 Update. Agency for Health Care Policy and Research (AHCPR Pub. No. 96-0682). Rockville, MD: Public Health Service.

Wagner, E., Grothaus, L. Hecht, J., & LaCroix, A. (1991). Factors associated with participation in a senior health promotion program. *Gerontologist, 31*(5), 598–602.

CHAPTER 8

Prevention of Cancer in the Elderly

Robert B. Wallace

undamentally, cancer is a disease of older people. While it is not one but several related conditions, cancer is responsible for about 25% of all deaths in the United States (Anonymous, 1993), most occurring after 65 years of age. Cancer incidence increases with age in almost all organs and anatomic sites. With the great increase in the number of older persons, particularly within industrialized countries, it is now possible to more accurately determine cancer occurrence rates for the eighth, ninth, and tenth decades of life, confirming the age-related increased occurrence. As a corollary, increased population aging has allowed the conduct of preventive and treatment trials that inform cancer management in elders, something never previously possible.

Great advances in understanding the epidemiology, pathogenesis and natural history of various cancers have revealed that the biologic onset of many cancers occurs years or decades before they become clinically apparent. For example, breast cancer risk in older women has been related to age-at-menarche (Hunter, Spiegelman, Adami, van den Brandt, Folsom et al., 1997) and the accumulation exposure to hazardous environmental chemicals in the workplace may have an impact many years later. On the surface, this seems to suggest that primary prevention of cancer in older people may be challenging because the disease process has already been set in motion. However, we also know that cancer development and progression can be altered at many points, and that screening programs at least have the potential to intercept cancers before they are destructive to the individual. Yet, it is also clear that effective cancer prevention among elders must often begin at an early age.

Aging and the Biology of Cancer

While this chapter is not about the biology either of cancer or aging, it is worth noting that these processes fundamentally concern the same set of cell machinery and functions, and pursuit of knowledge in each area informs the other. Several examples are worth noting. The function of telomeres, the endmost segments of chromosomes that change as cells divide, has important implications for both age-related physiological changes and for cancer pathogenesis (Dahse, Fiedler, & Ernst, 1997). One theory holds that errors in chromosomal DNA accumulate over time, particularly during cell replication, leading to both cellular aging and a propensity for cancer development (Knight, 1995). In fact, the ability of cells to repair errors in DNA may decrease with age and that ability has been explored as a risk factor for cancer development (Schantz, Zhang, Spitz, Sun, & Hsu, 1997). In another example, age-related changes in drug metabolism are well-described, but this may also be true for the metabolism of environmental chemicals. The net effect of these changes are uncertain and likely diverse, but could work in a health or unhealthy direction, either decreasing or enhancing the risk of cancer among those exposed, depending on whether the toxins are more or less available. This issue becomes important as more persons stay in the workplace longer. One important conclusion from all of these examples is that biomarkers of aging may also be biomarkers of cancer risk and occurrence.

A final example of the intersection of cancer and aging biology is the established principle of homeostasis, the ability of the body to respond to physiologic stresses and maximize survivorship (Childs & Egan, 1996; Parsons, 1996). With increasing age, this ability declines, and it is possible that nascent and clinical cancers, and their detection and treatment procedures, represent greater stresses to less resilient older people, leading to more difficulty in both cancer prevention and management. This may in part explain, for example, why stage-specific survival rates are often lower among elders.

Maintaining Vitality and the Primary Prevention of Cancer

Primary prevention is the prevention of a disease or undesired condition before its biologic onset. The primary prevention of cancer at all ages occurs in many settings. Promoting lower exposures to workplace carcinogens and medical x-rays are important examples of how primary prevention can work. Of course, the most important general carcinogen in the environment is tobacco smoke, and this is a continuing problem for older smokers. While the hazards of tobacco are widely appreciated, it has now been demonstrated that continued cigarette smoking leads to more frequent disease events even in the seventh and eighth decades (Corti, Guralnik, & Bilato, 1996), and smoking is also a risk factor for decreased physical function (LaCroix, Guralnik, Berkman, Wallace, & Satterfield, 1993). The effects of cigarette smoke may be biologically diverse. For example, exposure of aging mice to tobacco smoke altered the general immune response to test antigens (Beregi, Regius, Rajczy, Boross, & Penzes, 1991). Recent research has led to other examples of primary cancer prevention. Vaccination for hepatitis B infection will likely prevent some liver cancer that is related to chronic hepatitis B infection (Sherman, 1995). In the future, it is possible that the antibiotic treatment of *Helicobacter* species may lead to the primary prevention of gastric cancer (O'Connor, Buckley, & O'Morain, 1996). Prevention of excess sun exposure will likely decrease the incidence of skin cancers among older persons and even the oldest old.

However, much more problematic is the issue of dietary interventions for cancer prevention among older persons. General dietary recommendations for cancer prevention usually include lower fat, higher fiber diets that emphasize vitamins and "anti-oxidants" from fruit and vegetable sources. However, these diets have never been tested in a randomized trial of primary prevention among elders, although that is now occurring in the Women's Health Initiative (Greenwald, Sherwood, & McDonald, 1997). There are several problems with dietary recommendations for prevention in older persons, including the costs of various foods, the ability to chew and digest some foods, the frequent occurrence of specially prescribed diets for concurrent co-morbid conditions, altered taste and olfactory function, the increasing rates of lactose intolerance and the complexity of preparing many recipes. There is also the general issue of maintaining nutritional adequacy, as optimal requirements may differ for older people.

Because of epidemiological and supporting experimental animal research suggesting that some micronutrients are associated with lower rates of some cancers, there have been clinical trials of some of these agents as cancer preventives or of deferring the progression of premalignant lesions, such as adenomatous polyps of the colon. Findings so far have been incomplete and mixed. There is some preliminary evidence that, in separate studies, selenium (Clark, Combs, Turnbull, Slate, Chalker et al., 1996) and Vitamins C and E (Rock, Jacob, & Bowen, 1996) supplementation and calcium and Vitamin D intake (Kleibeuker, Cats, van der Meer, Lapre, & de Vries, 1994) have been associated with prevention of various cancers, but more work is clearly needed. However, adverse effects on lung cancer rates has been seen in trials of beta-carotene supplements (Palmgren, Freedman, Haapakoski, Barrett, Pietinen et al., 1996), suggesting at the very least that all such supplementation practices should be subject to rigorous clinical trials, with cancer outcomes, despite the "promise" of such agents. Similarly, a rush to "alternative medicine" may not always have the desired effects.

Body weight and obesity also subsume diet-related issues relevant to cancer prevention. Obesity is related to increased risk of breast and endometrial cancers among older women (Ballard-Barbash, Birt, Kestin, & King, 1997); thus, maintaining normative body weight may have a role in primary cancer prevention. Body weight is also in part related to exercise practices, and while exercise is not often thought of as a cancer preventive, it may well have an important role. Exercise speculatively may also be a preventive in that it promotes bowel motility, and may alter large intestinal contents in a favorable way (Thune, Brenn, Lund, & Gaard, 1997). That obesity is a risk factor for certain cancers highlights the problem that a harmful risk factor for one condition may be protective for another. In this case, obesity is associated with protection from hip fracture. Thus, understanding the net health and vitality impact of various preventive interventions seems essential for making hygienic and other preventive recommendations.

Secondary Prevention: The Early and Asymptomatic Detection of Cancer in Elders

This has been a somewhat controversial area but also one in which there have been substantial successes in cancer control. There is little question that certain universally applied screening tests have prevented deaths from breast, colon, and uterine cervical cancer. Much of this has been documented in the "Guide to Clinical Preventive Services," produced by the U.S. Department of Health and Human Services (U.S. Preventive Services Task Force, 1996). The problem for older persons is that there are few randomized trials to evaluate the outcomes of even successful screening *maneuvers that began with persons over 70 years of age at baseline.* The reasons for this lack of research findings are generally well known: there were fewer elders to study in prior years; informed consent was sometimes hard to obtain; elder health issues previously did not receive a high priority; frequent co-morbidity made recruitment into trials difficult and the interpretations of trial outcomes complex; and, there were logistical problems in maintaining the oldest old in long-term trials (e.g., difficulties with caregiving burden and lack of transportation).

Thus, an evidence-based assessment of cancer screening efficacy for persons over 70 years generally finds little to support the screening maneuvers, and the screening activities are often performed under the assumption that they can be extrapolated from evidence in younger age groups. For example, there is little direct evidence for the efficacy of screening for breast cancer with mammography in women over age 70 years. A similar situation pertains for colon cancer screening. An interesting issue is the emerging, but incomplete, evidence that if a woman has had at least three normal pap smears at annual intervals, there may be no reason to screen for cervical cancer after age 65 years (U.S. Preventive Services Task Force, 1996, p. 105). There are also some cancer screening maneuvers whose efficacy for preventing death from various tumors has not been demonstrated in any age group, such as screening for prostate cancer with prostate-specific antigen, and screening for ovarian, pancreatic, oral, bladder, or lung cancers (U.S. Preventive

Services Task Force, 1996). Randomized trials of several promising screening activities are in place, but clearly the biggest problem is that there have been too few longitudinal studies of the natural histories of various cancers and too few clinical trials of preventive interventions performed among older persons, particularly those over 70 years of age. Clinical preventive guidelines will continue to emerge, and on occasion different groups will offer different and contradictory recommendations. However, it is likely that even the most divergent recommendations would converge if solid evidence were available.

Even as evidence for the efficacy of various cancer screening maneuvers is being sought, an equally important problem is encouraging older people to avail themselves of existing cancer screening services. There is clear underutilization of proven screening services, and a variety of reasons have been suggested. Several factors associated with this underutilization have been identified:

Poor perception of the meaning of health
Little understanding of the role of cancer in health and mortality
Ongoing medical conditions
Lack of geographic access to screening services
Lower socioeconomic status
Lack of insurance coverage for cancer screening
Fear of cancer and its treatments
Cultural and linguistic barriers
Lack of transportation to medical care
Caregiving activities

While it is not possible to elaborate each particular factor here, many are amenable to change through education or provision of specific services. Self-defeating attitudes about the value of and need for cancer-screening activities can be a deterrent to active participation. An example from a survey of Hispanic and non-Hispanic white women in Texas is shown in Table 8.1 (Tortolero-Luna, Glober, Villarreal, Palos, & Linares, 1995). Hopefully, attitudes and behaviors that dissuade older persons from attending these screening activities can be changed so that cancer prevention can be maximized. There is also a need to encourage health care professionals, who attend nearly all older persons each year, to emphasize the need for cancer screening (Main, Cohen, & DiClemente, 1995) and

TABLE 8.1   Health Beliefs and Knowledge,
Neuces County, Texas

| | Women 50 Years and Older (percent) | |
	Hispanic	Non-Hispanic
Concerned about personal health	92	86
Illness a matter of chance	63	38*
Fast recovery a matter of luck	47	5*
Doctors help people	86	96*
Chances of surviving cancer	51	53
Fear of cancer	72	58*

Based on Tortolero-Luna et al., 1995.
* = $p < 0.05$

for medical care systems to build in mechanisms to automatically signal the use of these interventions (Frame, Zimmer, Werth, Hall, & Eberly, 1994). Not all educational and social interventions to improve screening rates and other preventive interventions need occur at the individual level; the potential for intervention at the community level should also be considered (Farquhar, Fortmann, Maccoby, Haskell, Williams et al., 1985).

The Tertiary Prevention of Cancer

Tertiary prevention of cancer refers to the prevention of progression of cancer conditions after the disease has occurred and received initial management. Of course, preventing tumor progression involves effective clinical treatments, and the special problems of treating older cancer patients has been highlighted (DiMatteo, Hays, & Sherbourne, 1992). However, there may also be general preventive activities that could preserve life and function. Examples include maintaining influenza and pneumonia immunizations, and adequate general nutrition. There could be reason to continue to perform periodic screening for cancer at other, unrelated anatomic sites or other preventive interventions not related to cancer, such as hypertension or bone density screening. In certain instances, chemoprophylaxis to prevent tumor recurrence or secondary infections (Donnelly, 1995) may be indicated. In any case, a philosophy of prevention even in the face of overt clinical illness may improve overall health and functional status.

Cancer Prevention and Vitality

The contribution of primary and secondary cancer prevention to vitality should not be underestimated. The physical and mental toll of cancer on the patient, the family, and society is enormous, and it can begin years before the clinical onset of the illness, as "preclinical" symptoms such as weight loss, fatigue, and possibly depression can occur due to nascent cancers. Also, the hygienic behaviors that decrease cancer occurrence, such as exercise and low fat diet, have salient positive effects on deterring other conditions and improving functional status and affect. Perhaps the satisfaction of knowing that a cancer is not likely present, after attending a negative screen, may contribute to an improved outlook and quality of life. However, as noted throughout this report, the biggest problem is that effective preventives for most of the common western cancers have not been identified for older people, and in their absence, the burden on vitality may be great.

REFERENCES

Anonymous. (1993). From the Centers for Disease Control and Prevention. Mortality Patterns—United States, 1991. *Journal of the American Medical Association, 270*(24), 2916–2917.

Ballard-Barbash, R. A., Birt, D. F., Kestin, M., & King, I. B. (1997). Perspectives on integrating experimental and epidemiologic research on diet, anthropometry and breast cancer. *Journal of Nutrition, 127*(Suppl. 5), 936S–939S.

Beregi, E., Regius, O., Rajczy, K., Boross, M., & Penzes, L. (1991). Effect of cigarette smoke and 2-mercaptoethanol administration on age-related alterations and immunological parameters. *Gerontology, 37*(6), 326–334.

Childs, S. J., & Egan, R. J. (1996). Bacteriuria and urinary infections in the elderly. *Urology Clinics of North America, 23*(1), 43–54.

Clark, L. C., Combs, G. F. Jr., Turnbull, B. W., Slate, E. H., Chalker, D. K., Chow, J., Davis, S. L., Glover, R. A., Graham, G. F., Gross, E. G., Krongrad, A., Lesher, J. L. Jr., Park, H. D., Sanders, B. B. Jr., Smith, C. L., & Taylor, J. R. (1996). Effects of selenium supplementation for cancer prevention in patients with carcinoma of the skin. A randomized controlled trial. *Journal of the American Medical Association, 276*(24), 1957–1963.

Corti, M. C., Guralnik, J. M., & Bilato, C. (1996). Coronary heart disease risk factors in older persons. *Aging, 8*(2), 75–89.

Dahse, R., Fiedler, W., & Ernst, G. (1997). Telomeres and telomerase: Biologic and clinical importance. *Clinical Chemistry, 43*(5), 708–714.

DiMatteo, M. R., Hays, R. D., & Sherbourne, C. D. (1992). Adherence to cancer regimens: Implications for treating the older patient. *Oncology, 6*(Suppl. 2), 50–57.

Donnelly, J. P. (1995). Chemoprophylaxis for the prevention of bacterial and fungal infections. *Cancer Treatment & Research, 79*, 45–81.

Farquhar, J. W., Fortmann, S. P., Maccoby, N., Haskell, W. L., Williams, P. T., Flora, J. A., Taylor, C. B., Brown, B. W. Jr., Solomon, D. S, & Hulley, S. B. (1985). The Stanford five-city project: Designs and methods. *American Journal of Epidemiology, 122*(2), 323–334.

Frame, P. S., Zimmer, J. G., Werth, P. L., Hall, W. J., & Eberly, S. W. (1994). Computer-based vs. manual health maintenance tracking. A controlled trial. *Archives of Family Medicine, 3*(7), 581–588.

Greenwald, P., Sherwood, K., & McDonald, S. S. (1997). Fat, caloric intake, and obesity: Lifestyle risk factors for breast cancer. *Journal of the American Dietetic Association, 97*(Suppl. 7), S24–30.

Hunter, D. J., Spiegelman, D., Adami, H. O., van den Brandt, P. A., Folsom, A. R., Goldbloom, R. A., Graham, S., Howe, G. R., Kushi, L. H., Marshall, J. R., Miller, A. B., Speizer, F. E., Willett, W., Wolk, A., & Yaun, S. S. (1997). Non-dietary risk factors for breast cancer, and as effect modifiers of the association of fat intake and risk of breast cancer. *Cancer Causes and Control, 8*(1), 49–56.

Kleibeuker, J. H., Cats, A., van der Meer, R., Lapre, J. A., & de Vries, E. G., (1994). Calcium supplementation as prophylaxis against colon cancer? *Digestive Diseases, 12*(2), 85–97.

Knight, J.A. (1995). The process and theories of aging. *Annals of Clinical and Laboratory Science, 25*(1), 1–12.

LaCroix, A. Z., Guralnik, J. M., Berkman, L. F., Wallace, R. B., & Satterfield, S. (1993). Maintaining mobility in late life. II. Smoking, alcohol consumption, physical activity and body mass index. *American Journal of Epidemiology, 137*(8), 858–869.

Main, D. S., Cohen, S. J., & DiClemente, C. C. (1995). Measuring physician readiness to change cancer screening: Preliminary results. *American Journal of Preventive Medicine, 11*(1), 54–58.

O'Connor, F., Buckley, M., & O'Morain, C. (1996). Helicobacter pylori: The cancer link. *Journal of the Royal Society of Medicine, 89*(12), 674–678.

Palmgren, J., Freedman, L. S., Haapakoski, J., Barrett, M. J., Pietinen, P., Malila, N., Tala, E., Liippo, K., Salomaa, E. R., Tangrea, J. A., Teppo, L., Askin, F. B., Taskinen, E., Erozan, Y., Greenwald, P., & Huttunen, J. K. (1996). Alpha-Tocopherol and beta-carotene supplements and lung cancer incidence in the alpha-tocopherol, beta-carotene cancer prevention study: Effects of baseline characteristics and study compliance. *Journal of the National Cancer Institute, 88*(21), 1560–1570.

Parsons, P. A. (1996). Rapid development and a long life: An association expected under a stress theory of aging. *Experimentia, 52*(7), 643–646.

Rock, C. L., Jacob, R. A., & Bowen, P. E. (1996). Update on the biologic characteristics of the antioxidant micronutrients. *Journal of the American Dietetic Association, 96*(7), 693–702.

Schantz, S. P., Zhang, Z. F., Spitz, M. S., Sun, M., & Hsu, T. C. (1997). Genetic susceptibility to head and neck cancer: Interaction between nutrition and mutagen sensitivity. *Laryngoscope, 107*(6), 765–781.

Sherman, M. (1995). Hepatocellular carcinoma. *Gastroenterologist, 3*(1), 55–66.

Thune, I., Brenn, T., Lund, E., & Gaard, M. (1997). Physical activity and the risk of breast cancer. *New England Journal of Medicine, 336*(18), 1269–1275.

Tortolero-Luna, G., Glober, G. A., Villarreal, R., Palos, G., & Linares, A. (1995). Screening practices and knowledge, attitudes and beliefs about cancer among Hispanic and non-Hispanic white women 35 years and older in Neuces County, Texas. *Journal of the National Cancer Institute,* Monographs(18), 49–56.

U.S. Preventive Services Task Force. (1996). *Guide to clinical preventive services* (2nd ed.). Baltimore: Williams & Wilkins.

CHAPTER 9

Premature Coronary Heart Disease: A Family Affair

Diane M. Becker and Raphael Yook

THE CURRENT STATE OF CARDIOVASCULAR DISEASE IN THE UNITED STATES

Violence, AIDS, substance abuse, and infectious diseases have received considerable attention as public health concerns in the past decade. These problems are eclipsing the importance of continuing high rates of chronic diseases, which are particularly significant as the lifespan increases in the U.S. population. Cardiovascular disease (CVD) remains highly prevalent in the United States (Figure 9.1) (American Heart Association [AHA], 1996). In 1996, an estimated 57,490,000 Americans had some form of CVD including high blood pressure (50,000,000), coronary heart disease (13,670,000), stroke (3,890,000), and rheumatic heart disease (1,380,000) (AHA, 1996).

Given the progress made in primary and secondary prevention, it is remarkable that nearly 1 million deaths still occur from CVD per year, with approximately equal rates in men and women. The sheer numbers of persons with CVD make it a major problem at both the individual and community level. Premature CVD is particularly troubling; 37% of CVD deaths occur prior to 75 years of age and 17% before 65 years of age (AHA, 1996).

Women are closing the well-known male-female gaps in CVD mortality rates, albeit at an older age. One in two women will die of heart disease or stroke, in comparison with the 4% who will die from breast cancer (AHA, 1996).

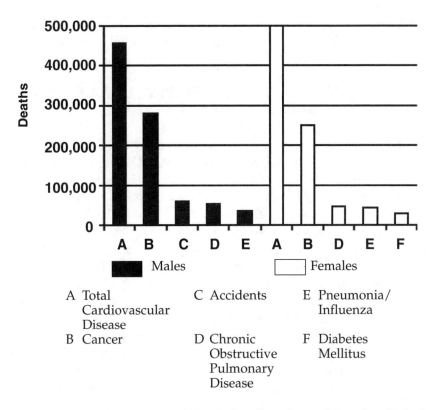

Figure 9.1 A Total Cardiovascular Disease B Cancer C Accidents D Chronic Obstructive Pulmonary Disease E Pneumonia/Influenza F Diabetes Mellitus

Figure 9.1 Leading causes of death for all males and females. United States: 1993 Mortality Data.
Source: National Center for Health Statistics; adapted from the American Heart Association *(1997 Heart and Stroke Statistical Update).*

Coronary heart disease (CHD) is the most frequent cause of CVD. CHD has well-characterized remediable risk factors which can be easily identified and treated. Maintaining vitality through-out the lifespan can be an achievable goal if persons at high risk for CHD can be identified and treated prior to experiencing a CHD event. Some risk factors are immutable but assist in identifying persons who need aggressive risk factor management. A family history of premature CHD (women <65 years of age and men <55 years of age) confers a potent increased risk in both men and women (Hunt, Williams, & Barlow, 1986; Nora, Lortscher, Spangler, Nora, & Kimberling, 1980; Rissanen, 1979). This paper will focus on CHD, risk factors, the effects of risk factor modification, and on our own studies of premature familial-aggregated CHD.

FAMILIAL-CLUSTERED PREMATURE CORONARY HEART DISEASE

First degree relatives of people with premature CHD have a 2 to 12 fold excess risk of developing premature CHD compared with the general population (Hunt et al., 1986; Rose, 1964; Shea, Ottman, Gabrieli, Stein, & Nichols, 1984; Slack & Evans, 1966; Snowden, McNamara, Garrison, Feinleib, Kannel et al., 1982). Familial-clustered CHD accounts for 55% to 60% of total documented CHD before 60 years of age (Williams, 1984). Specifically, siblings (SIBS) of persons with clinically manifest CHD are at the highest risk for developing future CHD events and also exhibit similar CHD risk factors. SIBS share both genetic material and sociocultural environments (Williams, 1988). Studies have demonstrated that individuals at the highest risk of developing CHD have clustering of multiple risk factors; only 3% to 35% of persons with CHD have ≤ two risk factors (Genest & Cohn, 1995; Sacco, Kargman, Gu, & Zamanillo, 1995), suggesting a need for multiple simultaneous interventions.

REMEDIABLE CHC RISK FACTORS

Lipids

Studies have established that elevated concentrations of serum total cholesterol and low density lipoprotein cholesterol (LDL-C) are independent predictors of increased CHD risk and that high-density lipoprotein cholesterol (HDL-C) demonstrates a strong inverse association to CHD risk (Frick, Elo, Haapa, Heinonen, Heinsalmi et al., 1987; Gartside & Glueck, 1995; Kannel, 1983; National Cholesterol Education Program [NCEP], 1994; National Institutes of Health Consensus Development Panel on Triglyceride High-Density Lipoprotein and Coronary Heart Disease, 1993). Increased levels of plasma triglycerides (TG) have been independently associated with CHD risk in some studies, but there is evidence that this may be dependent on concordance with other factors, mainly female sex, oral contraceptive use, and low HDL-C levels (Austin, 1989; Sprecher, Hein, & Laskarzewski, 1994). Two distinct types of familial lipoprotein disorders have been established: 1) genetic lipoprotein disorders, in which the molecular defect has been identified, and 2) familial clustering of lipoprotein abnormalities, in which the precise molecular defect is unknown and the interaction between genetic predisposition and environmental variables is more complex (Genest, Martin-Munley, McNamara, Ordovas, Jenner et al., 1992; Schaefer, Genest, Ordovas, Salem, & Wilson, 1993). The prevalence of familial lipoprotein disorders of any type is >57% in kindreds with premature CHD (Schaefer, 1994).

Hypertension

Results from longitudinal studies establish both high systolic and diastolic blood pressure (BP) as major risk factors for CHD, at all ages and in both sexes (Kannel, Castelli, Gordon, & McNamara, 1971). Epidemiological studies show that hypertension represents more than 25% of the attributable risk for first myocardial infarction (MI) (Kannel, 1993). Hypertension aggregates in families and BP levels reflect strong genetic determinants (Burke & Motulsky, 1992; Ward, 1990). Persons with elevated BP have a high prevalence of associated CHD risk factors, including hyperlipidemia and obesity. Williams, Hopkins, Hunt, Schumacher, Elbein et al. (1992) identified a coaggregation of hypertension and lipid abnormalities as one of the most common clinical syndromes within siblings of premature CHD families. The National Heart, Lung, and Blood Institute (NHLBI) Twin Study demonstrated that persons with this pattern had a 16-year mortality rate that was four times greater than in persons with a single lipid abnormality (Selby, Newman, Quiroga, Christian, Austin et al., 1991).

Smoking

Cigarette smoking is a major risk factor for CHD (Kannel, 1987) and may even be the single strongest discriminator of CHD events in some subsets (Beard, Griffin, Offord, & Edwards, 1986; Genest & Cohn, 1995; Willett, Green, Stampfer, Speizer, Colditz et al.,

1987). At least 25% of all CHD deaths are attributable to smoking (Hahn, Folsom, Sprafka, & Norsted, 1990). Studies have shown that smoking behavior aggregates within families (Fisher, Jr., Lichtenstein, & Haire-Joshu, 1993).

Obesity, Sedentary Lifestyle, and Dietary Factors

Thirty-two percent of CHD deaths are attributable to obesity (Hahn et al., 1990). An upper-body pattern of adipose tissue distribution, specifically high waist-to-hip ratio, has been associated with increased coronary morbidity (Lapidus, Bengtsson, Larsson, Pennert, Rybo et al., 1984; Larsson, Svardsudd, Welin, Wilhelmsew, Bjorntorp et al., 1984). Obesity is known to be associated with other cardiovascular risk factors, including hypertension, blood lipid abnormalities, and diabetes (Folsom, Burke, Byers, Hutchinson, Heiss et al., 1991; Lapidus & Bengtsson, 1988; National Institutes of Health, 1985). Physical activity has been associated with low rates of CHD (Donohue, Abbott, Reed, & Yano, 1988; Levy, Savage, Garrison, Anderson, Kannel et al., 1987; Paffenbarger, Jr., Hyde, Wing, & Hsieh, 1986) and other risk factors for CHD (Folsom, Caspersen, Taylor, Jacobs, Luepker et al., 1985). Diet has been associated with risk factor levels in several large populations but its role in CHD may be primarily mediated through other variables such as obesity and lipids (Esrey, Joseph, & Grover, 1996; Nicklas, 1995). In patients with known CHD in the Cholesterol Lowering Atherosclerosis Study (CLAS), each quartile of increased consumption of dietary total fat and polyunsaturated fat was associated with a significant increase of new atherosclerotic lesions at 2-year follow-ups (Blankenhorn, Johnson, Mack, el Zein, & Vailas, 1990).

Psychosocial Risk Factors

Several studies have demonstrated an inverse association of education and social class with CHD mortality (Kaplan & Keil, 1993). Low socioeconomic status and low educational attainment have also been associated with biological and behavioral risk factors for CHD. More educated persons have lower total cholesterol and lower systolic BP, and are less overweight, more physically active, smoke less, and have less atherogenic food habits than less educated individuals (American College of Sports Medicine [ACSM], 1993; Helmert, Mielck, & Classen, 1992; Matthews, Kelsey, Meilahn,

Kuller, & Wing, 1989). Persons with psychological morbidity or poor coping mechanisms also show a higher rate of CHD (Booth-Kewley & Friedman, 1987; Matthews, 1988). General psychological well-being may be an additional mediator for lifestyle related to CHD risk (Van Diest & Appels, 1991).

Race and Sex

Mortality rates from CHD under 55 years of age are approximately 35% higher in African Americans compared to their white counterparts (AHA, 1993). Explanations for these racial differences include socioeconomic factors, access to care (Maryland Department of Health and Mental Hygiene, 1986), health care provider bias (Keller, Fleury, & Bergstrom, 1995), major lifestyle differences, and a high prevalence of known risk factors in the African American population (Rotimi, Cooper, Cao, Sundarum, & McGee, 1994). True CHD incidence rates in African Americans remains unknown. Incidence of CHD in post-menopausal women escalates ten-fold compared with younger women of 35–54 years of age (Lerner & Kannel, 1986). In general, traditional risk factors are similar between men and women; smoking, elevated cholesterol level, hypertension, and sedentary lifestyle. However, unique risk factors to women include menopause and the use of oral contraceptives (Brezinka & Padmos, 1994).

THE EFFECTS OF RISK FACTOR MODIFICATION

Lipid-Lowering

A recent meta-analysis of 35 randomized trials concluded that reduced risk for CHD mortality is associated with reduction in serum cholesterol; there is a 13% to 14% reduction in CHD mortality for every 10-percentage-point net reduction in serum cholesterol (Gould, Rossouw, Santanello, Heyse, & Furberg, 1995). Another meta-analysis of 13 studies and 28 randomized controlled trials found that a reduction in serum cholesterol concentration of 0.6 mmol/L lowers the risk of CHD by 20% to 50% (Law, Wald, & Thompson, 1994). Clinical trials involving coronary angiography have demonstrated that CHD may stabilize or regress with aggressive lipid lowering therapy. Lifestyle, including diet, exercise, smoking, medications, and other factors are known to affect plasma lipoproteins. Guidelines for the identification and treatment of lipoprotein disorders have been established by the Adult Treatment Panels (ATP) of the National Cholesterol Education Program (1988).

Hypertension Control

Treatment for high BP has been associated with a decrement in CHD mortality and morbidity in long-term clinical trials. However, given the high prevalence of associated CHD risk factors in hypertensives, treatment contingencies need to be considered in the composite CHD risk profile. Failure to reduce cholesterol in hypertensives has been linked to limited efficacy of antihypertensive treatment in the reduction of CHD (Heyden, Schneider, & Fodor, 1987a). Furthermore, smoking has a greater deleterious effect on those hypertensives whose cholesterol levels are elevated (Heyden, Schneider, & Fodor, 1987b). Lifestyle and pharmacologic treatment guidelines have been outlined by the Joint National Committee on Detection, Evaluation, and Treatment of High Blood Pressure (JNC) and strongly recommend multiple risk factor screening and modification (JNC, 1988, 1993, 1997).

Smoking Cessation

Studies have shown that individualized smoking cessation counseling with or without nicotine replacement therapy can lead to substantial quit rates among participants (LeFebvre, Cobb, Goreczny, & Carleton et al., 1990). A meta-analysis of 39 controlled trials demonstrated highest quit rates were achieved in individualized face-to-face strategies that provided motivational messages (Kottke, Battista, DeFriese, & Brekke, 1988). Trials have shown that intensive advice, encouragement, and support to stop smoking are particularly effective in patients at high risk for CHD (Law & Tang, 1995). The effectiveness of nurse-mediated interventions in smoking cessation is well established in CHD patients (Taylor, Houston-Miller, Killen, & DeBusk, 1990). The recent availability and efficacy of different nicotine replacement therapies with individualized interventions may result in higher quit rates. The importance of multiple risk factor modification concomitant with smoking cessation has been demonstrated in the Multiple Risk Factor Intervention Trial (MRFIT); there was significant weight gain and a higher prevalence of new hypertension among quitters (Gerace, Hollis, Ockene, & Svendsen, 1991).

Obesity and Sedentary Lifestyle

Regular physical activity is associated with reduced incidence of hypertension (ACSM, 1993; Hagberg, Montain, Martin, & Ehsani, 1989), diabetes (Manson & Spelsberg, 1994), and obesity (Andersson, Xu, Rebuffe-Scrive, Terning, Krotkiewski et al., 1991; Gibbons, Blair, Cooper, & Smith, 1983), all risk factors for CHD. Physical activity and diet interventions are often associated with decreased BP (ACSM, 1993), improved HDL-C (Ewart, Loftus, & Hagberg, 1995; Wood, Stefanick, Williams, & Haskell, 1991), decreased TG levels, lower body weight (Holloszy, Skinner, Toro, & Cureton, 1964; Wood, Stefanick, Dreon, Frey-Hewitt, Garay et al., 1988), and improved glucose metabolism (Eriksson & Lindgarde, 1991). The Multiple Risk Factor Intervention Trial, along with other prospective and case-control studies, demonstrates that regular leisure time physical activity is associated with a reduced rate of CHD, independent of other risk factors (Leon & Connett, 1991).

NURSE CASE MANAGEMENT OF CHD RISK FACTORS

Observational studies and randomized trials indicate that nurses with specialty training can effectively alter cardiovascular risk factors in high-risk populations (Groves, Miller, & Cannell, 1987; Hill & Reichgott, 1979; Runyan, Jr. 1975; Safreit, 1997; Spitzer, Sackett, Sibley, Roberts, Gent et al., 1974). In a recent trial comparing a nurse-led team caring for persons with hyperlipidemia, those treated by the nurse team were four times more likely to reach the goal levels of 130 mg/dl than were persons treated by primary care physicians (Shaffer & Wexler, 1995). The model was a flexible one where nurses met weekly with dietitians, pharmacists, the psychologist, and the physician to review the progress of each case. The nurse caregivers applied the Adult Treatment Panel's guidelines through assessing progress and encouraging the next step in the ready patient. Typical of nurse-management, this approach appeared to identify barriers, enhancers, and readiness to make changes. A similar study using a team of physician and nurse with the nurse performing the lipid-lowering counseling and monitoring, implemented a stepped care approach suggested by the current ATP guidelines in 86 high risk patients. The trial showed that compliance to nurse treatment resulted in reductions in cholesterol level of 18% (Blair, Bryant, & Bocuzzi, 1988). The nurse-managed pharmacotherapy and patients' progresses were reviewed only every 6 months with the physician. Again the hallmark of the nurse-management model appeared to be the ability to spend time counseling and assessing barriers in the context of the social environment.

In nurse versus usual care studies of comprehensive risk reduction in first degree relatives of persons with sudden CHD death, the nursing intervention was associated with favorable shifts in BP and cholesterol levels and fatty meat consumption as well as beliefs about risk in siblings of persons with the disease (McCance, Eutropius, Jacobs, & Williams, 1985). Improved smoking cessation rates have been well-documented in post-MI patients treated by a nurse compared with usual care (Taylor et al., 1990). There are also a number of studies where nurses have been shown to effectively manage hypertension using the Joint National Committee on Detection, Evaluation, and Treatment of High Blood Pressure guidelines (Gilliland, 1979; Milne, Logan, & Campbell, 1979).

Organized nurse management clinics for multiple risk factor intervention have been more effective than usual care when focused on more than one risk factor simultaneously (Miller, Wikoff, Garrett, McMahon, & Smith, 1990; Robson, Boomla, Fitzpatrick, Jewell, Taylor et al., 1989). In a trial of post-MI patients, where nurses were trained to manage physical activity, smoking, and diet, 89% of patients in the nurse group showed dietary fat and cholesterol improvements compared with 62% of the primary care physician group (p = 0.008) while 50% of smokers stopped smoking in the nurse intervention group compared with 29% in the usual physician care group (Carlsson, Lindberg, Westin, & Israelsson, 1997). This is notable given the fact that the usual care group had access to the same rehabilitation program as the nurse group. Several earlier studies suggested that physicians in traditional medical care environments did not carry out cholesterol lowering very effectively (Block, Banspach, Gans, Harris, Lasater et al., 1988; Roberts, 1993). Nurse-management has been shown to be an alternative or complement to usual care, eminently reproducible across populations with a high prevalence of cardiovascular risk factors (Duryee, 1992; O'Neill, 1994; Persson, Lindstrom, Lingfors, & Bengtsson, 1996; Scalzi, Burke, & Greenland, 1980).

THE JOHNS HOPKINS SIBLING STUDIES: A PARADIGM FOR PRESERVING VITALITY THROUGHOUT THE LIFESPAN

Sibling investigations have been conducted by our team since 1982. The studies have progressed from simple observations of behavior and known risk factor distributions to more complex biological studies and interventions. These are briefly summarized.

Risk Factor Knowledge and Attitudes of Siblings of People with Premature CHD

We examined whether asymptomatic SIBS of people with premature CHD: 1) perceived their own high relative risk for premature CHD: 2) made changes in their own risk behaviors, or 3) sought medical advice to lower risk. Over 67% of siblings perceived their risk as the same or less than the general population. Virtually no siblings made self-initiated changes in lifestyle or risk factors after the index event (Becker & Levine, 1987).

The Prevalence of Risk Factors and Occult CHD in Siblings of People with Premature CHD

The next question was whether SIBS actually had a high prevalence of modifiable risk factors. In 150 SIBS screened at Johns Hopkins, we demonstrated that 70% had one or more modifiable risk factors, 25% had total cholesterol levels above the 90th percentile adjusted for sex and age, and the prevalence of hypertension was nearly double that found in the age and gender adjusted general population. Smoking rates were higher than the general population. Almost 50% of apparently healthy men 45–59 years of age exhibited a positive exercise test (Becker & Levine, 1987; Becker, Becker, Pearson, Fintel, Levine et al., 1988).

Detection of Risk and Incidence of CHD
in Siblings of People with Premature CHD

In 264 members of the earliest SIB cohort, abnormal exercise tests, and/or thallium scans predicted future CHD events; 64% of persons with a double positive (exercise test and scan) test developed a CHD event over an average of 6.5 years of follow-up, with 19 events including MI, sudden death, bypass surgery, or angioplasty (Blumenthal, Becker, Moy, Coresh, Wilder et al., 1996). The rate far exceeds the numbers predicted by any other long-term population-based study in persons who were healthy at baseline including the Framingham and Western Collaborative Group studies (Kannel & Larson, 1993; Stamler, Dyer, Shekelle, Neaton, & Stamler, 1993).

Coronary Disease Mechanisms
in African American and White Siblings

In 1993, we initiated a study to examine racial differences in CHD characteristics and risk factors. We have shown disparities in levels of some risk factors but a surprising concordance of many other risk factors between African American and white siblings. Among African American siblings, 16% had positive exercise tests and/or thallium tests; the highest risk subset being males with ages ≥ 45 years (56% were positive). Importantly, coronary angiography in SIBS with abnormal exercise tests and/or thallium tests has shown that there is a marked difference in the extent (modified Gensini score) of CHD between African Americans and whites (Aversano, Zhou, Moy, Becker, & Becker, 1995). African Americans have much greater scores of global severity while whites have less extensive disease but more focally severe stenoses.

A Randomized Trial of Nurse Management
Compared with Enhanced Primary Care

Between 1991 and 1996, a trial of nurse interventions for high LDL-C, high TG, hypertension, and cigarette smoking was initiated in apparently healthy 30–59 year old SIBS of people with premature CHD (< 60 years of age). SIBS were identified from index patients with angiographically documented CHD, screened for risk factors, and those with remediable criterion risk factors were randomized by family to care by their own physician provider (enhanced with recommendations from the screening) or to care provided by a specially trained registered nurse. On screening, SIBS in both groups had high levels of BP, lipids, and body mass index (BMI) and had a high prevalence of most CHD risk factors (Table 9.1). Trial entry criterion risk factors at screening included: LDL-C $\geq$ 160 mg/dl, BP $\geq$ 140/90 mmHg (on or off antihypertensives), and/or current (within the last month) smokers. Both groups received care for 2 years.

The specially trained registered nurse (NURS) group significantly lowered their LDL-C and decreased total dietary fat, whereas the physician provider enhanced with recommendations from screening (EPC) group showed minimal changes between baseline and both 1- and 2-year follow-ups. Declines were seen in BP and smoking in the NURS group. More NURS participants were taking and adhering to standard pharmacotherapy than in the EPC group (45% and 17% respectively, $p < 0.01$). While both NURS and EPC groups lowered their LDL-C levels, the NURS group demonstrated a statistically significant greater magnitude of change using an "intention-to-treat" analysis. In this analysis, there is an assumption that all of those "lost to attrition" did not favorably alter any outcomes. Additional analysis revealed those risk factor changes seen in the NURS group at 1-year was retained at 2-year follow-up. Most importantly, more SIBS in the NURS group were able to achieve nationally recommended goal levels of lipid and BP, and more were able to stop smoking successfully (Table 9.2). In addition, at baseline, the number of times that persons exercised for 30 minutes or more at baseline was 2 per month. At 2 years, this number in both groups was increased only a fraction.

CONCLUSION

Cardiovascular disease is a major cause of premature morbidity and mortality in the United States. Coronary heart disease, the single largest category of cardiovascular diseases, is eminently preventable or at least delayed through risk factor management over the lifespan. Some groups, such as those with a family history of premature CHD, bear a marked excess risk for CHD at a young age themselves. Such families are readily accessible to nurses and

TABLE 9.1   Characteristics of Sibling Participants by Treatment Contingency at Baseline Screening

	Randomized group	
	NURS (n = 135)	EPC (n = 132)
Age (yrs.)	46 ± 7	46 ± 7
Education (yrs.)	12 ± 3	13 ± 2
Systolic BP (mmHg)	136 ± 15	135 ± 15
Diastolic BP (mmHg)	86 ± 10	86 ± 10
LDL-C (mg/dl)	180 ± 52	165 ± 44
HDL-C (mg/dl)	48 ± 15	47 ± 15
Triglycerides (mg/dl)	192 ± 193	186 ± 168
Body Mass Index	28 ± 5	29 ± 7
Diabetics	5%	8%
Current Smokers	40%	49%
Daily Kcal	1946 ± 803	1987 ± 735
Dietary Fat (g)	84 ± 43	85 ± 38
Kcal as Fat %	38 ± 7	38 ± 8

NURS = nursing risk factor management
EPC = enhanced primary care risk factor management

easily identifiable at the time of a CHD event in an index patient under 60 years of age. Screening is likely to yield a high prevalence of previously undetected and untreated risk factors in these families. We have demonstrated that nurses with special training can effectively treat these risk factors. Since familial-clustered premature CHD accounts for a large percentage of the total pool of persons with CHD, models of family care that incorporate aggressive risk factor management have the potential of markedly lowering rates of CHD, providing an opportunity for longer healthier lives for an aging U.S. population.

TABLE 9.2 Overall Percentage of Siblings Meeting Risk Factor Goal Levels One and Two Years After Treatment Initiation

					Goals				
	LDL-C < 130 mg/dl		*BP < 140/90 mmHg*		*Smoking cessation*		*TG < 250 mg/dl*		
	1 yr	*2 yr*	*1 yr*	*2 yr*	*1 yr*	*2 yr*	*1 yr*	*2yr*	
NURS	26%	38%	50%	48%	27%	24%	48%	68%	
EPC	5%	11%	38%	38%	12%	14%	41%	56%	
p-value	< 0.01	< 0.01	0.27	0.38	0.09	0.27	0.69	0.46	

NURS = nursing risk factor management
EPC = enhanced primary care risk factor management

169

REFERENCES

American College of Sports Medicine (1993). Physical activity, physical fitness, and hypertension. *Medicine and Science in Sports and Exercise, 25*, i–x.

American Heart Association (1993). *Heart and stroke facts.* Dallas: American Heart Association.

American Heart Association (1996). *1997 Heart and stroke statistical update.* Dallas: American Heart Association.

Andersson, B., Xu, X., Rebuffe-Scrive, M., Terning, K., Krotkiewski, M., & Bjorntorp, P. (1991). The effects of exercise training on body composition and metabolism in men and women. *International Journal of Obesity, 15*(1), 75–81.

Austin, M. A. (1989). Plasma triglyceride as a risk factor for coronary heart disease: The epidemiologic evidence and beyond. *American Journal of Epidemiology, 129*(2), 249–259.

Aversano, T., Zhou, W., Moy, T. F., Becker, D. M., & Becker, L. C. (1995). Extent of occult coronary artery disease in high risk African American and white families. [Abstract]. *Circulation, 92*, I–75.

Beard, C. M., Griffin, M. R., Offord, K. P., & Edwards, W. D. (1986). Risk factors for sudden unexpected cardiac death in young women in Rochester, Minnesota. *Mayo Clinic Proceedings, 61*(3), 186–191.

Becker, D. M., Becker, L. C., Pearson, T. A., Fintel, D. J., Levine, D. M., & Kwiterovich, P. O. (1988). Risk factors in siblings of people with premature coronary heart disease. *Journal of the American College of Cardiology, 12*(5), 1273–1280.

Becker, D. M., & Levine, D. M. (1987). Risk perception, knowledge, and lifestyles in siblings of people with premature coronary disease. *American Journal of Preventive Medicine, 3*(1), 45–50.

Blair, T. P., Bryant, J., & Bocuzzi, S. (1988). Treatment of hypercholesterolemia by a clinical nurse using a stepped-care protocol in a nonvolunteer population. *Archives of Internal Medicine, 148*(5), 1046–1048.

Blankenhorn, D. H., Johnson, R. L., Mack, W. J., el Zein, H. A., & Vailas, L. I. (1990). The influence of diet on the appearance of new lesions in human coronary arteries. *Journal of the American Medical Association, 263*(12), 1646–1652.

Block, L., Banspach, S. W., Gans, K., Harris, C., Lasater, T. M., LeFebvre, R. C., & Carleton, R. A. (1988). Impact of public education and continuing medical education on physician attitudes and behavior concerning cholesterol. *American Journal of Preventive Medicine, 4*(5), 255–260.

Blumenthal, R. S., Becker, D. M., Moy, T. F., Coresh, J., Wilder, L. B., & Becker, L. C. (1996). Exercise thallium tomography predicts future coronary heart disease events in a high risk asymptomatic population. *Circulation, 93*(5), 915–923.

Booth-Kewley, S., & Friedman, H. S. (1987). Psychological predictors of heart disease: A quantitative review. *Psychological Bulletin, 101*(3), 343–362.

Brezinka, V., & Padmos, I. (1994). Coronary heart disease risk factors in women. *European Heart Journal, 15*(11), 1571–1584.

Burke, W., & Motulsky, A. G. (1992). Hypertension. In R. A. King, J. I. Rotter, & A. G. Motulsky (Eds.), *The genetic basis of common diseases* (pp. 507–528). New York: Oxford University Press.

Carlsson, R., Lindberg, G., Westin, L., & Israelsson, B. (1997). Influence of coronary nursing management follow up on lifestyle after acute myocardial infarction. *Heart, 77*(3), 256–259.

Donohue, R. P., Abbott, R. D., Reed, D. M., & Yano, K. (1988). Physical activity and coronary heart disease in middle-aged and elderly men: The Honolulu Heart Program. *American Journal of Public Health, 78*(6), 683–685.

Duryee, R. (1992). The efficacy of inpatient education after myocardial infarction. *Heart Lung, 21*(3), 217–227.

Eriksson, K., & Lindgarde, F. (1991). Prevention of type 2 (non-insulin-dependent) diabetes mellitus by diet and physical exercise: The 6-year Malmo feasibility study. *Diabetologia, 34*(12), 891–898.

Esrey, K. L., Joseph, L., & Grover, S. A. (1996). Relationship between dietary intake and coronary heart disease mortality: Lipid research clinics prevalence follow-up study. *Journal of Clinical Epidemiology, 49*(2), 211–216.

Ewart, C. K., Loftus, K. S., & Hagberg, J. M. (1995). School-based exercise to lower blood pressure in high-risk African-American girls: Project design and baseline findings. *Journal of Health Education, 26,* S99–S105.

Fisher, E. B., Jr., Lichtenstein, E., & Haire-Joshu, D. (1993). Multiple determinants of tobacco use and cessation. In C. T. Orleans & J. Slade (Eds.), *Nicotine addiction principles and management.* New York: Oxford University Press.

Folsom, A. R., Burke, G. L., Byers, C. L., Hutchinson, R. G., Heiss, G., Flack, J. M., Jacobs, D. R., & Caan, B. (1991). Implications of obesity for cardiovascular disease in Blacks: The CARDIA and ARIC studies. *American Journal of Clinical Nutrition, 53*(6 Suppl.), 1604S–1611S.

Folsom, A. R., Caspersen, C. J., Taylor, H. L., Jacobs, D. R., Jr., Luepker, R. V., Gomez-Marin, O., Gillum, R. F., & Blackburn, H. (1985). Leisure time, physical activity and its relationship to coronary risk factors in a population-based sample. *American Journal of Epidemiology, 121*(4), 570–579.

Frick, M. H., Elo, O., Haapa, K., Heinonen, O. P., Heinsalmi, P., Helo, P., Huttunen, J. K., Kaitaniemi, P., Koskinen, P., Manninen, V., Maenpaa,

H., Malkonen, M., Manttari, M., Norola, S., Pasternack, A., Pikkarainen, J., Romo, M., Sjoblom, T., & Nikkila, E. A. (1987). Helsinki Heart Study: Primary-prevention trial with gemfibrozil in middle-aged men with dyslipidemia: Safety of treatment, changes in risk factors, and incidence of coronary heart disease. *New England Journal of Medicine, 317*(20), 1237–1245.

Gartside, P. S., & Glueck, C. J. (1995). The important role of modifiable dietary and behavioral characteristics in the causation and prevention of coronary heart disease hospitalization and mortality: The prospective NHANES I Follow-up Study. *Journal of the American College of Nutrition, 14*(1), 71–79.

Genest, J., & Cohn, J. S. (1995). Clustering of cardiovascular risk factors: Targeting high-risk individuals. *American Journal of Cardiology, 76*(2), 8A–20A.

Genest, J., Martin-Munley, S., McNamara, J. R., Ordovas, J. M., Jenner, J. L., Meyers, R., Silberman, S. R., Wilson, P. W. F., Salem, D. N., & Schaefer, E. J. (1992). Familial lipoprotein disorders in patients with premature coronary artery disease. *Circulation, 85*(6), 2025–2033.

Gerace, T. A., Hollis, J., Ockene, J. K., & Svendsen, K. (1991). Smoking cessation and change in diastolic blood pressure, body weight, and plasma lipids. MRFIT Research Group. *Preventive Medicine, 20*(5), 602–620.

Gibbons, L. W., Blair, S. N., Cooper, K. H., & Smith, M. (1983). Associations between coronary heart disease risk factors and physical fitness in healthy adult women. *Circulation, 67*(5), 977–983.

Gilliland, M. M. (1979). A nurse managed hypertension clinic. Preventive Medicine, 8, 165.

Gould, A. L., Rossouw, J. E., Santanello, N. C., Heyse, J. F., & Furberg, C. D. (1995). Cholesterol reduction yields clinical benefit: A new look at old data. *Circulation, 91*(8), 2274–2282.

Groves, R. M., Miller, P. V., & Cannell, C. F. (1987). Differences between the telephone and personal interview data. In Anonymous, *An experimental comparison of telephone and personal health interview surveys* (pp. 11–19). Washington D.C. National Center for Health Statistics, Series 2, No. 106.

Hagberg, J. M., Montain, S. J., Martin, W. H., & Ehsani, A. A. (1989). Effect of exercise training on 60–69 year old persons with essential hypertension. *American Journal of Cardiology, 64*(5), 348–353.

Hahn, L. P., Folsom, A. R., Sprafka, J. M., & Norsted, S. W. (1990). Cigarette smoking and cessation behaviors among urban blacks and whites. *Public Health Reports, 105*(3), 290–295.

Helmert, U., Mielck, A., & Classen, E. (1992). Social inequities in cardiovascular disease risk factors in East and West Germany. *Social Science and Medicine, 35*(10), 1283–1292.

Heyden, S., Schneider, K. A., & Fodor, G. J. (1987a). Failure to reduce cholesterol as explanation for the limited efficacy of antihypertensive treatment in the reduction of CHD. Examination of the evidence from six hypertension intervention trials. *Klinische Wochenschrift, 65*(17), 828–832.

Heyden, S., Schneider, K. A., & Fodor, J. G. (1987b). Smoking habits and antihypertensive treatment. *Nephron, 47*(Suppl. 1), 99–103.

Hill, M. N., & Reichgott, M. J. (1979). Achievement of standards for quality care of hypertension by physicians and nurses. *Clinical and Experimental Hypertension, 1*(5), 665–684.

Holloszy, J. O., Skinner, J. S., Toro, G., & Cureton, T. K. (1964). Effects of a six month program of endurance exercise on lipids of middle-aged men. *American Journal of Cardiology, 14*, 753–760.

Hunt, S. C., Williams, R. R., & Barlow, G. K. (1986). A comparison of positive family history: Definitions for defining risk of future disease. *Journal of Chronic Disease, 39*(10), 809–821.

Joint National Committee on Detection, Evaluation, and Treatment of High Blood Pressure. (1988). The 1988 Report of the Joint National Committee on Detection, Evaluation, and Treatment of High Blood Pressure. *Archives of Internal Medicine, 148*(5), 1023–1038.

Joint National Committee on Detection, Evaluation, and Treatment of High Blood Pressure (1993). The Fifth Report of the Joint National Committee on Detection, Evaluation, and Treatment of High Blood Pressure (JNC V). *Archives of Internal Medicine, 153*, 154–183.

Joint National Committee on Detection, Evaluation, and Treatment of High Blood Pressure (1997). The Sixth Report of the Joint National Committee on Prevention, Detection, Evaluation, and Treatment of High Blood Pressure. *Archives of Internal Medicine, 157*, 2413–2446.

Kannel, W. B. (1983). High-density lipoproteins: Epidemiologic profile and risks of coronary artery disease. *American Journal of Cardiology, 52*(4), 9B–12B.

Kannel, W. B. (1987). New perspectives on cardiovascular risk factors. *American Heart Journal, 114*(1pt2), 213–219.

Kannel, W. B. (1993). Hypertension as a risk factor for cardiac events—Epidemiological results of long-term studies. *Journal of Cardiovascular Pharmacology, 21*(Suppl. 2), S27–S37.

Kannel, W. B., Castelli, W. P., Gordon, T., & McNamara, P. M. (1971). Serum cholesterol, lipoproteins, and the risk of coronary heart disease: The Framingham Study. *Annals of Internal Medicine, 74*(1), 1–12.

Kannel, W. B., & Larson, M. (1993). Long-term epidemiologic prediction of coronary disease. *Cardiology, 82*(2-3), 137–152.

Kaplan, G. A., & Keil, J. E. (1993). Socioeconomic factors and cardiovascular disease: A review of the literature. *Circulation, 88*(4 pt 1), 1873–1998.

Keller, C., Fleury, J., & Bergstrom, D. L. (1995). Risk factors for coronary heart disease in African-American women. *Cardiovascular Nursing, 31*(2), 9–14.

Kottke, T. E., Battista, R. N., DeFriese, G. H., & Brekke, M. L. (1988). Attributes of successful smoking cessation interventions in medical practice: A meta-analysis of 39 controlled trials. *Journal of the American Medical Association, 259*(19), 2882–2889.

Lapidus, L., & Bengtsson, C. (1988). Regional obesity as a health hazard in women—a prospective study. *Acta Medica Scandinavica Supplementum, 723,* 53–59.

Lapidus, L., Bengtsson, C., Larsson, B., Pennert, K., Rybo, E., & Sjostrom, L. (1984). Distribution of adipose tissue and risk of cardiovascular disease and death: A 12 year follow-up of participants in the population study of women in Gothenburg, Sweden. *British Medical Journal (Clinical Research Ed.), 289*(6454), 1257–1261.

Larsson, B., Svardsudd, K., Welin, L., Wilhelmsen, L., Bjorntorp, P., & Tibblin, G. (1984). Abdominal adipose tissue distribution, obesity, and risk of cardiovascular disease and death: 13 year follow-up of participants in the study of men born in 1913. *British Medical Journal, 228*(6428), 1401–1404.

Law, M., & Tang, J. L. (1995). An analysis of the effectiveness of interventions intended to help people stop smoking. *Archives of Internal Medicine, 155*(18), 1933–1941.

Law, M. R., Wald, N. J., & Thompson, S. G. (1994). By how much and how quickly does reduction in serum cholesterol concentration lower risk of ischaemic heart disease? *British Medical Journal, 308*(6925), 367–373.

LeFebvre, R. C., Cobb, G. D., Goreczny, A. J., & Carleton, R. A. (1990). Efficacy of an incentive-based community smoking cessation program. *Addictive Behaviors, 15*(5), 403–411.

Leon, A. S., & Connett, J. (1991). Physical activity and 10.5 year mortality in the Multiple Risk Factor Intervention Trial (MRFIT). *International Journal of Epidemiology, 20*(3), 690–695.

Lerner, D. J., & Kannel, W. B. (1986). Patterns of coronary heart disease morbidity and mortality in the sexes: A 26-year follow-up of the Framingham population. *American Heart Journal, 111*(2), 383–390.

Levy, D., Savage, D. D., Garrison, R., Anderson, K. M., Kannel, W. B., & Castelli, W. P. (1987). Echocardiographic criteria for left ventricular hypertrophy: The Framingham Heart Study. *American Journal of Cardiology, 59*(9), 956–960.

Manson, J. E., & Spelsberg, A. (1994). Primary prevention of non-insulin-dependent diabetes mellitus. *American Journal of Preventive Medicine, 10*(3), 172–184.

Maryland Department of Health and Mental Hygiene (1986). *Variations in the Use of Medical Surgical Services by the Maryland Population. Report of the Division of Medical Practice Patterns Analysis.* Baltimore: Author.

Matthews, K. A. (1988). Coronary heart disease and type A behaviors: Update on the alternative to the Booth-Kewley and Friedman quantitative review. *Psychological Bulletin, 104*(3), 373–380.

Matthews, K. A., Kelsey, S. F., Meilahn, E. N., Kuller, L. H., & Wing, R. R. (1989). Educational attainment and behavioral and biologic risk factors for coronary heart disease in middle-aged women. *American Journal of Epidemiology, 129*(6), 1132–1144.

McCance, K. L., Eutropius, L., Jacobs, M. K., & Williams, R. R. (1985). Preventing coronary heart disease in high-risk families. *Research in Nursing & Health, 8*(4), 413–420.

Miller, P., Wikoff, R., Garrett, M. J., McMahon, M., & Smith, T. (1990). Regimen compliance two years after myocardial infarction. *Nursing Research, 39*(6), 333–336.

Milne, B. J., Logan, A. C., & Campbell, W. P. (1979). Cost effectiveness of utilizing nurses to control hypertension at work. *Preventive Medicine, 8,* 197.

National Cholesterol Education Program (1994). Second report of the expert panel on detection, evaluation, and treatment of high blood cholesterol in adults (Adult Treatment Panel II). *Circulation, 89,* 1329–1445.

National Cholesterol Education Program Expert Panel (1988). Report of the National Cholesterol Education Program Expert Panel on Detection, Evaluation, and Treatment of High Blood Cholesterol in Adults. *Archives of Internal Medicine, 148,* 36–69.

National Institutes of Health (1985). Health implications of obesity: National Institutes of Health Consensus Development Conference Statement. *Annals of Internal Medicine, 103,* 1073–1077.

National Institutes of Health Consensus Development Panel on Triglyceride High-Density Lipoprotein and Coronary Heart Disease (1993). Triglyceride, high-density lipoprotein, and coronary heart disease. *Journal of the American Medical Association, 269,* 505–510.

Nicklas, T. A. (1995). Dietary studies of children and young adults (1973–1988): The Bogalusa Heart Study. *American Journal of Medical Science, 310*(Suppl. 1), S101–S108.

Nora, J. J., Lortscher, R. H., Spangler, R. D., Nora, A. H., & Kimberling, W. J. (1980). Genetic epidemiologic study of early-onset ischemic heart disease. *Circulation, 61*(3), 503–508.

O'Neill, C. (1994). The OXCHECK Study: A nursing perspective. Oxford and Collaborators Health Check. *Health Reports, 6*(1), 160–165.

Paffenbarger, R. S.,Jr., Hyde, R. T., Wing, A. L., & Hsieh, C. (1986). Physical activity, all-cause mortality, and longevity of college alumni. *New England Journal of Medicine, 314*(10), 605–613.

Persson, L. G., Lindstrom, K., Lingfors, H., & Bengtsson, C. (1996). Results from an intervention programme dealing with cardiovascular risk factors. Experiences from a study of men aged 33-42 in Habo, Sweden. *Scandinavian Journal of Primary Health Care, 14*(3), 184–192.

Rissanen, A. M. (1979). Familial occurrence of coronary heart disease: Effect of age at diagnosis. *American Journal of Cardiology, 44*(1), 60–66.

Roberts, W. C. (1993). Getting cardiologists interested in lipids. *American Journal of Cardiology, 72*(9), 744–745.

Robson, J., Boomla, K., Fitzpatrick, S., Jewell, A. J., Taylor, J., Self, J., & Colyer, M. (1989). Using nurses for preventive activities with computer assisted follow up: A randomised controlled trial. *British Medical Journal, 298*(6671), 433–436.

Rose, G. (1964). Familial patterns in ischemic heart disease. *British Journal of Preventive and Social Medicine, 18,* 75–80.

Rotimi, C., Cooper, R., Cao, G., Sundarum, C., & McGee, D. (1994). Familial aggregation of cardiovascular diseases in African-American pedigrees. *Genetic Epidemiology, 11*(5), 397–407.

Runyan, W. S., Jr. (1975). The Memphis Chronic Disease Program: Comparisons in outcome and the nurse's extended role. *Journal of the American Medical Association, 231*(3), 264–267.

Sacco, R. L., Kargman, D. E., Gu, Q., & Zamanillo, M. C. (1995). Race-ethnicity and determinants of intracranial atherosclerotic cerebral infarction: The Northern Manhattan Stroke Study. *Stroke, 26*(1), 14–20.

Safreit, B. J. (1997). Health care dollars and regulatory sense: The role of advanced practice nursing. *Yale Journal on Regulation, 9,* 417–487.

Scalzi, C., Burke, L., & Greenland, S. (1980). Evaluation of an inpatient educational program for coronary patients and families. *Heart Lung, 9*(5), 846–853.

Schaefer, E. J. (1994). Familial lipoprotein disorders and premature coronary artery disease. *Medical Clinics of North America, 78*(1), 21–39.

Schaefer, E. J., Genest, J., Ordovas, J. M., Salem, D. N., & Wilson, P. W. F. (1993). Familial lipoprotein disorders and premature coronary artery disease. *Current Opinions of Lipidology, 4,* 288–298.

Selby, J. V., Newman, B., Quiroga, J., Christian, J. C., Austin, M. A., & Fabsitz, R. R. (1991). Concordance for Dyslipidemic Hypertension in Male Twins. *Journal of the American Medical Association, 265*(16), 2079–2084.

Shaffer, J., & Wexler, L. F. (1995). Reducing low-density lipoprotein cholesterol levels in an ambulatory care system. Results of a multidisciplinary collaborative practice lipid clinic compared with traditional physician-based care. *Archives of Internal Medicine, 155*(21), 2330–2335.

Shea, S., Ottman, R., Gabrieli, C., Stein, Z., & Nichols, A. (1984). Family history as an independent risk factor for coronary heart disease. *Journal of the American College of Cardiology, 4*(4), 793–801.

Slack, & Evans, K. A. (1966). The increased risk of death from ischemic heart disease in first degree relatives of 121 men and 96 women with ischemic heart disease. *Journal of Medical Genetics, 3,* 239–257.

Snowden, C. B., McNamara, P. M., Garrison, R. J., Feinleib, M., Kannel, W. B., & Epstein, F. H. (1982). Predicting coronary heart disease in siblings—a multivariate assessment: The Framingham Heart Study. *American Journal of Epidemiology, 115*(2), 217–222.

Spitzer, W. O., Sackett, D. L., Sibley, J. C., Roberts, R. S., Gent, M., Kergin, D. J., Hacket, B. C., & Oynich, A. (1974). The Burlington randomized trial of the nurse practitioner. *New England Journal of Medicine, 290*(5), 251–256.

Sprecher, D. L., Hein, M. J., & Laskarzewski, P. M. (1994). Conjoint high triglycerides and low HDL cholesterol across generations: Analysis of proband hypertriglyceridemia and lipid/lipoprotein disorders in first-degree family members. *Circulation, 90*(3), 1177–1184.

Stamler, J., Dyer, A. R., Shekelle, R. B., Neaton, J., & Stamler, R. (1993). Relationship of baseline major risk factors to coronary and all-cause mortality, and to longevity: Findings from long-term follow-up of Chicago cohorts. *Cardiology, 82*(2–3), 191–222.

Taylor, C. B., Houston-Miller, N., Killen, J. D., & DeBusk, R. F. (1990). Smoking cessation after acute myocardial infarction: The effects of a nurse-managed intervention. *Annals of Internal Medicine, 113*(2), 118–123.

Van Diest, R., & Appels, A. (1991). Vital exhaustion and depression: A conceptual study. *Journal of Psychosomatic Research, 35*(4–5), 535–544.

Ward, R. (1990). Familial aggregation and genetic epidemiology of blood pressure. In J. H. Laragh & B. M. Brenner (Eds.), *Hypertension: Pathophysiology, diagnosis, and management* (pp. 81–100). New York: Raven Press.

Willett, W. C., Green, A., Stampfer, M. J., Speizer, F. E., Colditz, G. A., Rosner, B., Monson, R. R., Stason, W. B., & Hennekens, C. H. (1987). Relative and absolute excess risks of coronary heart disease among women who smoke cigarettes. *New England Journal of Medicine, 317*(21), 1303–1309.

Williams, R. R. (1984). Understanding genetic and environmental risk factors in susceptible persons. *Western Journal of Medicine, 141*(6), 799–806.

Williams, R. R. (1988). Nature, nurture, and family predisposition (editorial). *New England Journal of Medicine, 318*(12), 769–771.

Williams, R. R., Hopkins, P. N., Hunt, S. C., Schumacher, M. C., Elbein, S. C., Wilson, D. E., Stults, B. M., Wu, L. L., Hasstedt, S. J., & Lalouel, J.

(1992). Familial dyslipidaemic hypertension and other multiple metabolic syndromes. *Annals of Medicine, 24*(6), 469–475.

Wood, P. D., Stefanick, M. L., Dreon, D. M., Frey-Hewitt, B., Garay, S. C., Williams, P. T., Superko, H. R., Fortmann, S. P., Albers, J. J., Vranizan, K. M., Ellsworth, N. M., Terry, R. B., & Haskell, W. L. (1988). Changes in plasma lipids and lipoproteins in overweight men during weight loss through dieting as compared with exercise. *New England Journal of Medicine, 319*(18), 1173–1179.

Wood, P. D., Stefanick, M. L., Williams, P. T., & Haskell, W. L. (1991). The effects on plasma lipoproteins of a prudent weight-reducing diet, with or without exercise, in overweight men and women. *New England Journal of Medicine, 325*(7), 461–466.

CHAPTER *10*

Immunizations

Jurgis Karuza

T his chapter reviews the published scientific literature on the delivery of immunization services for at-risk adults to provide an understanding of current immunization practices and how to improve them.

The review focuses on four major topic areas:

- effectiveness of immunization for adulthood diseases
- current immunization rates in adults
- barriers and facilitating factors that influence adult immunization rates
- outcomes of interventions that have improved adult immunization rates

While immunization patterns for influenza, pneumonia, tetanus, and hepatitis B will be considered, the primary focus will be on influenza and pneumonia vaccination of older adults.

Arguably, in the prevention literature the effectiveness of adult immunization is accepted with less controversy compared to other interventions. Immunization guidelines for influenza, pneumonia, tetanus, and hepatitis B are well publicized, clear and, for most practitioners, non-controversial (Miller, 1997; U.S. Preventive Services Task Force, 1989; Zimmerman & Clover, 1995), yet, ironically, vaccination rates historically have fallen short of goals, such as Healthy People 2000 (Public Health Service, 1990). The guidelines are summarized in Table 10.1.

179

TABLE 10.1   Summary of Vaccination Guidelines

Influenza

When:	Annually (administered preferably in the autumn)
Selected risk groups:	Older adults age 65 and over, those with chronic respiratory or cardiovascular disorders, institutionalized long-term care residents, health care workers. Vaccination should not be given to persons who had anaphylactic reaction to eggs.

Pneumonia

When:	Once (with revaccination after 6 years)
Selected risk groups:	Older adults age 65 and over, persons who are immunocompromised, persons with chronic respiratory or cardiovascular disorders, institutionalized long-term care residents

Tetanus

When:	Initial series of three toxoid doses (6–12 months) with a booster shot every 10 years
Selected risk groups:	All adults, especially those with pressure ulcers

Hepatitis B

When:	Series of three doses
Selected risk groups:	Homosexual men, recipients of blood products, hemodialysis patients, health workers where exposure to hepatitis B is probable

INFLUENZA AND PNEUMOCOCCAL IMMUNIZATION

Recent studies and reviews have documented the costs of influenza and the effectiveness of influenza vaccination in community and institutionalized populations (Fedson, 1992; Fiebach & Beckett, 1994; Gross, Hermogens, Sacks, Lau, & Levandowski, 1995; Mullooly, Bennett. Hornbrook, Barker, Williams et al., 1994; Nichol, Margolis, Wuorenma, & Von Sternberg, 1994). Influenza is estimated to cause 10,000–40,000 deaths annually in the United States, with most of the deaths (80%) occurring in older adults, age 65 and older (Fedson, 1992; Fiebach & Beckett, 1994). Depending on the severity of the influenza outbreak, the number of excess hospitalizations is estimated at between 172,000 and 500,000 during the influenza season (Barker, 1986; Fiebach & Beckett, 1994). The annual economic cost of influenza has been pegged at $12 billion (Nichol, 1992). Annual hospitalizations for pneumonia have been estimated at 40,000–120,000. Hospitalization risk is greater for patients with chronic cardiopulmonary disease, stroke, diabetes mellitus, and cancer (Fedson, 1992). An estimated 40,000 deaths from pneumococcal infections occur annually (Fiebach & Beckett, 1994).

Interestingly, as Fedson (1992) and others (Fiebach & Beckett, 1994) point out, influenza vaccine is 65% to 85% protective against influenza illness in young adults, but there is little conclusive evidence that influenza vaccination protects older adults against influenza illness. Among older adults, immunization is effective in reducing negative consequences of influenza, such as hospitalization (Barker & Mullooly, 1980). The effectiveness of the immunization varies with the degree to which the vaccine antigen matches the influenza virus during an epidemic (Barker & Mullooly, 1986). While the efficacy of influenza vaccination has been demonstrated in several randomized control studies with young adults (Spika, Fedson, & Facklam, 1990), only the randomized control study of Govaert, Tnijis, Masurel, Sprenger, Dinant et al. (1994) shows the efficacy of the immunizations with an older adult population.

The evidence for the effectiveness of influenza immunization for older adults primarily rests on a series of observational studies. Several studies examine the effectiveness of influenza vaccination in institutional settings (Gross, Quinnan, Rodstein, LaMontagne, Kaslow et al., 1988; Patriarca, Weber, Parker, Hall, Kendal et al., 1985; Saah, Neufeld, Rodstein, LaMontagne, Blackwelder et al., 1986). In general, immunization was found to be 50% to 60% effective in preventing hospitalization and 60% to 70% effective in reducing death in nursing home populations (Fedson, 1992).

Additional studies have examined the efficacy of influenza vaccination in community dwelling older adults. Barker and Mullooly (1986) did a retrospective study of older adult enrollees in a health maintenance organization (HMO) in Oregon. They focused on four influenza A epidemics that occurred between 1968 and 1981. High risk older adults with chronic conditions who were vaccinated had a 70% reduction of hospitalization and death during two of four influenza epidemics compared to unvaccinated high risk older adults. Nichol et al. (1994) followed older adults enrolled in a Minneapolis-based HMO for three influenza seasons in a serial cohort study. In all three influenza seasons, she found significant reductions in hospitalization for pneumonia, influenza, and chronic respiratory conditions, and death among older adults who were vaccinated compared with the rates of the unvaccinated older adults. During the 1991–92 season, when there was an influenza A epidemic, she also found a significant reduction in hospitalization for congestive heart failure, and lower costs of hospitalization for all illness among vaccinated older adults compared to non-vaccinated older adults. She estimated that vaccination produces average direct savings per year of $117 per person vaccinated. This study replicates previous case control studies with community based older adults in Manitoba (Fedson, Wadja, Nichol, Hammond, Kaiser et al., 1993) and the United States (Foster, Talsma, Furumoto-Dawson, Ohmit, Marguiles et al., 1992). Both studies showed vaccination was associated with reduced hospitalization rates for pneumonia and influenza.

Concerns are sounded concerning the limits of observational studies and the absence of randomized control designs. Uncontrolled biases can make the drawing of conclusions equivocal. Outcomes may be biased by differences in health status, health promotion behavior, immunological response, and influenza susceptibility between the vaccinated and unvaccinated patients. It is important to adjust for these and other risk factors when considering the efficacy of immunization using retrospective case control types of studies. It is not surprising, then, that the grade the U.S. Preventive Task Force gives the influenza vaccination is a "B" (Goldberg & Chavin, 1997).

Among younger adults, randomized control studies (Douglas, 1990) demonstrate the effectiveness of pneumococcal vaccination in prevention of pneumococcal infections. A mixed picture emerges for the effectiveness of the vaccine for older adults. A randomized control study of pneumococcal vaccination in older adult veterans by Simberkoff, Cross, and Al-Ibrahim, Baltech, Geiseler et al. (1986) did not find any vaccination effect on the number of pneumococcal infections. However, the results of the study need to be interpreted with caution, given problems with case definitions and with an inadequate sample size. Several case control studies (Shapiro, Berg,

Austrian, Schroeder, Parcells et al., 1991; Sims, Steinmann, & McConnville, King, Zwick et al., 1988) have examined the effectiveness of pneumococcal vaccination by comparing the vaccination status of patients hospitalized with pneumococcal infections to hospitalized controls without pneumococcal infection. Based on these studies' findings, the vaccine is estimated to be about 60% effective in preventing pneumococcal bacterimia in elderly persons (Fedson, 1992; Fiebach & Beckett, 1994). The grade the U.S. Preventive Task Force gives pneumococcal vaccination is a "B" (Goldberg & Chavin, 1997).

TETANUS VACCINATION

With the widespread immunization of children against tetanus the occurrence of the disease has been dramatically reduced. Currently, about 70–100 cases of adult tetanus are reported annually. According to Centers for Disease Control (1985, 1987), the incidence and fatality rates increase with age. Among those adults age 60 and older, the case fatality rate was 39%. With booster doses every 10 years, tetanus vaccine is nearly 100% effective in preventing tetanus (Williams, Hickson, & Kane, 1986). While the prevalence of tetanus is not great among older adults, the effectiveness of the vaccination earns the tetanus vaccination an "A" grade from the U.S. Preventive Task Force (Goldberg & Chavin, 1997).

HEPATITIS B VACCINATION

The incidence of hepatitis B infection is estimated at 300,000 individuals, primarily young adults, each year (Centers for Disease Control, 1987). Of these patients, 10,000 require hospitalization and 400 die from the disease. The attack rate of the virus varies. In the general population the annual attack rate is .01%, in health professionals the rate varies from 1% to 20%, in homosexual men the rate varies from 4% to 33%, and in intravenous drug users the rate varies from 12% to 33% (Williams et al., 1986). Each year, 4000 persons die from hepatitis B–related cirrhosis of the liver and 1000 persons die from hepatitis B–related liver cancer. Randomized control trials (Hadler, Francis, Maynard, Thompson, Judson et al., 1986) show that hepatitis B vaccination can be 85 to 95% effective in preventing the disease in high risk populations.

IMMUNIZATION RATES

Data on immunization rates come from a variety of sources. A primary source is the periodic reports vaccine manufacturers make to the Centers for Disease Control on the number of doses distributed and returned. Additional data on immunization patterns can be found in published results of more "micro" studies and demonstration projects of immunization practice and outcomes in specific settings and populations.

Macro epidemiological data suggest that only about 30% of older adults are vaccinated (Fedson, 1992; Fiebach & Beckett, 1994). Overall vaccination levels, as reflected by the influenza vaccination distribution in the United States, at best, reflect a modest gain (Fiebach & Beckett, 1994) over the past 10 years, and still fall far short of the national goal of 60% of older adults set forth in Healthy People 2000 (Public Health Service, 1990). The pneumococcal vaccination rate is estimated to be 10% to 15% in older adults and other high risk persons (Fedson, 1992; McBean, Babish, & Prihoda, 1991). Based on data from pharmaceutical firms, hepatitis B vaccination rate in high risk groups is estimated at 30% (Williams et al., 1986). While general temporal trends may be reflected by macro data, more fine-grained analysis of regional differences or analysis of at-risk sub-groups is difficult, if not impossible using these gross indicators of immunization practice.

"Micro" epidemiological data from specific studies and demonstration projects indicate higher estimates of influenza vaccination rates, especially among high-risk frail and chronically ill older adults. In nursing homes, influenza vaccination rates of over 80% have been obtained, especially when informed consent is not required (Patriarca et al., 1985; Setia, Serventi, & Lorenz, 1985). In community-based retrospective studies, vaccination rates of 40% to 50% have been reported (Buchner, Larson, & White, 1987; Gillick & Ditzion; 1992; Margolis, Nichol, Wuorenma, & Von Sternberg, 1992; Nichol et al., 1994).

It is important to note that in these studies, the vaccination rates were determined by examination of clinical and administrative data sets. Physician estimates of their vaccination behavior have been shown to be invalid (Fedson, 1992; Nichol, 1992). For example, in a survey by the Centers for Disease Control, 90% of internists reported that they typically gave influenza vaccination to their older adult patients. In comparison, another survey found that only 10% of the older adult patients actually were given the vaccination (Fedson, 1987a, 1987b). Several studies (Buchner et al., 1987; Buffington & LaForce, 1991) indicate a theoretical upper limit of 70% vaccination rate in community-based older adults.

FACTORS INFLUENCING IMMUNIZATION RATES

Multiple factors influence immunization rates. Barriers and facilitators of immunization include:

- practice-based factors
- practitioner-based factors
- patient-based factors

Practice Factors

Most immunizations (70%) are given in physician offices (Fedson, 1987a). However, as seen below, many of the innovations in improving immunization delivery are taking place in alternative practice settings. While health services research has not specifically tested how medical organization impacts on immunization rates, several studies provide anecdotal data suggestive of differences in immunization practice among practice settings. In general, the highest reported immunization rates (70% and higher) have been found in nursing homes with instituted immunization policies and no required informed consent policy (Patriarca et al., 1985; Setia et al., 1985), Veteran Affairs Medical Centers (Nichol, Korn, Margolis, Poland, Petzel et al., 1990), and staff model Health Maintenance Organizations (Barton & Schoenbaum, 1990; Margolis et al., 1992). Immunization rates of 30% to 70% have been found for physicians working in private practice, and outpatient clinic settings, with the highest vaccination rates obtained in practices that developed organized programs for vaccine delivery to ensure that high risk patients are offered immunizations (Bennett, Lewis,

Doniger, Bell, Kovides et al., 1994; Fedson, 1987b, 1992; Margolis, Lofgren, & Korn, 1988). Underutilized, as vaccination sites, are hospitals and emergency rooms (Fedson, 1992; Fiebach & Beckett, 1994). While they hold much promise as immunization sites, especially for pneumococcal vaccinations (Fedson, Harward, Reid, & Kaiser, 1990; Rodriquez & Baraff, 1993), potential barriers to their use include the difficulty of maintaining records of the patient's vaccination status, focus on acute care, and a lack of an economic incentive for hospitals to immunize, since an expected outcome is *reduced* future hospitalization rates.

Comparisons of immunization rate data across sites suggest that a potential facilitating factor in immunization practice may be a more structured and organized group medical setting that can help set and reinforce immunization practice (Fedson, 1987a, 1987b, 1992; Nichol, 1992). The results from the Medicare Influenza Vaccination Demonstration—Selected States 1999–1992 study (Centers for Disease Control, 1993) also suggest that a lack of orchestrated immunization policy in the community is a major barrier to increased immunization vaccination rates.

Physician Factors

The relatively low immunization rates by primary care physicians reflect the general problem of low compliance with prevention guidelines (Schwartz, Lewis, Clancy, Kinosian, Radany et al., 1991). Part of the difficulty rests with the problems of maintaining a busy primary care practice where primary prevention competes with acute care demands and management of chronic conditions (Frame, 1979). Under those conditions, preventive practice, such as immunization, may receive lower priority.

Considerable evidence has emerged that suggests physician lack of knowledge about adult immunization is *not* a major barrier to immunization practice (Fedson, 1987b). Typically, differences are not found in physician attitudes toward influenza and pneumococcal immunization among the primary care disciplines (Fedson, 1987b) or among medical provider type, for example, nurse practitioner, physician, (Fiebach & Viscoli, 1991). In other studies, the immunization rates of physicians in general internal medicine clinics were much higher than in specialty clinics (Margolis, Lofgren, & Korn, 1988; Ratner & Fedson, 1983). The fundamental reason that immunization rates are not higher is that physicians fail to translate their knowledge into clinical practice.

Patient Factors

A variety of patient-related factors have been examined to determine what effects, if any, they have on immunization rates.

Reviews (Fedson, 1987a, 1987b, 1992; Fiebach & Beckett, 1994) suggest three important patient-based experiences that facilitate immunization behavior:

- obtaining recommendation for immunization by the health care professional (Centers for Disease Control, 1988; Fedson, 1992; Fiebach & Viscoli, 1991; Nichol, Lofgren, & Gapinski, 1992)
- appointment record with the physician. The number of previous visits (Nichol et al., 1994), having a medical checkup within the past year (Stehr-Green, Sprauer, Williams, & Sullivan, 1990) and having an appointment scheduled during the influenza vaccination season (Gillick & Ditzion, 1992) all were related to being vaccinated.
- history of previous vaccination (Carter, Beach, Inui, Kirscht, & Prodzinski, 1986; Frank, McMurray, & Henderson, 1985; Nichol et al., 1992; Ratner & Fedson, 1983)

The power of physician recommendation for vaccination can be seen in the results from the Centers for Disease Control study (1988) that interviewed 867 older adults in DeKalb and Fulton counties in Georgia (metro Atlanta). When the physician recommended influenza vaccination, the vaccination rates were 87% among patients with a positive attitude toward vaccination and 70% among patients with a negative attitude. In contrast, 8% of patients with a positive attitude and 7% of patients with a negative attitude were vaccinated when the physician did not recommend vaccination. Parallel findings were found for pneumococcal vaccination.

Some previous case control studies suggest that immunization rates are greater among adults who have more chronic disease (Barker & Mullooly, 1980; Nichol et al., 1994; Ohmit, Furumoto-Dawson, Monto, & Fasano, 1995; Petersen, Saag, Wallace, & Doebbeling, 1999), although other studies found no relationship between chronic disease diagnosis and immunization (Fiebach &

Viscoli, 1991). Mixed results have been found in the relationship between patient age and vaccination status. Nichol et al., (1994) found an inverse relationship between age and vaccination status, Fiebach and Viscoli (1991) found no relationship between age and vaccination status, and Petersen et al. (1999) found age 70 or greater associated with receipt of vaccination. Gender does not seem to affect vaccination rates (Centers for Disease Control, 1988; Fiebach & Viscoli, 1991; Nichol et al., 1994).

The race of the patient was not related to the actual receipt of pneumococcal and/or influenza vaccination in some studies (Centers for Disease Control, 1985, 1988, 1995; Fiebach & Viscoli, 1991). Other studies (e.g., Stehr-Green et al., 1990) report lower influenza vaccination rates among African Americans and individuals who identify with Spanish-speaking cultures. In a related vein, Gemson, Elinson, and Messeri (1988) found that the prevention practices, including influenza vaccinations, with patients differed with the composition of the physician's practice panel. Physicians with a predominantly white practice panel were more likely to follow prevention guidelines than physicians with practices that had a majority of African American patients or patients who identify with Spanish-speaking cultures.

Several studies find that patient's health beliefs and attitudes toward immunization affect their vaccination status. In the Centers for Disease Control (1988) study of older adults in Fulton and DeKalb Counties, most older adults were aware of the availability of influenza vaccination (90%) and pneumococcal vaccines (53%). Only 50% of patients with a negative attitude and 70% of patients with a positive attitude toward influenza vaccination reported receiving the vaccine; however, as pointed out above, the physician's recommendation for vaccination was an important mediating variable for predicting whether the patient was vaccinated.

Fear of side effects from being vaccinated has been found to have an impact on whether the patient is vaccinated (Buchner, Carter, & Inui, 1985; Buffington & LaForce, 1991; Carter et al., 1986; Fiebach & Viscoli, 1991; Frank et al., 1985; Larson, Bergman, Heidrich, Alvin, & Schneeweiss, 1982; Nichol et al., 1992). In an interesting study, Margolis, Nichol, Poland, and Pluhar (1990) tested whether influenza vaccination produced negative symptoms using a randomized double blind control study. Fever, myalgia, and malaise, common symptoms putatively associated with vaccination, in fact, occurred in only 4% to 7% of the study subjects. There were no significant differences in the rate of occurrence of these negative symptoms in the vaccine and saline placebo groups.

Health beliefs about whether influenza was serious and the extent to which patients felt to be susceptible to disease were found to be related to vaccination status in a case control study done by Larson, Olsen, Cole, & Shortell (1979). Buchner et al. (1985) found, that while specific attitudes toward vaccination may shift from year to year, the behavioral intent to be vaccinated and the actual patient vaccination behavior was stable from year to year. In a related vein, data from the 1987 Behavioral Risk Factor Surveillance System Survey (Stehr-Green et al., 1990) indicated that patients who exhibited a preventive pattern of behavior (e.g., used seat belts, did not smoke, were not obese) were more likely to be vaccinated.

STRATEGIES TO INCREASE IMMUNIZATION

Many specific studies report on interventions designed to increase vaccination rates among adults. Interventions are broken down into three general classes: patient focused, provider focused, and system focused. In a review of studies evaluating strategies to increase influenza vaccination, Gyorkos, Tannenbaum, Abrahamowitz, Bedard, Carsley et al. (1994) found 21 studies using client-oriented approaches, seven using provider-oriented approaches, and four using system-oriented approaches. The average size of the intervention effect, for example, the percentage increase of vaccination resulting from the intervention, ranged from 12.2% for client-oriented approaches and 18.1% for provider-oriented approaches to 39.4% for system-oriented approaches. Gyorkos et al. (1994) also found evidence that the baseline vaccination rate may constrain the intervention's effect. A 20% increase in vaccination was found when the baseline rate was under 20%, but this dropped to a 14.8% increase in vaccination rate when the baseline rate was over 50%. A major concern with these intervention studies is that, all too often, they focus on short-term changes and do not provide data on the long-term effectiveness of the intervention in boosting immunization rates.

Patient-Focused Interventions

Patient-focused interventions typically are implemented in outpatient settings and have the goal of informing or reminding patients of the need to be vaccinated. Common methods that have been used include:

- mailed reminders
- telephone reminders

Mailed reminders, either postcard or letter, to patients have been found to be effective in increasing influenza vaccination rates in university and community-based clinics (Frank, McMurray, & Henderson, 1985; Larson et al., 1979; Larson et al., 1982; Mullooly, 1987; Pearson & Thompson, 1994; Turner, Day, & Borenstein, 1989). The effectiveness of mail reminders by themselves in HMOs (Barton & Schoenbaum, 1990) and private practices (Buchner et al., 1987) is equivocal. An alert is sounded in some studies (Hutchison & Shannon, 1991; McDowell, Newell, & Rosser, 1990) that continued use of patient reminder may be counter-productive in the long run by creating a dependency on the reminder. Several studies have examined the use of telephone-based patient reminders (Frank et al., 1985; McDowell, Newell, & Rosser, 1986, 1990). While their use increased vaccination rates, their cost/effectiveness in comparison to mailed reminders is debatable. Leirer, Morrow, Pariante, and Doksum (1988) found a voice mail reminder system for patients was effective in boosting vaccination rates.

Physician-Focused Interventions

Several intervention studies with physicians have shown that the vaccination rates of physicians can be increased. Physician-focused interventions typically include:

- checklists or reminders attached to patient charts
- computer reminders at the time of the patient's visit
- feedback on physician performance either as a group or individually

Some evidence suggests that combinations of interventions are more likely to have an impact on physician immunization practice, although the evidence is mixed. The use of reminders and feedback mechanisms for physicians can help the physician to re-prioritize the importance of prevention practices within the primary care setting.

A study by Cohen, Littenberg, Wetzel, and Neuhauser (1982) examined physician compliance with preventive medicine guidelines as a function of implementing a checklist reminder system and scheduling physician information seminars. McDonald, Hui, and Tierney (1992) found use of a computerized reminder system, not only improved vaccination rates, but also reduced patient mortality rates during an influenza epidemic. Chambers, Balaban, Carlson, and Grasberger (1991) found that physician computer-generated reminders were effective in increasing influenza vaccination, and that the effect was more pronounced when reminders were generated for all the relevant patients in the panel than only for some of the patients. Tierney, Hui, and McDonald, (1986) found a seven-fold enhancement of compliance with pneumococcal vaccine guidelines was achieved by the implementation of a computerized reminder system for physicians. Clancy, Geffman, and Poses (1992) replicated this finding in a university hospital. Ornstein, Garr, Jenkins, Rust, and Arnon (1991) found that computer-generated physician reminders in combination with patient reminders increased tetanus immunizations from 23% to 35% in a family medicine clinic.

Barton and Schoenbaum (1990) attempted to increase the rate of influenza vaccination performance in an HMO setting by using both computer-generated reminders and peer comparison feedback. This study was conducted at the Health Centers Division of Harvard Community Health Plan in Boston. This project collected data during 1983–87. Three different interventions were implemented sequentially over 3 years. In 1983, the year before the influenza vaccination program began, chart review of patients aged 65 and over revealed immunization rates of 24% to 22% in the centers. The results demonstrated that it is possible to improve annual influenza vaccination performance in a practice setting using a combination of patient reminder and physician feedback techniques. Additional evidence for the usefulness of feedback mechanisms can be found in the Monroe County portion of Medicare Influenza Vaccination Demonstration Selected States 1999–1992 project (Bennett et al., 1994). Their coordinated community-wide program to increase influenza vaccination included the posting, in the intervention practices, of a target-based poster that tracked physicians' immunization rates. The vaccination rate was significantly higher among those physicians who were given feedback by the tracking poster compared to control physicians.

System-Focused Interventions

Examples of system-focused strategies include:

- written policy
- standing orders
- flexible informed consent procedures for vaccination
- dedicated nurse
- dedicated vaccination clinics

In nursing home settings, the development of standing orders for vaccination of nursing home patients resulted in dramatic increases in vaccination rates (Setia et al., 1985). Klein and Adachi (1986) found similar success using standing orders to increase pneumococcal vaccination. Ethical questions regarding patient rights and informed consent are raised when developing a standing orders policy and should be considered carefully. Rodriquez and Baraff (1993) demonstrated the feasibility of administering influenza and pneumococcal vaccine to older adult patients in a hospital emergency department. The importance of increasing hospital-based vaccinations is underscored by the fact that discharged patients are much more likely to be rehospitalized for respiratory conditions (Fedson, Wajda, Nichol, & Roos, 1992) and pneumonia (Fedson et al., 1990).

Demonstration projects that establish vaccination clinics in the community have met with success (Centers for Disease Control, 1991). Maricopa County portion of Medicare Influenza Vaccination Demonstration Selected States 1988–1992 project arranged for primary care physicians to conduct vaccination clinics in shopping malls. Nearly a majority (43%) of the older adults' Medicare beneficiaries who were vaccinated during that influenza season were vaccinated in the mall clinics.

Perhaps the most effective organizational/community intervention is the development of organized programs for vaccine delivery. Examples of organized programs for vaccine delivery can be seen at the hospital level (Nichol, 1998; Nichol et al., 1990) and in staff model HMOs (Margolis et al., 1992). The Margolis and colleagues

(1992) study suggests that intensive organizational-based intervention that includes informational mailing to patients, standing order policies allowing nurses to administer vaccine, and a vaccination reminder system can be translated from an academic to a community setting. Another example of such an organized approach at the community level is Medicare Influenza Vaccination Demonstration Selected States 1988–1992 project (Centers for Disease Control, 1993). Published data from the Monroe County segment of the program (Bennett et al., 1994) revealed that such a comprehensive approach, was able to push immunization rates over 70%. Selected strategies used in the Medicare Influenza Vaccination Demonstration Selected States 1988–1992 project included provision of free vaccine to providers, central claims processing, community outreach and comprehensive education programming, including public awareness campaigns using print and radio media, and patient and professional education. These educational efforts highlight the role of nurses in educating both professionals and patients to effect immunization rates among older adults. Extensive education efforts focused on health care professionals, primarily providing education to nurses (Bottum, Bacall, Balsam, Ellis, Etkind et al., 1995). Sessions given in a variety of settings provided information about why older adult patients should be encouraged to receive the vaccine and how nurses could motivate the patients. In addition, special material packets were prepared for distribution to older adults. Educational efforts also targeted nurses' aides. A 20-minute program of slide and tape recapping basic information about influenza, the vaccine, infection control procedures, and the importance of being vaccinated was prepared and presented in nursing homes. Although immunization service delivery is predominantly under the purview of the physician, this project demonstrates the unique opportunity nurses have to impact the health of the elderly through health education about influenza immunization.

TWO QUESTIONS: WHAT WORKS? AND HOW TO IMPLEMENT IT?

The above review illustrates a variety of techniques that have the potential to enhance vaccination rates. We are beginning to get an answer to the question "What works?" Several general strategies from the literature are highlighted as especially promising:

- using multiple approaches aimed at both patient and practitioner
- getting patients to see primary care practitioners
- implementing a systemic approach to vaccination at the practice site or in the community
- opportunistic vaccination—use every opportunity

But, a second question remains: *how to get these interventions to work, that is, how to implement them.* The challenge is to take these good ideas and to bring them into practice, regardless of which strategy is chosen. As the continuing medical education and guidelines dissemination literature highlight, merely informing practitioners of a guideline or of an innovative technique does not guarantee that the practitioner will adopt it and put it into practice (Davis Thompson, Oxman & Haynes, 1992; Kossecoff, Kanouse, Rogers, McCloskey, Wislow et al., 1987). It is essential that the practitioner "buy into" changing his or her practice pattern.

In a recent review of the continuing medical education literature, Davis Thompson, Oxman and Haynes, (1995) point out that it is possible for continuing educational efforts to result in a practitioner changing his or her practice pattern. However, not all efforts are equally effective. Continuing education that used traditional dissemination formats, such as lectures, conferences, written pamphlets, and so on, were not effective in bringing about practice change. Far more effective in changing practice patterns were innovative continuing educational efforts that went beyond spreading information and focused on ways to enable physicians to change their practice (e.g., employing office facilitators) or to reinforce practice pattern changes. Also effective were a variety of approaches that involved the practitioner more intimately in the educational process, such as outreach visits, use of opinion leader education, and peer discussion.

Other interventions suggested are most relevant for the practice of nursing and can serve to facilitate the work of physicians and other health professionals to maximize the rate of influenza immunization. These interventions include patient education whether it may be written or verbal. In addition, nurses can provide support through the implementation of mailed or telephoned immuniza-tion reminders. The development of health care provider educa-tional programs and accompanying materials has also been shown to be under the auspice of the nurse.

Some of the interventions reviewed above, such as use of chart reminders for vaccination or providing physicians with feedback on vaccination performance, by their nature, enable and reinforce physician vaccination practice. Also promising is the work of Karuza, Calkins, Feather, Hershey, Katz et al. (1995) on the use of peer discussion type format for boosting vaccination performance in group practices. Physicians enrolled in a small group process intervention, designed to lead to physician "buy into" vaccination guidelines for older adults, increased their vaccination rates of older adults to 63%. This represented a significant 34% increase in vaccination rate compared to the vaccination rate of physicians in the control arm of the study.

Not to be overlooked is nursing's role in enhancing and rein-forcing the work of physicians and other health professionals to maximize the rate of influenza immunization. As seen above, one important nursing-based intervention is patient education, whether it be written or verbal (Schofield, 1999). Nurses can provide support through the implementation of mailed or telephoned immunization reminders. Also effective is the development of health care provider educational programs and accompanying materials under the aus-pices of the nurse. As the research of Rhew, Glassman, and Goetz (1999) suggests, implementing nurse-initiated standing order vac-cine protocols, in addition to physician and patient reminder sys-tems, may be an additional strategy to increase vaccination rates.

Finally, while the vaccination guidelines are well-known among practitioners, their actual rates of performance are not. As Nichol, Grimm, and Peterson (1996) point out:

> Without measurements of current performance and a method for evaluating ongoing efforts, personnel in facilities may be unaware of the inadequacy of current level of activities and have little or no motivation to introduce programs for improving immunization rates. Measures of performance are critical for establishing the need for improvement. (pp. 349–355)

This suggests the value of using a continuous quality improve-ment framework (Barwick, 1989) within the practice site to guide the development of a comprehensive systemic approach to enhancing vaccination performance.

REFERENCES

Barker, W. H. (1986). Excess pneumonia and influenza associated hospitalization during influenza epidemics in the United States, 1970–78. *American Journal of Public Health, 76*(7), 761–765.

Barker, W. H., & Mullooly, J. P. (1980). Influenza vaccination of elderly persons. Reduction in pneumonia and influenza hospitalizations and death. *Journal of the American Medical Association, 244*(22), 2547–2549.

Barker, W. H., & Mullooly, J. P. (1986). Effectiveness of inactive influenza vaccine among non institutionalized elderly person. In A. P. Kendal & P. A. Patriarca (Eds.), *Options for the control of influenza.* New York: Alan R. Liss.

Barton, M. B., & Schoenbaum, S. C. (1990). Improving influenza vaccination performance in an HMO setting: The use of computer-generated reminders and peer comparison feedback. *American Journal of Public Health, 80*(5), 534–536.

Barwick, D. (1989). Continuous improvement as an ideal in health care. *New England Journal of Medicine, 320*(1), 53–56.

Bennett, N. M., Lewis, B., Doniger, A. S., Bell, K., Kouides, R., LaForce, F. M., & Barker, W. (1994). A coordinated, community wide program in Monroe County, New York, to increase influenza immunization rates in the elderly. *Archives of Internal Medicine, 154*(15), 1741–1745.

Bottum, C. L., Bacall, D., Balsam, A., Ellis, C., Etkind, P., & Gardiner, C. (1995). Better than chicken soup: Encouraging older patients to receive influenza immunization. *Caring, 14*(11), 70–73.

Buchner, D. M., Carter, W. B., & Inui, T. S. (1985). The relationship of attitude change to compliance with influenza immunization. A prospective study. *Medical Care, 23*(6), 771–779.

Buchner, D. M., Larson, E. B., & White, R. F. (1987). Influenza vaccination in community elderly. A controlled trial of postcard reminders. *Journal of the American Geriatrics Society, 35*(8), 755–760.

Buffington, J., & LaForce, F. M. (1991). Achievable influenza immunization rates in the elderly. *New York State Journal of Medicine, 91*(10), 433–435.

Carter, W. B., Beach, L. R., Inui, T. S., Kirscht, J. P., & Prodzinski, J. C. (1986). Developing and testing a decision model for predicting influenza vaccination compliance. *Health Services Research, 20*(6 pt 2), 897–932.

Centers for Disease Control (1985). Tetanus—United States, 1982–1984. *Morbidity and Mortality Reports, 34*(39), 602, 607-611.

Centers for Disease Control (1987). Tetanus—United States, 1985–1986. *Morbidity and Mortality Reports, 36*(29), 477–481.

Centers for Disease Control (1988). Adult immunization: Knowledge, attitudes and practices—DeKalb and Fulton Counties, Georgia, 1988. *Morbidity and Mortality Reports, 37*(34), 657–661.

Centers for Disease Control (1991) Successful strategies in adult immunization. *Morbidity and Mortality Reports, 40*(41), 700–703.

Centers for Disease Control. (1993). Final results: Medicare influenza vaccine demonstration—Selected states, 1988–1992. *Morbidity and Mortality Reports, 42*(31), 301–304.

Centers for Disease Control (1995). Race specific differences in influenza vaccination levels among Medicare beneficiaries—United States, 1993. *Morbidity and Mortality Reports, 44*(2), 24–27, 33.

Chambers, C., Balaban, D., Carlson, B., & Grasberger, D. (1991). The effect of microcomputer-generated reminders on influenza vaccination rates in a university based family practice center. *Journal of the American Board of Family Practice, 4*(1), 19–26.

Clancy, C. M., Geffman, D., & Poses, R. M. (1992). A strategy to improve the utilization of pneumococcal vaccine. *Journal of General Internal Medicine, 7*(1), 14–18.

Cohen, D., Littenberg, B., Wetzel, C., & Neuhauser, D. (1982). Improving physician compliance with preventive medicine guidelines. *Medical Care, 20*(10), 1040–1045.

Davis, D. A., Thompson, M. A., Oxman, A. D., & Haynes, R. B. (1992). Evidence for the effectiveness of CME: A review of 50 randomized trials. *Journal of the American Medical Association, 268*(9), 1111–1117.

Davis, D. A., Thompson, M. A., Oxman, A. D., & Haynes, R. B. (1995). Changing physician performance: A systematic review of the effect of continuing medical education strategies. *Journal of the American Medical Association, 274*(9), 700–705.

Douglas, R. G. (1990). Prophylaxis and treatment of influenza. *New England Journal of Medicine, 322*(7), 443–450.

Fedson, D. S. (1987a). Influenza prevention and control past practices and future prospects. *The American Journal of Medicine, 82*(6a), 42–47.

Fedson, D. S. (1987b). Influenza and pneumococcal immunization strategies for physicians. *Chest, 91*(3), 436–434.

Fedson, D. S. (1992). Clinical practice and public policy for influenza and pneumococcal vaccination of the elderly. *Clinics in Geriatric Medicine, 8*(1), 183–199.

Fedson, D. S., Harward, M. P., Reid, R. A., & Kaiser, D. L. (1990). Hospital based pneumococcal immunization. Epidemiologic rationale from the Shenandoah Study. *Journal of the American Medical Association, 264*(9), 1117–1122.

Fedson, D. S., Wajda, A., Nichol, J. P., Hammond, G. W., Kaiser, D. L., & Roos, L. L. (1993). Clinical effectiveness of influenza vaccination in Manitoba. *Journal of the American Medical Association, 270*(16), 1956–1961.

Fedson, D., Wajda, A., Nichol, J. P., & Roos, L. L. (1992). Disparity between influenza vaccination rates and risks for influenza-associated discharge and death in Manitoba in 1982–1983. *Annals of Internal Medicine, 116*(7), 550–555.

Fiebach, N., & Beckett, W. (1994). Prevention of respiratory infections in adults. Influenza and pneumococcal vaccines. *Archives of Internal Medicine, 154*(22), 2545–2557.

Fiebach, N. H., & Viscoli, C. M. (1991). Patient acceptance of influenza vaccination. *American Journal of Medicine, 91*(4), 393–400.

Foster, D. A., Talsma, A., Furumoto-Dawson, A., Ohmit, S. E., Marguiles, J. R., Arden, N. H., & Monto, A. S. (1992). Influenza vaccine effectiveness in preventing hospitalization for pneumonia in the elderly. *American Journal of Epidemiology, 136*(3), 296–307.

Frame, P. S. (1979). Periodic health screening in a rural private practice. *Journal of Family Practice, 9*(1), 57–64.

Frank, J. W., McMurray, L., & Henderson, M. (1985). Influenza vaccination in the elderly: The economics of sending reminder letters. *Canadian Medical Association Journal, 132*(5), 516, 8, 521.

Gemson, D. H., Elinson, J., & Messeri, P. (1988). Differences in physician prevention practice patterns for white and minority patients. *Journal of Community Health, 13*(1), 53–64.

Gillick, M. R., & Ditzion, B. (1992). Influenza vaccination. Are we doing better than we think? *Archives of Internal Medicine, 151*(9), 1742–1744.

Goldberg, T. H., & Chavin, S. I. (1997). Preventive medicine and screening in older adults. *Journal of the American Geriatrics Society, 45*(3), 344–354.

Govaert, T. M., Thijis, C. T., Masurel, N., Sprenger, M. J., Dinant, G. J., & Knottnerus, J. A. (1994). The efficacy of influenza vaccination in elderly individuals. A randomized double blind placebo controlled trial. *Journal of the American Medical Association, 272*(21), 1661–1665.

Gross, P. A., Hermogens, A. W., Sacks, H. S., Lau, J., & Levandowski, R. A. (1995). The efficacy of influenza vaccine in elderly persons: A meta analysis and review of the literature. *Annals of Internal Medicine, 123*(7), 518–527.

Gross, P. A., Quinnan, G. V., Rodstein, M., LaMontagne, J. R., Kaslow, R. A., Saah, A. J., Wallenstein, S., Neufeld, R., Denning, C., & Gaerlan, P. (1988). Association of influenza immunization with reduction in mortality in an elderly population. A prospective study. *Archives of Internal Medicine, 148*(3), 562–565.

Gyorkos, T. W., Tannenbaum, T. N., Abrahamowitz, M., Bedard, L., Carsley, J., Franco, E. D., Delage, G., Miller, M. A., Lamping, D. L., & Grover, S. A. (1994). Evaluation of the effectiveness of immunization delivery methods. *Canadian Journal of Public Health, 85,* Suppl 1, S14–S30.

Hadler, S. C., Francis, D. P., Maynard, J. E., Thompson, S. E., Judson, F. N., Echenberg, D. F., Ostrow, D. G., O'Malley, P. M., Penley, K. A., & Altman, N. L. (1986). Long term immunogenicity and efficacy of hepatitis B vaccine in homosexual men. *New England Journal of Medicine, 315*(4), 209–214.

Hutchison, B. G., & Shannon, H. S. (1991). Effect of repeated annual reminder letters on influenza immunization among elderly patients. *Journal of Family Practice, 33*(2), 187–189.

Karuza, J., Calkins, E., Feather, J., Hershey C. O., Katz, L., & Majeroni, B. (1995). Enhancing physician adoption of practice guidelines: Dissemination of influenza vaccination guideline using a small-group consensus process. *Archives of Internal Medicine, 155*(6), 625–632.

Klein, R. S., & Adachi N. (1986). An effective hospital based pneumococcal immunization program. *Archives of Internal Medicine, 146*(2), 327–329.

Kosecoff, J., Kanouse, D. E., Rogers, W. H., McCloskey, L., Wislow, C. M., & Brook, R. H. (1987). Effects of the National Institutes of Health Consensus Development Program on physician practice. *Journal of the American Medical Association, 258*(19), 2708–2713.

Larson, E. B., Bergman, J., Heidrich, F., Alvin, B. L., & Schneeweiss, R. (1982). Do postcard reminders improve influenza vaccine compliance? *Medical Care, 20*(6), 639–648.

Larson, E. B., Olsen, E., Cole, W., & Shortell, S. (1979). The relationship of health beliefs and a postcard reminder to influenza vaccination. *Journal of Family Practice, 8*(6), 1207–1211.

Leirer, V. O., Morrow, D. G., Pariante, G., & Doksum, T. (1988). Increasing influenza vaccination adherence through voice mail. *Journal of the American Geriatrics Society, 37*(12), 1147–1150.

Margolis, K. L., Lofgren, R. P., & Korn, J. E. (1988). Organization strategies to improve influenza vaccine delivery: A standing order in a general medicine clinic. *Archives of Internal Medicine, 148*(10), 2205–2207.

Margolis, K. L., Nichol, K. L., Poland, G. A., & Pluhar, R. E. (1990). Frequency of adverse reactions to influenza vaccine in the elderly. A randomized placebo controlled trial. *Journal of the American Medical Association, 264*(9), 1139–1141.

Margolis, K. L., Nichol, K. L., Wuorenma, J., & Von Sternberg, T. L. (1992). Exporting a successful influenza vaccination program from a teaching hospital to a community outpatient setting. *Journal of the American Geriatrics Society, 40*(10), 1021–1023.

McBean, A. M., Babish, J. D., & Prihoda, R. (1991). The utilization of pneumococcal polysaccharide vaccine among elderly Medicare beneficiaries, 1985 through 1988. *Archives of Internal Medicine, 151*(10), 2009–2016.

McDonald, C. J., Hui, S. L., & Tierney, W. M. (1992). Effects of computer reminders for influenza vaccination on morbidity during influenza epidemics. *MD Computing, 9*(5), 304–312.

McDowell, I., Newell, C., & Rosser, W. (1986). Comparisons of three methods of recalling patients for influenza vaccination. *Canadian Medical Association Journal, 135*(9), 991–997.

McDowell, I., Newell, C., & Rosser, W. (1990). A follow-up study of patients advised to obtain influenza immunizations. *Family Medicine, 22*(4), 303–306.

Miller, C. (1997). Preventive care should address the immunizations for older adults. *Geriatric Nursing, 18*(1), 42–43.

Mullooly, J. P. (1987). Increasing influenza vaccination among high risk elderly: A randomized control trial of a mail cue in an HMO setting. *American Journal of Public Health, 77*(5), 626–627.

Mullooly, J. P., Bennett, M. D., Hornbrook, M. C., Barker, W. H., Williams, W. W., Patriarca, P. A., & Rhodes, P. H. (1994). Influenza vaccination program for elderly persons: Cost effectiveness in a health maintenance organization. *Annals of Internal Medicine, 121*(12), 947–952.

Nichol, K. L. (1992). Preventing influenza: The physician's role. *Seminars in Respiratory Infections, 7*(1), 71–77.

Nichol, K. L. (1998). Ten year durability and success of an organized program to increase influenza and pneumococcal vaccination rates among high risk adults. *American Journal of Medicine, 105*(5), 385–392.

Nichol, K. L., Grimm, M. B., & Peterson, D. C. (1996). Immunizations in long term care facilities: Policies and practice. *Journal of the American Geriatrics Society, 44*(4), 349–355.

Nichol, K. L., Korn, J. E., Margolis, K. L., Poland, G. A., Petzel, R. A., & Lofgren, R. P. (1990). Achieving the nation health objective for influenza immunization: Success of an institution wide vaccination program. *The American Journal of Medicine, 89*(2), 156–160.

Nichol, K. L., Lofgren, R. P., & Gapinski, J. (1992). Influenza vaccination: Knowledge, attitudes and behavior among high-risk outpatients. *Archives of Internal Medicine, 152*(1), 106–110.

Nichol, K. L., Margolis, K. L., Wuorenma, J., & Von Sternberg, T. (1994). The efficacy and cost effectiveness of vaccination against influenza among elderly persons living in the community. *New England Journal of Medicine, 331*(12), 778–784.

Ohmit, S., Furumoto-Dawson, A., Monto, A. S., & Fasano, N. (1995).

Influenza vaccine use among an elderly population in a community intervention. *American Journal of Preventive Medicine, 11*(4), 271–276.

Ornstein, S. M., Garr, D. R., Jenkins, R. G., Rust, P. F., & Arnon, A. (1991). Computer-generated physician and patient reminders: Tools to improve population adherence to selected preventive services. *Journal of Family Practice, 32*(1), 82–90.

Patriarca, P. A., Weber, J. A., Parker, R. A., Hall, W. N., Kendal, A. P., & Bergman, D. J. (1985). Efficacy of influenza vaccine in nursing homes: Reduction of illness and complications during an influenza A (H3N2) epidemic. *Journal of the American Medical Association, 253*(8), 1136–1139.

Pearson, D. C., & Thompson, R. S. (1994). Evaluation of Group Health Cooperative of Puget Sound's senior influenza immunization program. *Public Health Reports, 109*(4), 571–578.

Petersen, R., Saag, K. W., Wallace, R. B., & Doebbeling, B. N. (1999). Influenza and pneumococcal vaccine receipt in older persons with chronic illness: A population based study. *Medical Care, 37*(5), 502–509.

Public Health Service (1990). *Healthy People 2000. National Health Promotion and Disease Prevention Objectives.* Washington, DC: Department of Health and Human Services.

Ratner, E. R., & Fedson, D. S. (1983). Influenza and pneumococcal immunization in medical clinics, 1978–1980. *Archives of Internal Medicine, 143*(11), 2066–2069.

Rhew, D. C., Glassman, P. A., & Goetz, M. B. (1999). Improving pneumococcal vaccine rates. Nurse protocols versus clinical reminders. *Journal of General Internal Medicine, 14*(6), 351–356.

Rodriquez, R. M., & Baraff, L. J. (1993). Emergency department immunization of the elderly with pneumococcal and influenza vaccines. *Annals of Emergency Medicine, 22*(11), 1729–1732.

Saah, A. J., Neufeld, R., Rodstein, M., LaMontagne, J. R., Blackwelder, W. C., Gross, P. A., Quinnan, G., & Kaslow, R. A. (1986). Influenza vaccine and pneumonia mortality in a nursing home population. *Archives of Internal Medicine, 146*(12), 2353–2357.

Schofield, I. (1999). Influenza vaccination. *Elder Care, 11,* 19–23.

Schwartz, J. S., Lewis, C. E., Clancy, C., Kinosian, M. S., Radany, M. H., & Koplan, J. P. (1991). Internists' practices in health promotion and disease prevention. *Annals of Internal Medicine, 114*(1), 46–53.

Setia, U., Serventi, I., & Lorenz, P. (1985). Factors affecting the use of influenza vaccine in the institutionalized elderly. *Journal of the American Geriatric Society, 33*(12), 856–858.

Shapiro, E. D., Berg, A. T., Austrian, R., Schroeder, D., Parcells, V., Margolis, A., Adair, R. K., & Clemens, J. D. (1991). The protective efficacy of polyvalent pneumococcal polysaccharide vaccine. *New England Journal of Medicine, 325*(21), 1453–1460.

Simberkoff, M. S., Cross, A. P., Al-Ibrahim, M., Baltech, A. L., Geiseler, P. J., Nadler, J., Richmond, A. S., Smith, R. P. , Schiffman, G., & Shepard, D. S. (1986). Efficacy of pneumococcal vaccine in high-risk patients. *New England Journal of Medicine, 315*(21), 1318–1327.

Sims, R. V., Steinmann, W. C., McConnville, J. H., King, L. R., Zwick, W. C., & Schwartz, J. S. (1988). The clinical effectiveness of pneumococcal vaccine in the elderly. *Annals of Internal Medicine, 108*(5), 653–657.

Spika, J. S., Fedson, D. S., & Facklam, R. R. (1990). Pneumococcal vaccination. Controversies and opportunities. *Infectious Disease Clinics in North America, 4*(1), 11–27.

Stehr-Green, P. A., Sprauer, M. A., Williams, W. W., & Sullivan, K. M. (1990). Predictors of vaccination behavior among persons ages 65 years and older. *American Journal of Public Health, 80*(9), 1127–1129.

Tierney, W. M., Hui, S. L., & McDonald, C. J. (1986). Delayed feedback of physician performance versus immediate reminders to perform preventive care. *Medical Care, 24*(8), 659–666.

Turner, B. J., Day, S. C., & Borenstein, B. (1989). A controlled trial to improve preventive care: Physician or patient reminders. *Journal of General Internal Medicine, 4*(5), 403–409.

U. S. Preventive Services Task Force (1989). *Guide to clinical preventive services*. Baltimore: Williams & Wilkins.

Williams, W. W., Hickson, M. A., & Kane, M. A. (1986). Immunization policies and vaccine coverage among adults. *Annals of Internal Medicine, 108*, 616–625.

Zimmerman, R. K., & Clover, R. D. (1995). Adult immunizations—A practical approach for physicians: Part I. *American Family Physician, 51*(4), 859–867.

CHAPTER 11

Interventions with Elderly African American Diabetics

Barbara Holder

INTERVENTION RESEARCH WITH ELDERLY AFRICAN AMERICAN DIABETICS

Effective diabetic management is a primary goal of diabetic interventions with patients. Among African American diabetics, the difficulty in achieving this goal has been associated with patient belief about the diabetes and psychological distress in and negative feelings shared between patients and their family members (Kumanyika & Ewart, 1990; Stevens, Kumanyika, & Keil, 1994; Weatherspoon, Kumanyika, Ludlow, & Schatz, 1994; Wing & Anglin, 1996). Although important for continued and successful diabetic management, the effects of diabetic interventions on these factors are seldom investigated systematically in African American samples. More important, the few studies that address these factors focus primarily on diabetic education and generally exclude the patient's family. In addition, the studies generally use small samples of African American diabetics and seldom address the cultural appropriateness or the focus and approach of the diabetic intervention.

This chapter summarizes the research literature concerned with diabetic interventions with African American diabetics. Emphasis will be the effect of diabetic education intervention and family-focused intervention on patient beliefs about their diabetes and the level of psychological distress in diabetic patients and their family members, and the negative feelings shared between patients and their family members. A summarized description of an ongoing longitudinal intervention study with elderly African American diabetics and their families will be presented followed by a description of the short- and long-term effects of a diabetic educational intervention and a family-centered intervention. Discussion will focus on the implications of the findings for nursing practice and research.

ISSUES OF INTERVENTION RESEARCH

Patients' beliefs about their diabetes and the quality of feelings in their families have been associated with African American diabetics' participation in lifestyle changes that are important for effective diabetic management.

Diabetic Beliefs

Cultural beliefs about being overweight also influence African American diabetics' effectiveness at diabetic management. For some African Americans, obesity is a sign of good health. Health reasons serve as motivation for weight loss among African American women. Negative beliefs may decrease this motivation and promote a more fatalistic attitude leading to decrease dietary adherence (Stevens et al., 1994; Weatherspoon et al., 1994). African American diabetics who fail to follow nutritional recommendations feel negative about their lives and perceived their diabetes as a negative influence on their social and personal lives (Fitzgerald, Anderson, Funnell, Arnold, Davis et al., 1997).

Wing and Anglin (1996) found that African American diabetics were initially compliant with a yearlong weight reduction intervention program. However, attendance at fewer meetings was associated with rapid weight regain during the last 6-month period of the intervention. Negative feelings and eating behaviors have also been linked to poor attendance at intervention sessions and weight regain in diabetic patients, particularly among female and young adult diabetics. Adult diabetics who eat more or inappropriate food have been found to be angry, depressed, and anxious or nervous (psychological distress). In contrast, those who attend initial and follow-up educational sessions follow their nutritional regimen (Travis, 1997).

Skelly, Marshall, Haughey, Davis, and Dunford (1995) found that the belief regarding the performance of diabetic tasks effects different components of inner city African American diabetics' diabetic regimen at different points over time. Although this finding suggests that patients' beliefs change over time, the timing of this change is unclear. Also unclear is the link between changes in patients' belief and the type of diabetic intervention (diabetic education or combination of education, support, and problem solving) between patients' belief and the focus of a diabetic intervention (patient-focus versus family-focus). The absence of information on the timing of changes in patients' beliefs about their diabetes is an additional concern.

Family Social Support and Negative Family Feelings

Kumanyika and Ewart (1990) link family or other close relationships to the ability of African American diabetics to follow their diabetic regimen effectively. African Americans who are externally oriented placed more emphasis on social support systems and the importance of following instructions of health providers (Bell, Summerson, & Konen, 1995). These patients were also more stressed and had families who were dysfunctional and disengaged (Bell et al., 1995; Konen, Summerson, & Dignan, 1993).

Kumanyika and Ewart's (1990) research also link patient stress and family conflict to African American diabetics' difficulty in following their diabetic regimen. Other research suggests that African American diabetics who are overweight expect family and friends to approve their personal goals (Anderson, Janes, Ziermer, & Philips, 1997). Social interactions of African American diabetic patients—such as the church and church-related meal functions, and sharing of food-influence their ability to adhere to their diabetic regimen (Kumanyika & Ewart, 1990). Although family and friends also encourage African American diabetics to follow their diet (Travis, 1997), long-term diabetic adherence requires social skills in negotiation and self-assertion (Kumanyika & Ewart, 1990). These findings suggest that the use of interventions that incorporate family support and family problem solving into diabetic interventions are a means for reducing family conflict and negative feelings between African American diabetics and their families.

Research suggests constructing diabetic interventions that include self-efficacy training and, for females, incorporate social support. Female diabetics are more likely to follow their diabetic regimen if they participate in interventions that focus on significant others, reduce barriers, and follow their health beliefs (Uzoma & Feldman, 1989). Although interventions for specific age groups are suggested, there is little information on the effects of a diabetic intervention with either a patients only focus or a family focus on patients' beliefs about their diabetes and the quality of feelings shared between patients and their family members. Also, the timing and the long-term effects of a diabetic education intervention and a family-focused diabetic intervention on patients' beliefs about their diabetes and shared negative feelings and psychological distress among patients, family members and families remain unclear. Thus, there is a need to examine the differential effects and timing (immediate and long-term) of a patient-only diabetic education intervention and a family-focused intervention on the level of psychosocial distress, patients' beliefs about their diabetes, and the negative feelings of adult African American diabetic patients and their families.

ELDERLY AFRICAN AMERICAN DIABETICS: A FAMILY INTERVENTION STUDY

The elderly African American diabetics study is an ongoing, longitudinal study investigating the effects of a patient-centered intervention and a family-centered intervention on patients' perceptions of their diabetes, the quality of family relationships, and metabolic control and diabetic adherence. The study focuses on the immediate and long-term effects of a diabetic education intervention and a multiple family discussion group (MFDG) intervention on 101 community-residing elderly African American Type II diabetics 60 years and older and one or more of their family members over a 7-month period.

Human subject approval was obtained from the university and all collaborating clinical agencies. We recruited the sample from three inner city clinical facilities, a large municipal medical center, a freestanding municipal neighborhood family care center, and a voluntary medical center. Patients and family members completed baseline data collection and were then sequentially assigned to either a family-centered intervention group (n = 40 families), a patient-centered intervention group (40 = families), or a control group (n = 21 families). Data were also collected at 1, 4, and 7 months after completion of a 6-week intervention period. All data were collected during a home visit. Eight families from the family-centered intervention group participated in two post-intervention focus groups (patient and one family member from four families per focus group). The focus groups were held after the 7-month data collection was completed to elicit families' perception of their experience in family-focused intervention and its impact on the families' identity and relationships.

Study Measures

A geriatric survey identified eligible families and provided information on patients' age at diabetic diagnosis, length of time of being diabetic, and current and past diabetic treatment. The demographic questionnaire provided information on the patient and family members' age, gender, employment status, educational level, and living arrangement. The psychological distress subscale of the Psychosocial Adjustment to Illness Scale's (PAIS) measured psychological distress (depression, anxiety, guilt, worry, hostility, self-devaluation, and body image distortion) (Derogatis & Derogatis, 1990). The Inventory of Family Feelings' (IFF) negative affect subscale measured patients and family members' negative feelings towards each other and the degree of negative feelings shared in the family as a whole (Lowman, 1981). A modified version of the Illness Effect Questionnaire (IEQ) measured the extent to which the patient perceived the diabetes as disrupting his or her life (Greenberg, Peterson, & Heilbronner, 1984). Only the patient completed the IEQ. The patient and family members both completed the other measures.

Diabetic Education Intervention

A masters prepared geriatric nurse practitioner led the diabetic education intervention, which focused on diabetic monitoring, diabetic education, and diabetic management skills. Diabetic monitoring included a physical assessment and diabetic and hypertensive monitoring. The physical assessment included a baseline history and physical examination and a profile of the patient's medication, diet, exercise, and diabetic concerns. Blood glucose and blood pressure were monitored weekly. Diabetic education focused on providing patients with information to facilitate their understanding of their diabetes, identification of acute diabetic complications, and the performance of diabetic management skills. The development of diabetic management skills focused on teaching patients physical activity, foot care, and acute diabetic complications. Teaching strategies included didactic instructions (lecture, discussion, and audiovisual media) as well as the practice and return demonstration of diabetic management skills. Patients attended 6 weekly group meetings that included only diabetic patients.

Multiple Family Discussion Group Intervention

The family-focused intervention consisted of a multiple family discussion group (MFDG) led by two masters prepared psychiatric mental health clinical specialists with experience as group and/or family therapists. Each MFDG group had four to five families, each with an elderly African American diabetic patient and one or more family members, who attended 6 weekly group meetings. The MFDG intervention focused on education, social support, and problem solving via sharing of experiences among families and between family members (Table 11.1). Three premises provided a framework for the MFDG intervention: (1) a community of families who share common experiences related to a chronic illness of a family member; (2) the families must include both patient and non-patient family members; and (3) the establishment of a non-blaming, nonjudgmental atmosphere. Emphasis was on sharing feelings, agreements, and disagreements related to the patient's diabetes and collaborative problem solving within the family, between families, and between families and the clinical team (Gonzalez, Steinglass, & Reiss, 1987, 1989; Steinglass & Holder, 1993).

RESULTS

Sample

The elderly African American patients were mostly widowed (44.4%) or married (27.2%) and uneducated (66%), retired (64.6%)

TABLE 11.1. Diabetic Education and Multiple Family Discussion Group (MFDG) Interventions

Diabetic education intervention	*MFDG intervention*
Components	
Diabetic monitoring	Family education
Diabetic education	Family social support
Diabetic management skills	Family problem solving

Intervention strategies

Diabetic monitoring	Intervention environment
– Physical assessment	– Use community of families
– Weekly monitoring of	with shared experiences related
diabetes and hypertension	to patient's diabetes
Diabetic patient group minus	– Include patient and non-patient
family members	family members
– Shared group experience	– Establish non-blaming and
– Group support	non-judgmental environment
– Incorporate African	Multiple families discussion group
American values	– Incorporate African American
• independence	values and behaviors
• education	• extended family
Didactic instructions	• collaboration
– Lecture	• interdependence
– Discussion	• education
– Audiovisual media	• story telling
Diabetic management skills	– Use relational learning style
– Diabetic skills	(education)
• diabetic and hypertensive	• shared teaching and learning
medications	about diabetes
• blood glucose testing	• shared assignments in-session
• diet and activity	and at home
• foot care	• shared decision making
– Return demonstration of	– Emphasize shared family
diabetic skills	beliefs and experiences
– Diabetic knowledge	(family social support)
• acute diabetic complications	• diabetes experience among
	families and between
	family members
	• impact of diabetes on family
	identity and family rituals
	– Use collaborative family
	problem solving
	• within the family
	• between families
	• between families and clinical
	team

females with an average age of 68.7 years (s.d. = 6.1) (Table 11.3). The patients lived either with adult children (36.5%), a spouse (30.2%), or alone (29.2%). Almost 83% of the patients described their ethnicity as either African American or Black American and 11.5% as Caribbean American. They were diagnosed with Type II diabetes at an average age of 53.99 (s.d. = 12.03) years and were diabetic an average of 14.9 years (s.d. = 11.31). At the time of entry in the study, 47% of the patients were treated with insulin and diet; 21.8% of the patients had one or more diabetic family members living with them (Table 11.2).

Family members were mostly married (39.5%) or single (25.4%), educated (59.1% high school or higher) females (77%) who were either employed (48.7%) or unemployed (32.2%). The family members were on the average 46.5 years of age (s.d. = 16.8), and described themselves as Black American (49.6%) or Caribbean American (32.7%). Almost 50% of the family members lived with children only; another 40.2% lived with a spouse.

Attrition rates were 5%, 10%, and 7.5% for completion of the 6-week intervention period for the family-centered intervention group, the patient-centered intervention group, and the control group, respectively. Reasons for non-completion of the intervention period include family problems, conflicting work schedule, and dissatisfaction with subject compensation. The post-intervention attrition rates were 12.9%, 16.8%, and 20.8% at 1, 4, and 7 months post-intervention, respectively, for the entire sample.

Diabetic Education Intervention

At 1-month post-intervention, patients in the diabetic education group had not experienced a significant change in their perception of their diabetes ($t = -1.14$, $p < .26$, $n = 32$). There was also a trend for perceived illness effect to decrease at 4 months post-intervention ($t = -1.79$, $p < .08$, $n = 25$) and to decrease significantly at 7 months post-intervention ($t = -2.78$, $p = .01$, $n = 26$) (Table 11.3).

Negative feelings towards each other did not change significantly for patients, their family members, and the families as a whole at 1, 4, and 7 months post-intervention, respectively ($t = 0.84$, $p < .40$, $n = 30$ and $t = 0.99$, $p < .33$, $n = 19$; $t = 1.14$, $p < .26$, $n = 25$ and $t = -0.46$, $p < .65$, $n = 11$; $t = 0.94$, $p < .36$, $n = 25$ and $t = -0.12$, $p < .91$, $n = 11$). Similarly, there was also no significant change in

TABLE 11.2   Characteristics of Patients and Family Members

Intervention group	Patient	Family member
Age	*Mean (SD)*	*Mean (SD)*
Family	68.8 yrs (6.3)	50.7 yrs (18.2)
Patient	67.9 yrs (6.3)	41.8 yrs (15.1)
Control	70.1 yrs (5.7)	46.4 yrs (15.2)
Total	68.7 yrs (6.1)	46.5 yrs (16.8)
Gender	*N (%)*	*N (%)*
Female	76 (77.6%)	92 (79.3%)
Male	22 (22.4%)	24 (20.7%)
Marital Status	*N (%)*	*N (%)*
Single	9 (9.1%)	29 (25.4%)
Married	27 (27.2%)	45 (39.5%)
Divorced/Separated	19 (19.2%)	23 (20.2%)
Widowed	44 (44.4%)	15 (13.2%)
Ethnicity	*N (%)*	*N (%)*
African American[2]	17 (17.7%)	8 (7.1%)
Black American[3]	53 (55.2%)	56 (49.6%)
Colored/Negro	8 (8.3%)	–
Caribbean American[4]	11 (11.5%)	37 (32.7%)
Other	5 (5.2%)	12 (10.6%)
Education	*N (%)*	*N (%)*
< HS	64 (66.0%)	47 (40.9%)
High School	25 (25.8%)	41 (35.7%)
Some College	3 (3.1%)	15 (13.0%)
≥ 4 years College	5 (5.2%)	12 (10.4%)
Employment status	*N (%)*	*N (%)*
Employed	9 (9.4%)	56 (48.7%)
Unemployed	25 (26.0%)	37 (32.2%)
Retired	62 (64.6%)	19 (16.5%)
Student	–	3 (2.6%)
Living arrangements	*N (%)*	*N (%)*
Live with spouse	29 (30.2 %)	43 (40.2%)
Live alone	28 (29.2%)	9 (8.4%)
Live with children	35 (36.5%)	53 (49.5%)
Live with roommate	4 (4.2%)	2 (1.9%)

[1] Information missing on 5 subjects; [2] includes African and American; [3] includes Black; [4] includes Caribbean, Haitian, Jamaican, Panamanian, West Indian, and Barbadian

TABLE 11.3 Paired T-Test for Psychological Distress and Family Negative Feelings in Patients and Family Members, and Patients' Perceived Illness Effect: Baseline to 1, 4, and 7 Months by Intervention Groups

Intervention group	Psychological distress			Negative feelings			Perceived illness effects		
	N	T	p	N	T	p	N	T	p
Family-centered patients									
Baseline to 1 Month	28	−0.58	.57	36	1.55	.13	32	−2.21	.03
Baseline to 4 Months	21	−0.23	.82	24	−0.12	.90	21	−2.70	.03
Baseline to 7 Months	26	0.54	.59	35	1.16	.25	33	−2.73	.01
Family members									
Baseline to 1 Month	29	−4.80	.0001	34	1.16	.25			
Baseline to 4 Months	20	−3.74	.001	23	−0.87	.39			
Baseline to 7 Months	24	−2.15	.04	31	0.31	.76			
Patient-centered patients									
Baseline to 1 Month	29	−2.09	.05	30	0.85	.40	29	−1.14	.26
Baseline to 4 Months	24	−1.94	.05	25	1.15	.26	25	−1.79	.08
Baseline to 7 Months	25	0.48	.63	25	0.94	.36	26	−2.78	.01
Family members									
Baseline to 1 Month	19	−3.33	.004	19	1.00	.33			
Baseline to 4 Months	13	−2.83	.01	11	−0.46	.65			
Baseline to 7 Months	10	0.23	.82	11	−0.12	.90			

negative feelings for the families as a whole at 1, 4, and 7 months post-intervention, respectively (t = 1.30, p < .20, n = 31; t = 1.23, p < .23, n = 26; t = 0.98, p < .34, n = 26) (Table 11.3).

Psychological distress decreased significantly for patients and their family members in the diabetic education intervention at 1 and 4 months post-intervention, respectively (t= –2.09, p ≤ .05, n = 29 and t = –3.33, p < .004, n = 19; t = –1.94, p ≤ .05, n = 24 and t = –2.83, p ≤ .01, n = 13), but not at 7 months post-intervention, respectively (t = 0.48, p ≤ .63, n = 25 and t = 0.23, p < .82, n = 10).

Multiple Family Discussion Group Intervention

Perceived illness effect decreased significantly for patients in the family-centered intervention at 1, 4, and 7 months post-intervention, respectively (t = –2.21, p = .03, n = 32; t = –2.70, p = .03 n = 21; t = –2.73, p < .01, n = 33). There was no significant change in negative feelings for diabetic patients and their family members in the MFDG intervention group at 1, 4, and 7 months post-intervention, respectively (t = 1.55, p < .13, n = 36 and t = 1.0, p < .33, n = 19; t = –0.12, p < .90, n = 24 and t = –0.46, p < .65, n = 11; t = 1.16, p < .25, n = 35 and t = –0.12, p < .90, n = 11) (Table 11.3). However, family members did experience a significant decrease in psychological distress at 1, 4, and 7 months post-intervention, respectively (t = –4.80, p = .0001, n = 29; t = –3.74, p < .001, n = 20; t = –2.15, p < .04, n = 24). Psychological distress did not change significantly for patients at 1, 4, and 7 months post-intervention, respectively (t = –0.58, p < .57, n = 28; t = –0.23, p < .82, n = 21; t = 0.54, p < .59, n = 26) (Table 11.3).

Focus Data

Focus group data from the two focus groups revealed that patients and family members in the MFDG intervention learned that people viewed and responded to diabetes differently. Patients and family members also described learning more about diabetes and how families deal with diabetes. The families also described several changes that continued to influence their lives as a result of their participation in the MFDG intervention. Some patients were following their diabetic regimen more closely, particularly the nutritional regimen. Most family members became more involved in assisting their patient family member with their diabetic management. The daughter of a patient described her mother as being better at taking her medication and managing her diabetes. The patient responded that, since attending the meetings, her daughter no longer allowed her to have sweets; she (the patient) also cut down the size of pieces of cake. Her daughter also described keeping one of the in-meeting family tasks in her home (she lived separately from the patient) as a reminder and for teaching her children about their grandmother's diabetes—what she could and could not eat.

DISCUSSION

The diabetic education intervention and the MFDG intervention were both effective in changing the elderly African American diabetics' beliefs about their diabetes. However, the interventions differed in the timing and persistence of this change. Patients in the MFDG intervention developed a more positive view of their diabetes immediately after completing the intervention that continued for a 7-month period. Similar to those in the MFDG intervention, patients in the diabetic education intervention group had a more positive view of their diabetes at 7 months post-intervention. However, this change in belief did not begin to occur until 4 months post-intervention.

The diabetic education intervention and the MFDG intervention also changed the level of psychological distress post-intervention. However, these changes differed in the timing and the strength of their effect and, in some instances, in the family member effected. The MFDG intervention appears to have its greatest effect on family members who experienced a sustained decrease in psychological distress throughout the entire 7-month post-intervention period. The diabetic education intervention appears to have its greatest effect on both patients and family members, particularly during the first 4 months post-intervention. Finally, the diabetic education intervention and the MFDG intervention had no effect on negative feelings shared between patients and family members. These findings provide little support for findings in Kumanyi and Ewart's (1990) research, which link family conflict and problems in diabetic management in African American diabetics. However, the study's findings, together, provide support for findings in Skelly and associates' (1995) findings regarding the differential timing of effects from diabetic interventions. The data also suggest that family-focus diabetic interventions are more effective in bringing about sustained yet unique changes in diabetic patients and their family members.

Differential Effects of Interventions

The differential effects of the diabetic education intervention and the MFDG intervention may be due to differences in the interventions' focus and intervention strategies (Table 11.1). Both interventions use a group format as a context for their respective intervention strategies. However, the diabetic education intervention uses a diabetic patient-only group as the context for facilitating patients' acquisition of diabetic knowledge and diabetic management skills. The strategies in the diabetic education intervention were designed to enhance patients' sense of self-effectiveness and confidence in managing their diabetic symptoms (Bell et al., 1995). However, the intervention strategies (monitoring of the patient's diabetic and hypertensive status, providing didactic information on diabetes, and becoming efficient in diabetic management skills) required patients to focus more on their diabetes. Given the intervention's de-emphasis on the family, an interesting finding is the decrease in psychological distress in diabetic patients and their family members, particularly during the first 4 months post-intervention. This finding may be related to the patient's achievement of diabetic management skills and, thus, a sense of empowerment and less psychological distress (Bell et al., 1995). However, the lack of persistence of these changes is unclear.

The MFDG intervention builds on and incorporates African American values and behaviors of kinship, education, collaboration, and interdependence. It includes intervention strategies of family education, storytelling, and problem-solving style (Butler, 1993; Gonzalez et al, 1987). Emphasis is on using a relational learning style to acquire knowledge and maximize learning about the patients' diabetes through family sharing of experiences with diabetes. Storytelling acknowledges the diabetic experiences of patients and their family members while encouraging them to interact with each other and other families. It provides patients and family members a means to share their beliefs, feelings, and knowledge about diabetes and the impact of the diabetes on the patient and the family's identity (changes in diet and significantly family relationships) (Boyd-Franklin, 1989). In the process, family members collectively shared their past and current experience of coping with diabetes in a family member. This collective sharing appeared to increase the family's knowledge about diabetes and allows family members to support each other. The data also indicate that family members experience an immediate decrease in psychological distress that continues over time. However, the extent to which the intervention increased family members' knowledge of diabetes and facilitated the integration of the patient's diabetes into the family's identity and experiences remains unclear. Also unclear is the efficacy of the MFDG intervention in facilitating the patient's achievement of effective diabetic management skills.

CONCLUSION

The study's findings suggest that nurses need to consider the type and the differential timing and effect of diabetic interventions on patients and their family members. Before initiating interventions, nurses should assess the diabetic experience and determine the beliefs of African American patients and their family members. When possible, family members should be included in an intervention that is culturally appropriate for African American diabetics. Structural aspects and the timing effects of the intervention should be incorporated in its implementation and evaluation. Emphasis should be on both the patient and family's response and, for the patient, achievement of diabetic management skills. Implementation of successful interventions with African American diabetics may depend partially on the psychosocial orientation of these patients' beliefs. African American diabetics may be more receptive to diabetic interventions that incorporate strategies, which simultaneously address their beliefs and enhance their sense of self-effectiveness and confidence in managing their diabetes. Given this study's findings, a recommendation is to develop a diabetic intervention that combines MFDG intervention and the diabetic education intervention.

The study's sample limits generalizations of the findings to other diabetics who differ by age, ethnic group, and geographic location. Given these limitations, future research should include

Type II diabetics who are younger and from other ethnic groups. There is also a need to examine systematically the impact of diabetic education and the MFDG intervention on patient diabetic adherence and changes in psychological stress, family negative feelings, and the patient's view of the diabetes. Given this study's findings regarding the differential timing of changes, future studies should compare the immediate and long-term benefits of participating in either a diabetic education intervention, a MFDG intervention, or a combined diabetic education intervention and the MFDG interventions on health outcomes in the patients and their family members and diabetic management.

REFERENCES

Anderson, L. A., Janes, G. R., Ziermer, D. C., & Phillips, L. S. (1997). Diabetes in urban African Americans. Body image, satisfaction with size, and weight change attempt. *The Diabetes Educator, 23*(3), 301–308.

Bell, R. A., Summerson, J. H., & Konen, J. C. (1995). Racial differences in psychosocial variables among adults with non-insulin dependent diabetes mellitus. *Behavioral Medicine, 21*, Summer, 69–73.

Boyd-Franklin, N (1989). *Black families in therapy, A multisystem approach.* New York: Guilford Press.

Butler, J. P. (1993). Of kindred people: The ties that bind. In Orlandi, M. A., Weston, R., & Epstein, L. G. (Eds), *Cultural competence for evaluators, A guide for alcohol and other drug abuse prevention practitioners working with ethnic/racial communities.* Office of Substance Abuse Prevention, U.S. Department of Health and Human Services, Public Health Service, ADMAHA, OSAP Cultural Competence Series.

Derogatis, L. R., & Derogatis, M. F. (1990). *The psychological adjustment to illness scale (PAIS & PAIS-SR): Administration, scoring and procedure manual-II.* Townson, MD: Clinical Psychometric Research, Inc.

Fitzgerald, J. T., Anderson, R. M., Funnell, M. M., Arnold, M. S., Davis, W. K., Aman, L. C., Jacober, S. J., & Grunberger, G. (1997). Differences in the impact of dietary restrictions on African Americans and Caucasians with NIDDM. *The Diabetic Educator, 23*(1), 41–47.

Gonzalez, S., Steinglass, P., & Reiss, D. (1987). *Family-centered intervention for people with chronic disabilities: The eight-session Multiple Family Discussion Group Program.* Washington, DC: Rehabilitation Research and Training Center, Department of Psychiatry and Behavioral Sciences, The George Washington University Medical Center.

Gonzalez, S., Steinglass, P., & Reiss, D. (1989). Putting the illness in its place: Discussion groups for families with chronic medical illnesses. *Family Process, 28,* 69–87.

Greenberg. G. B., Peterson, R., & Heilbronner, R. (1984). *Illness effect questionnaire, illness effect questionnaire medical rating-experimental, and treatment effect questionnaire-experimental.* Unpublished document.

Konen, J. C., Summerson, J. H., & Dignan, M. B. (1993). Family function, stress, and locus of control, Relationships to glycemia in adults with diabetes mellitus. *Archives of Family Medicine, 2*(4), 393–402.

Kumanyika, S. K., & Ewart, C. (1990). Theoretical and baseline consideration for diet and weight control of diabetes among Blacks. *Diabetes Care, 13*(11), 1154–1162.

Lowman, J. (1981). Love, hate, and the family: Measures of emotion. In E. E. Filsinger & R. A. Lewis (Eds.), Assessing marriage: New behavioral approaches (pp. 55–73). Beverly Hills, CA: Sage.

Skelly, A. H., Marshall, J. R., Haughey, B. P., Davis, P. J., & Dunford, R. G. (1995). Self-efficacy and confidence in outcomes as determinants of self-care practices in inner-city African-American women with non-insulin-dependent diabetes. *The Diabetic Educator, 21*(1), 38–46.

Steinglass, P., & Holder, B. (1993). The Six-Session Multiple Family Discussion Group Manual, Unpublished.

Stevens, J., Kumanyika, S. K., & Keil, J. E. (1994). *American Journal of Public Health, 84*(8), 1322–1325

Travis, T. (1997). Patient perceptions of factors that affect adherence to dietary regimens for diabetes mellitus. *Diabetes Care, 23*(2), 152–156.

Weatherspoon, L. J., Kumanyika, S. K., Ludlow, R., & Schatz, D. (1994). Glycemic control in a sample of Black and White clinic patients with NIDDM. *Diabetes Care, 17*(10), 1148–1153.

Wing, R. R., & Anglin, K. (1996). Effectiveness of a behavioral weight control program for Blacks and Whites with NIDDM. *Diabetes Care, 19*(5), 409–413.

Uzoma, C. U., & Feldman, R. H. (1989). Psychosocial factors influencing inner city black diabetic patients' adherence with insulin. *Health Education, 20*(5), 29–32.

CHAPTER 12

Health Promotion for Older Adults in a Managed Care Environment

Barbara A. Given and Charles W. Given

Given the changes in American demographics and the changes in the health care system, we need to consider, as Alford and Futrell (1992) indicated, that the concept of health promotion in older adults must be restructured. Filner and Williams (1979) suggested that health be defined "as the ability to live and function effectively in society and to exercise self-reliance and autonomy to the maximum extent feasible but not necessarily as total freedom from disease" (p. 365). If we reconceptualize "health," then our concept of health promotion for the elderly deserves to be reconsidered. The goal for care of the elderly should be to assist individuals to age well.

In addition to curing disease, preventing disease, and retarding the clinical progression of disease, postponing dysfunction and disability have become desired outcomes. Pope and Tarlov (1991) suggest that to accommodate the changing needs of an increasingly older society we must broaden the traditional goals of health that of curing disease and preventing its occurrence to include preventing the ill from becoming disabled. We must then help the disabled to cope with their disability and prevent further disability.

Given this perspective, health includes independence and function, not just disease-free status. Health can exist for those individuals with chronic conditions as we prevent or postpone impairments and seek ways to limit the disabilities that derive from those impairments. Health promotion for the aging population needs to be redirected toward a broader perspective of health and wellness. Concepts such as function preservation, disability prevention and postponement, chronic-disease management, and independence enhancement must become central concerns of our health system. This perspective and definition of health promotion needs to include the traditional health components of exercise, nutrition, weight control, substance abuse, smoking cessation, and stress management. This perspective on health must be integrated without losing emphases on prevention, screening, and early detection for conditions such as hypertension and cancer, and immunization for pneumonia and influenza. Health plans should be designed to cover health promotion and health maintenance activities targeted to protect the independence, self-reliance, and autonomy of older individuals, in addition to the usual acute or chronic illness care health-promotion activities (Amler & Eddins, 1987).

As managed care organizations contract to care for Medicare populations, they must be prepared to incorporate components of this broader perspective. Careful attention to disability prevention and adaptation will generate cost savings and high-quality care preferred by these consumers. The national movement which shows a rapidly increasing enrollment of the Medicare population into managed care plans will impact health promotion. The stated goals of managed care organizations focus on health orientation, access, coordination of care, quality of care, continuity, and cost containment. These goals should be compatible with the goals of care for the older adult. Managed care plans offer potential advantages over traditional delivery systems. Managed care could offer access to a full, broad range of care, offer less fragmentation of care, and thus provide for a more integrated holistic approach with appropriate service utilization. If managed care is to deal successfully with the aging population and be sensitive to cost containment, there must be a broader focus on health and health promotion than is currently seen. This focus moves care from an episode-driven approach to the broader perspective of health outlined above and also to the risk management and health management focus of a mature managed care organization. Managed care—with its economic bottom line based on risk—contracting and incentives to contain costs, control use, and emphasize prevention and early detection—provides incentives to compress morbidity curves. Given the complexity of health problems older adults face, mechanisms to provide risk management and health management need to be addressed.

To date, only a small proportion of Medicare recipients are enrolled in managed care organizations, and current enrollees are often healthy and middle class, for the most part coming from retired or retiring employer groups. In fact, two other groups of older adults will be added soon to the managed care enrollees— those who are chronically ill and those who are frail and require long-term care. It is likely that as greater numbers of older adults enroll in managed Medicare programs those who are frail elderly and chronically ill will bring new challenges to this system. Managed care organizations are experienced with care and services for acute care episodes, but have little experience with complex chronic illness or long-term care for the frail elderly and socioeconomically disadvantaged groups.

Some evidence exists that health-oriented services for the aging Medicare population can be relevant and can be implemented within managed care organizations. There are some successful models of health promotion in our aging population and thus we have to consider how we can draw upon the experiences of these model, managed care organizations that have proven to be effective in responding to the needs and preserving the health and well-being of older adult populations. It is important to ensure that the health care system consider the "health management" orientation and supportive care services to keep individuals functional, prevent or postpone disability, and enhance independence. This includes *concerns* for and linking with housing, transportation, social, and protective services (Alford & Futrell, 1992).

In the following sections, the characteristics of managed care organizations will be examined, descriptions and discussions of published research on health-oriented programs for older adults will be provided, and, finally, suggestions for opportunities to incorporate health promotion for the elderly within managed care organizations will be offered. Although the frail elderly must be considered, a discussion of the needs of this group is beyond the scope of this chapter. Nurses, especially those in advanced practice with expertise in gerontology and health promotion, can assume important roles in the design and implementation of health-promotion programs for the older adult within managed care organizations.

MANAGED CARE AND THE AGING
MEDICARE POPULATION

Five million of Medicare's 38 million beneficiaries have joined more than 350 managed care plans, accounting for 12% of the total Medicare population (Huntington, 1997) with another 80,000 joining each month. This represents an 87% increase in the enrollment of Medicare beneficiaries in managed care organizations since 1993. Additional Medicare choices recently were legislated by Congress based on successful demonstration projects and these will be expanded.

Health Maintenance Organizations (HMOs) have been contracting with the Medicare program for 2 decades to provide services to beneficiaries under what is commonly referred to as "Medicare risk-contracting" (risk programs include full risks, predetermined monthly, and prepayment plans). To date, Medicare risk-contract programs enroll about 11% of the eligible population. Typically these programs attract younger, healthier Medicare beneficiaries leaving older, sicker, and more costly Medicare patients in fee-for-service arrangements. Now, as more Medicare clients move to managed care organizations, creating a more diverse risk pool, we see the necessity of adjusting capitation rates to better reflect the risks of differing populations of Medicare patients.

Managed care options for Medicare beneficiaries are being expanded. The Health Care Financing Administration (HCFA) has eight demonstration plans to enroll seniors in the "Medicare Choices" demonstration projects during 1997. The Medicare Choices demonstration projects lets beneficiaries explore innovative managed care plans other than traditional options. Variations in these plans include: benefits packaged with reduced co-payments and expanded benefits, an option that allows a point of service plan external to the system upon payment of an additional monthly premium, and a high option plan with expanded benefits. The *high-option plan* is prospectively adjusted for beneficiaries' health status. This latter plan puts the onus on personal risk factors; the premium is based on an individual's degree of regular positive health habits practiced. Individuals with illnesses and/or conditions resulting from negative health behaviors and/or practices must pay higher insurance premiums.

Due to material factors inherent in aging, managed care organizations pose some challenges. In the Medicare program, for example, 10% of beneficiaries account for 75% of medical expenditures. Persons with activity limitations due to chronic conditions represented 17% of the general population in 1987, but accounted for 47% of medical expenditures. Individuals 85 and older also consume high rates of health care dollars due to chronic conditions. Persons with more than one chronic condition spent $4,672 per year on care, compared with $1,829 for persons with only one chronic condition (Moon, 1996). The managed care system will be challenged by the high cost of care for those with chronic illness and disabilities. High utilization rates of health care services among the elderly with chronic conditions make them less attractive to managed care plans. Successful cost-containment approaches within managed care organizations will have to address the needs of this group of older adults with extreme medical needs and higher costs of care. Well-designed managed care programs that focus on the broadened definition of health promotion have the potential to provide a range of services to promote independence, prevent disability (leading to lower utilization of services), and contain costs. In the next sections, we will review and summarize evidence on health promotion for the elderly—how health promotion and prevention fit into the framework of managed care, including the incentives for these activities—and conclude with how health management must be fit into a team approach within managed care organizations.

MANAGED CARE AND HEALTH PROMOTION

Although espousing a health orientation, managed care organizations have often not been sensitive to or concerned with broadened health promotion activities. To date, growth in services designed to maintain health and independent living—particularly for persons with nonfatal chronic conditions—remains subordinate to the provision of acute episodic care. Containment of cost for acute care episodes has been undertaken by shortening hospital stays and by controlling access to specialty and selected high-cost care. As more high-risk older, chronically ill, and frail adults enroll, managed care organizations will face the task of addressing and managing risk factors and maintaining independence as sources of cost containment. Managed care will be required to move from an "event" and "acute" care-driven system to a risk reduction and health management *model.*

Once managed care organizations reign in costs of specialty and episodic care, it will be necessary to focus on decreasing the cost of *primary care* through risk reduction efforts. Primary care will increasingly be delivered by *"health management"* focused teams that serve risk-defined populations. Political pressure (regulation) and consumer pressure (demands for quality care and disenrollment when unsatisfied) will encourage concerns beyond cost containment. As managed care price reductions approach their limits in the more integrated and consolidated markets, *patient* satisfaction, provider access, and documentable quality with specific outcomes are expected to take center stage (Gerstein, 1995).

Many managed care organizations have demand management programs either purchased from vendors or integrated into their care programs. Demand management enables and encourages enrollees to make appropriate use of medical care and to participate and share in health choices (McEacheren, 1995). It is a proactive approach that includes teaching enrollees to become skilled users of care through education seminars and printed materials, guidance, decision-making seminars, triage systems, toll-free phone services, and resource centers made available through the plan. As older patients enroll in managed care, demand management will need to receive greater attention and should focus on reducing resource utilization through programs that support "health and self-care" and on maintenance of physical functioning. This will be important as older adults enroll. Many managed care organizations currently do not have broad health promotion programs. However, we can examine some health-promotion activities and begin to project what will be useful for Medicare managed care organizations.

HEALTH PROMOTION AND THE ELDERLY— A REVIEW OF THE LITERATURE

A literature review examined successful health-promotion programs among the elderly. Although the results are mixed, the literature on participation by older adults in health-promotion programs reveal that older adults are not known for high levels of participation in health-promotion activities. Knowledge about what is effective for older adults is even more limited. These studies are few and mixed, but provide some context for health promotion among older adults enrolled in managed care organizations. Research results from health-promotion programs for the elderly do not appear to be markedly different from those for younger populations but some specific studies will be described.

Health-promotion programs are more likely to attract individuals at lower risk and higher education and income than the general population. In 1988, the Health Care Financing Administration (HCFA) began a series of health-promotion demonstrations to address the health issues related to older adults. COBRA mandated that the HCFA "test the feasibility of providing disease-prevention and health-promotion services to Medicare beneficiaries in a cost-effective manner" (U.S. Preventive Services Task Force, 1989). The University of Washington and the State of California conducted trials of HMO enrollees. John Hopkins University enrolled an inner-city group and Pennsylvania State University conducted its study in a rural area. Two of these will be described.

Schweitzer, Atchison, Lubben, Mayer-Oakes, De-Jong et al. (1994) report on program participation in one of the HCFA health-promotion demonstration sites. A University of California, Los Angeles trial enrolled urban middle-class Medicare beneficiaries receiving health care via fee-for-service. Over 1,900 community-dwelling Medicare beneficiaries who received their health care through fee-for-service providers were enrolled. Enrollees were randomly assigned to control and experimental groups. The experimental group was offered health-screening and promotion services via letter and follow-up phone call. Nine-hundred seventy-three of the experimental subjects and 938 of the control subjects completed telephone interviews that described the use of preventive services and health-promotion practices. The researchers analyzed 17 health behaviors of those in the experimental group who attended the first session and those who did not. Those who engaged in preventive behaviors were neither more nor less likely to attend the screening services. Thus, the researchers found neither "favorable" nor "unfavorable" selection bias in the use of these preventive services. Results of the logistic regression of the experimental group show that only four variables were significant predictors of Screening and Health Promotion Clinic (SHPC) attendance: (a) having no difficulty with instrumental activities of daily living (IADL); (b) having spent no days in bed in the past year; (c) having private health insurance; and (d) not having a smoke detector in the house. Those who participated in regular exercise were more likely to attend screening clinics.

As part of the Rural Health Promotion Project Medicare Demonstration (Ives, Kuller, Schulz, Traver, & Lave, 1992), community-based recruitment methods and participant characteristics were studied. A total of 3,884 individuals aged 65 to 79 were recruited using four sequential recruitment strategies varying in aggressiveness. The methods were: (a) mail only (14%); (b) mail with phone recruitment follow-up (21%); (c) mail with phone recruitment and scheduling (31%); and (d) mail with aggressive phone recruitment and scheduling (37%). The most aggressive methods (c and d) yielded recruitment of more educated individuals. The authors suggest that despite the high utilization of medical care within the "older population," only a fairly aggressive approach is likely to be successful in recruiting eligible individuals in a defined population for health promotion. Continued efforts will be needed to define the best methods of delivering prevention and health promotion for older individuals, especially the frail and socioeconomically disadvantaged.

This same research team then examined the *use* of such health-promotion and disease-prevention services (Lave, Ives, Traven, & Kuller, 1995, 1996). Individuals enrolled in the demonstration were eligible for specific risk-reduction interventions. Forty-one percent were eligible for a nutrition program, 11% for smoking cessation, and 2% for alcohol counseling. Few attended all of the risk-reduction sessions. Participation rates ranged from 16.8% for smoking cessation to 58% for influenza immunization. The authors concluded that older rural Americans will use *some* disease-prevention and health-promotion services if they are covered by Medicare. The more educated will try new services and overall service use will be higher. Enrolled individuals were more likely to use those services which required little involvement on their part and to do so if encouraged by their physicians rather than by a general referral.

Ohmit, Furumoto-Dawson, Monto, and Fasano (1995) conducted a study of a community intervention designed to promote influenza immunization in an elderly population as a Medicare-covered benefit. Results indicated that the intervention had a statistically significant impact on increasing immunization rates among the elderly population, especially those with preexisting chronic disease. Immunization rates improved from 40% to 56% (only 16%) in 3 years, but with only heavy community-wide and multiple-promotion strategies.

Morrissey, Harris, Kincade-Norburn, McLaughlin, Garrett et al. (1995) report on a randomized, control trial of patients 65 years of age and older to assess the effects of a financial *and* office-system intervention to increase preventive care in physicians' offices. Over 1,900 patients from 10 practices were randomized. The intervention included reimbursement to physicians for preventive care and health promotion, prompting of physicians, and a system where nurses carried out prevention and documentation of the preventive care. The performance of screening tests markedly increased in the intervention group. However, there was a lack of follow-up of abnormalities. At 2 years there were minimal differences in health-related quality-of-life for the participants. The program was basically cost neutral. They concluded that even reimbursing physicians to undertake preventive services would *not* lead to effective implementation of preventive services.

Wolinsky, Stump, and Clark (1995) report on the antecedents and consequence of exercise on the physical activities of 6,780 respondents in the Longitudinal Study on Aging. Those persons involved in exercise reported: fewer lower body limitations, better perceived health, more social support, less worry about health, and a greater sense of control over one's health. These four markers were statistically associated with mortality, nursing home placement, hospital resource utilization, and changes in functional status in the next 6 to 8 years. Clearly this would suggest value in these health-oriented behaviors.

Beck, Scott, Williams, Robertson, Jackson et al. (1997) compared 321 chronically ill members of an HMO aged 65 years and older in a randomized trial. Some members received a group out-patient visit while others received traditional physician-patient dyad care. They were compared on health service utilization and cost, self-reported health status, and patient and physician satisfaction. Patients with frequent health-services utilization and one or more chronic conditions had monthly group visits with their primary care physician and nurse. Visits included health education, prevention activities, opportunities for socialization, and for one-to-one consultations with their physician, if necessary. Outcome measures obtained after a 1-year follow-up period showed that group participants had fewer emergency room visits, fewer visits to subspecialists, and fewer repeat hospital admissions per patient. Group participants, however, did have more visits and calls to nurses than control-group patients but fewer calls to physicians. Group participants had greater satisfaction with care and physicians reported higher levels of satisfaction with the group compared to individual care. No differences were observed between groups on self-reported health and functional status. Cost of care per member per month was less for the participants.

The Kaiser Cooperative Health Care Clinic educates patients about illness, addresses their psychosocial needs, and assesses patients' care participation and satisfaction. Targeted to high health care users over the age of 60 who have a chronic illness but are not necessarily frail, group meetings are held monthly. Groups consist of 20 to 25 people and address six core topics. The influence of the group activities on patients' health status and health outcomes has not been reported.

Testifying before the Ways and Means Subcommittee on Health, Vladeck (1996) indicated that the PACE (Program for All Inclusive Care of the Elderly) and SHMO (Social Health Maintenance Organizations) programs were building blocks for customer-oriented community-based programs that promote independence for the frail elderly. The SHMO adds community care and short-term nursing care to the Medicare HMO basic acute-care benefits. In the PACE model, integrated funding between Medicaid and Medicare is available to provide comprehensive care for the most frail elderly eligible for institutional care—and the program uses extensive day-care services. Vladeck argued that these programs reduce the burden of informal care, improve patient social and psychological well-being, improve health status and functional independence, and increase longevity. A reduction in the need for *institutional* care, and controlled utilization of services were reported as the positive *results* of the PACE program by Eng, Pedulla, Eleazer, McCann, and Fox (1997). The SHMO's outcomes were reported to be less beneficial; but they continue to expand and will continue under the new legislation.

There are a few clinical trials of multiple risk factor interventions that have shown positive effects in preventing disability among community-dwelling older adults. Wagner, LaCroix, Gothamus, Leveille, Hecht et al. (1994) tested home-based screening of HMO enrollees age 65 and older. A home assessment by a nurse followed by referral for targeted interventions on risk factors showed a significantly lower functional decline in experimental versus controls, although there was no difference at 2 years. Interventions targeted inadequate exercise, excessive alcohol use, increased fall risk, high medication use, and vision and hearing impairments. Stuck, Aronow, Steiner, Alessi, Bula et al. (1995) report on a comprehensive geriatric assessment by nurse practitioners in a group 75 years of age and older. Recommendations were made to the patients and participants were followed for 3 months. At the end of 3 years, the intervention group was less likely to be dependent or to have been admitted to a nursing home. There were no differences in IADL dependencies.

In 1992, the *Journal of Family Practice* published a two-part article with an exhaustive review of the literature on prevention in the elderly (Klinckman, Zazove, Mehr, & Ruffin, 1992; Zazove, Mehr, Ruffin, Klinckman, Peggs et al., 1992). The authors argued that it is unknown whether the prevention and promotion programs are cost-effective or if they compress morbidity. Further, they point out that the U. S. Preventive Services Recommendations and Guidelines do not focus on the older adult. The investigators do argue for distinguishing between the young-old and old-old in discussions of prevention and health promotion for the elderly. For persons over the age of 75, the authors were unable to document support for mobility, nutrition, breast, lung, cervical, and colorectal cancer screening or for glaucoma or glucose screening. The most important contribution of the two-part series, however, was to specifically evaluate screening and prevention interventions by applying geriatric-specific effectiveness criteria. Proof of effectiveness for many common screening areas was clearly lacking. This report needs to be tested and challenged as new data emerge.

From this brief literature review, it appears that the elderly do not readily participate in these health-promotion programs and that education and income appear to be important predictors of participation in the programs. Differences exist among screening and prevention programs. Older adults require multiple and intense strategies for recruitment and participation in health-promotion and screening programs. Studies were few and mixed, but do provide some context to *consider* strategies for health promotion for older adults enrolled in managed care organizations.

Strategies to Encourage Health Promotion within Managed Care Organizations

Health promotion and maintenance in the older adult population have not achieved lofty goals. Many of the programs have shown limited results despite strong marketing and an intensive set of strategies. Chronic conditions with symptom distress and disability continue to occur. Arthritis, diminished hearing, loss of vision, incontinence, and hip fracture all continue to occur at the same age. Little evidence exists regarding which health-promotion strategies will consistently and positively impact patient health status outcomes. Butler (1995) addresses aging as a series of risk factors. "Postponement" of disability and dysfunction could be an effective means of prevention and promotion to overcome these risk factors for the older adult (Lawrence & Jette, 1996). As more older adults enter into managed care, including the frail elderly, disability postponement approaches should be considered. Regular exercise, smoking cessation, and weight control are important factors to prevent disability in the older adult (Fried & Guralnik, 1997). We must guide older adults through periods of age-dependent disease, postponing the age of onset of dysfunction and disability (Brody, 1995). Delay of dysfunction and risk-reduction of disability means reducing the length and amount of dependence; it means living longer in good health with vigor and vitality. The challenge is to delay dependence and dysfunction at a greater pace—a pace faster than the increase in life expectancy (Butler, 1995). Health promotion and prevention activities are a dual responsibility shared by the individual and society. Strategies may include buffers and professional interventions including physically therapy and occupational therapy, counseling, personal assistance, and environmental accommodations to avoid, retard, and minimize disability (Fried & Guralnik, 1997; Lawrence & Jette, 1996; Pope & Tarlov, 1991).

One method of encouraging appropriate utilization of managed care is to teach adults and patients to engage in their own health promotion and prevention activities. Demand management has been such an attempt. Use of health-oriented self-care manuals is becoming widely used and numerous managed care organizations market these to their membership. The Healthwise community project of Kaiser (funded by the Robert Wood Johnson Foundation), for example, prides itself in describing how they distributed copies of *The Heathwise Handbook,* a 334-page self-help book that covers 180 health problems (Mettler, 1996). These programs encourage appropriate utilization by providing access to nurse-telephone health counseling, home diagnostic kits, medical second-opinion services, education centers, CD-ROM computer software, telephone voice-response, workshops, self-care guides, and telecommunications and telemonitoring information resources. More and more of these strategies—electronic and communication-based— will need to be built into the managed care organizations of the future, but tailored to ensure they are appropriate and accepted by low-income, low-educated, and culturally diverse older populations. Providers must be taught further to support patients in their self-care efforts and to work in a shared decision-making environment, offering real choices and approaches to the consumer as a partner in care. This continuum from prevention to disease-stage management approach spurs confidence and self-care capability and teaches patients how to use the system. Healthwise published a survey in which members report avoiding trips to physician offices by utilizing health information provided in the booklet. Other programs with a similar approach include Aetna, United Health Care, and Access Health. All report success with this program.

These programs, however, need to be broader than the current managed care programs. These strategies are now marketed as health-promotion endeavors, but no rigorous testing, no clinical trials, and no longitudinal follow-up has been undertaken to examine the effectiveness of targeted strategies or cost savings, overall clinical outcomes, or health-status improvement for the health-promotion efforts. It is vital that specific research studies with objective outcomes be examined to identify the real influence of demand-management efforts upon older adults.

Perhaps health care professionals can alter disease, reduce risk, prevent disability, and promote health by using tools such as risk assessments designed to identify those at high risk and to deliver targeted risk-management and risk-reduction interventions. Risk assessments will need to go well beyond the health-risk assessments

of years gone by. Preventing disease and encouraging health promotion and health management means preventing "medical care"
and "disease" costs for an individual.

It is the domain of medical care and disease management, where
the focus is on minimizing disability, alleviating symptoms, and
detecting the signs of early illness. The domain of high-level wellness or peak performance, maximum reserve capacity, independence, creativity, flexibility, and adaptability. This focus seeks an
optimal state of health and well-being. To achieve this, a managed
care organization originating a health and wellness model for
older adults should shift responsibility from the provider of "medical" care to a partnership with the individual/the consumer. The
older adult working with the provider must be empowered to be
responsible for his or her own health through awareness, education, and personal growth. Included in this approach must also be
a focus on optimizing functional health, postponing disability,
(health status improvement), enhancing well-being, and minimizing health risks. This certainly falls within the range of knowledge
and skills of nurses in an advanced practice role. Containment of
health risk within a managed care system requires a broader
system-wide perspective to provide health management. Nurses
will need to take leadership roles and focus on the outcomes from
health promotion and health risk-reduction programs.

It is important that "health-promotion" programs within managed care organizations are more than "public relations" and
social events to satisfy and attract the consumer and retain their
enrollment in managed care organizations. Currently, information
may be disseminated but these efforts are not really directed to
behavior and lifestyle changes, and changes in outcomes are neither expected nor measured. It is important that outcomes are
examined. Likewise, these "events" will not attract the frail elderly
or the socioeconomically disadvantaged or those with few social
skills. Leadership roles in managed care organizations are needed
to ensure that educational, promotion, and prevention programs
with the goals of positive health behavior changes and clinical outcomes are established, implemented, and evaluated.

"Health risks" as well as medical care costs must be managed
for the older individual within a managed care organization. Health
management (health promotion, screening, health maintenance,
disease prevention, etc.) can be defined as the optimization of

clinical, financial, and quality-of-life outcomes accomplished by management of the entire range of health risks for the individual. This concept may be useful in achieving improved health status of the older adult within managed care organizations. Our health care system will have to identify and predict risk and try to manage it before managing illness and disability. Objectives and goals of health management include:

- To optimize functional health and well-being (delaying disability)
- To minimize health risk factors
- To prevent specific diseases in at-risk populations (e.g., hypertension, diabetes)
- To facilitate the early diagnosis of disease (e.g., cancer)
- To maximize clinical effectiveness and efficiencies
- To avoid preventable disease-related complications
- To eliminate or minimize ineffective or unnecessary care
- To maximize functioning and disability prevention
- To measure outcomes and provide continuous assessment and improvement that include nurse-sensitive outcomes

Health management within managed care organizations that focuses on health-oriented behaviors requires an integrated system of health care interventions, that include screening and early disease detection; health-risk assessment; behavioral approaches; economic and other incentives for both providers and consumers; and self-care management and maintenance of function, postponement of disability, and enhancement of independence. This will require important and new provider/patient relationships. An appropriate balance between the role of the formal health care system and older adults and their family members to manage these risks will be crucial (Goldsmith, 1996). This balance will be important as more chronically ill and frail elderly enroll in managed care organizations.

These health-management plans and objectives sound reasonable and appropriate, but current efforts in managed care organizations are limited to screening areas, as evidenced by HEDIS 3.0 criteria. Procedures for the healthy older adult population that HEDIS 3.0 has targeted include screening for hypertension, cholesterol levels, breast, cervical, and colorectal cancer. These are process and screening exams and do little to move us toward health promotion, health management, or disability postponement that will be needed for the Medicare population.

The U.S. Preventive Services Task Force Recommendations for those ages 65 and older include a broader list of items than HEDIS screening but do not include polypharmacy, incontinence, or disability. These recommendations include substance use, diet and exercise, injury prevention, dental health, sexual behavior, lifestyle counseling, and chemopaplylaxis. Both HEDIS and the U.S. Preventive Task Force omit other components included in a broader health definition: minimizing risk factors; allowing for early diagnosis; and promoting functioning, enhancing independence, and postponing and delaying disability or chronic disease. Concern for mental health care, polypharmacy, incontinence, and fall prevention is also needed.

Health care professionals can use known education and guidance applications of health-management strategies to increase knowledge, alter health attitudes, deal with self-efficacy, and engender skilled self-care. However, behavioral changes will require more than the distribution of books and pamphlets; it will require the dissemination of provider recommendations, follow-up, and in some instances, case management. Risk-reduction efforts will include tailored risk reduction designed and targeted to behavioral and lifestyle changes. Learning needs and learning styles of older adults must consider additional age-dependent variables.

For individuals at high risk, scheduling telephone calls or personal appointments based on provider recommendations at regular intervals, as well as general or aggressive and intensive follow-up, may be needed. We need to look for and test new approaches that go beyond the offerings tried to date. Although there are some benefits from community-wide programs, most benefits are riddled with ambiguities, skeptical not firm results, and small or restricted efforts. Efforts within managed care organizations need to be more tailored, targeted, and directed to the individual.

Criteria for evaluating and selecting useful prevention and promotion services should include those proposed by Klinckman et al. (1992) in the *Journal of Family Practice* (see Table 12.1). This calls for more research and cost-benefit analyses. In the absence of information on cost-benefit calculations, incidence and cost-effectiveness data for efforts will have to be used as an estimation in addition to

TABLE 12.1   Six Criteria for Evaluating Preventive Services in the Elderly

1. The condition must have a significant effect on health.
2. Acceptable methods of preventive intervention or treatment must be available for the condition.
3. For *primary* preventive services (counseling, chemoprevention, immunizations), the intervention must be effective in preserving health.
4. For *other* preventive services:
   (a) There must be a period before the individual (or his or her caretaker) is aware of the condition, or of its seriousness or implications, during which it can reliably be detected by providers;
   (b) Tests used to identify the condition must be able to reliably discriminate between cases and non-cases of the condition; and
   (c) Preventive services or treatment during this "pre-awareness" period must have greater effectiveness than care or treatment delayed until the individual or caretaker brings it to a provider's attention.
5. For individuals who are cared for by caregivers, the benefit offered by the preventive service must outweigh any negative effects on the quality of life of caregivers.
6. The relative value of the preventive service or intervention must be determined by a comparison of its costs with its expected health benefits.

Note: Zazove et al. (1992).

clinical outcomes. This will help clinicians to have an objective standard and allow comparisons to evaluate effective health-promotion programs. Ultimately, this approach should help managed care organizations determine how to spend health care dollars effectively for the older population.

SUMMARY

The fragmentary evidence available indicates that managed care is neither superior nor inferior to fee-for-service (Kassirer, 1995; Ware, Bayliss, Rogers, Kosinski, & Tarlov, 1996). Managed care enrollment by Medicare beneficiaries may be the crisis that precipitates innovative solutions to both new and long-standing delivery problems for the older adult population. The opportunities for improvement of care and health-oriented services for older adults presented through managed care delivery are extensive but are only beginning to come into focus. Agreement on the definition of "excess" or "inappropriate care" and curbing of practices falling within that definition are needed. Greater emphasis on psychosocial support, mental health, health management, disability prevention, and postponement-improved continuity and coordination of care and fit between patient and family need and practitioner behavior are important directions. Development of practice standards for major problems and conditions of the older adult and outcome measures that truly are relevant to functional independence and disability postponement may reduce expensive treatments and shift the focus to those interventions most effective in terms of cost and outcome.

The integrated nature of the managed care organization makes the possibility of delivery of high-quality care to the older adult possible. Providing health care professionals with constant peer review and performance reviews creates the potential to identify "poor" quality practices more rapidly and to maintain pressure for quality. Outcome measures and measures beyond HEDIS will be needed. Providers/insurers in managed care systems have a strong incentive (that will become stronger with enrollment of more older adults in general and the frail older adult) to examine how care is delivered, what care is delivered, and which type of provider is "best" for providing that care. This means an increased consideration of the various levels of care and skill levels of providers. Some of the past incentives have fostered "no care" since payment occurred whether patients were seen or not. Managed care can provide more integrated primary, preventive, and specialty care and can coordinate care among clinics, homes, and community-based services to the older adult. This is changing largely due to pressure from consumers and the need to reduce risk as large pools of higher-risk individuals—both Medicare and Medicaid—enter the system.

Nurses in advanced practice can come to the fore with "value added" evidence regarding strategies to achieve positive outcomes that can transform managed care. Managed care organizations that value quality and recognize the importance of prevention, health promotion, independence enhancement, wellness, and early intervention can benefit greatly from the expertise of nurses in advanced practice. In turn, nurses can help guide managed care to focus on providing a full range of quality, cost-effective health-management services targeted to risk reduction and disability postponement and following the health-promotion theme as described here. We have the knowledge and skills to take a leadership role.

Capitation can also compensate providers for investing in patient education, prevention, and health-promotion activities by reducing the liability for services associated with future episodes of illness. Capitated providers, as compared to fee-for-service providers, should be motivated to assure that patients receive health-oriented services (pap smears and mammograms, immunizations, disability prevention, independence enhancement, and routine screening for hypertension). General measures for the older adult to keep them functional and using health management should assist programs to achieve cost control and will need to be added to the repertoire of current managed care providers.

Managed care organizations provide an exciting opportunity to restructure service delivery in a way that potentially may improve the health and the quality of the lives of covered older populations. Providers may be rewarded (both financially and professionally) for becoming effective producers of improved health status and for delaying disability or dysfunction. Providers who make clinical decisions in the best interest of older patients based on evidence-based practice and knowledge of outcomes should do well for older adults within managed care organizations.

When care is integrated, quality and outcomes are easier to track. We should take advantage of the integration and tracking mechanisms of information systems and ensure that they include components relevant and sensitive to nursing practice. Hopefully, managed care organizations will recognize the cost-saving advantages of early detection over futile "curative" care and episodic "illness" care. We should also embrace prevention and early detection practices; disability postponement; and hospice, palliation, and psychosocial support when appropriate.

There are few systematic inquiries into the impact of managed care on the full spectrum of care for the elderly. In the absence of more complete data it is not yet possible to determine whether managed care generally is a "more efficient type of healthcare system, or whether it reflects the chronic problems that remain endemic to the U.S. health-care system" (Miller & Luft, 1994, p. 438).

The ideal health care system is one in which caretaking roles are based on the dominant needs of the patient and family, and care is rendered by a team that operates across constantly shifting care settings. Managed care may prove beneficial by breaking down entrenched resistance to care that have been compartmentalized not by patient need, but by the rigid focus on cost only. This will benefit older adult enrollees.

The new era in managed care organizations—a mature managed care model—broadens the focus from individuals to total populations of covered lives. This mature model balances concern for the numerator (few people with costly illness) with the denominator (many people who are well and not using the system) in the health care equation. In a mature managed care era, managed care organizations must integrate the management of medical costs with the management of health-risk reduction and health management. In this mature managed care organization model, the focus on health management makes perfect sense and has to be considered in the planning of care for the older adult.

Only if we work hard with the managed care systems and bring the nursing knowledge and value-added components to the care can we make major impact on the health and vitality of our older adults.

REFERENCES

Alford, D. M., & Futrell, M. (1992). Wellness and health promotion of the elderly. *Nursing Outlook, 40*(5), 221–226.

Amler, R., & Eddins, D. (1987). Cross sectional analysis of premature death in the United States. In R. Amler & H. Dull (Eds.), *Closing the gap: The burden of unnecessary illness* (pp. 181–187). New York: Oxford Press.

Beck, A., Scott, J., Williams, P., Robertson, B., Jackson, D., Gade, G., & Cowan, P. (1997). A randomized trial of group outpatient visits for chronically ill older HMO members: The cooperative health care clinic. *Journal of the American Geriatrics Society, 45*(5), 543–549.

Brody, J. A. (1995). Postponement as prevention in aging. In R. N. Butler & J. A. Brody (Eds.), *Delaying the onset of late-life dysfunction* (pp. 11–13). New York: Springer Publishing Co.

Butler, R. N. (1995). Introduction: Revolution in longevity. In R. N. Butler & J. A. Brody (Eds.), *Delaying the onset of late-life dysfunction* (pp. 1–8). New York: Springer Publishing Co.

Eng, C., Pedulla, J., Eleazer, G. P., McCann, R., & Fox, N. (1997). Program of All inclusive Care for the Elderly (PACE): An innovative model of integrated geriatric care and financing. *Journal of the American Geriatrics Society, 45*(2), 223–232.

Filner, B., & Williams, T. (1979). Health promotion for the elderly, reducing functional dependency. In *Healthy People 2000* (pp. 365–387). Washington: U. S. Government Printing Office.

Fried, L. P., & Guralnik, J. M. (1997). Disability in older adults: Evidence regarding significance, etiology, and risk. *Journal of the American Geriatrics Society, 45*(1), 92–100.

Gerstein, M. (Ed.) (1995). *Renaissance for health care: Environmental assessment 1995/1996.* Chicago: Society for Healthcare Planning and Marketing of the American Hospital Association.

Goldsmith, J. (1996). Risk and responsibility: The evolution of health care payment. In *2020 Vision: Health in the 21st Century* (pp. 49–57). Washington, DC: National Academy Press.

Huntington, J. A. (1997). Health care in chaos: Will we ever see real managed care? *Online Journal of Issues in Nursing.* Download from http://www.nursingworld/ojin/tpc2/ tpc2_.htm on April 7, 1997.

Ives, D., Kuller, N., Schulz, R., Traver, N., & Lave, J. (1992). Comparison of recruitment strategies and associated disease prevalence for health promotion in rural elderly. *Preventive Medicine, 21*(5), 582–591.

Kassirer, J. P. (1995). Managed care and the morality of the marketplace. *New England Journal of Medicine, 333*(1), 50–52.

Klinckman, M., Zazove, P., Mehr, D., & Ruffin, M. (1992). A criterion based review of preventive health in the elderly. Part I: Theoretical framework and development of criteria. *Journal of Family Practice, 34*(2), 205–224.

Lave, J. R., Ives, D. G., Traven, N. D., & Kuller, L. H. (1995). Participation in health promotion programs by the rural elderly. *American Journal of Preventive Medicine, 11*(1), 46–53.

Lave, J. R., Ives, D. G., Traven, N. D., & Kuller, L. H. (1996). Evaluation of a health promotion demonstration program for the rural elderly. *Health Services Research, 31*(3), 261–281.

Lawrence, R., & Jette, A. (1996). Disentangling the disablement process. *The Journals of Gerontology, Series B, 51*(4), S173–183.

McEacheren, S. (1995). Demand management will be a necessity, a baked-in utility. *Health Care Strategic Management, 13*(10), 19–23.

Mettler, M. (1996). Creating "smarter" patients: Preliminary results for the Healthwise Communities Project are in. Online: http://www.healthwise.org/ohsupr1.htm [4 June, 1996].

Miller, R. H., & Luft, H. S. (1994). Managed care plans: Characteristics, growth, and premium performance. *Annual Review of Public Health, 15,* 437–459.

Moon, M. (1996). What Medicare has meant to older Americans. (Medicare: Advancing Towards the 21st Century, 1966–1996). *Health Care Financing Review, 18*(2), 49–60.

Morrissey, J. P., Harris, R. P., Kincade-Norburn, J., McLaughlin, C., Garrett, J. M., Jackman, A. M., Stein, J. S., Lannon, C., Schwartz, R. J., & Patrick, D. L. (1995). Medicare reimbursement for preventive care: Changes in performance of services, quality of life, and health care costs. *Medical Care, 33*(4), 315–331.

Ohmit, S., Furumoto-Dawson, A., Monto, A. S., & Fasano, N. (1995). Influenza vaccine use among an elderly population in a community intervention. *American Journal of Preventive Medicine, 11*(4), 271–276.

Pope, A. M., & Tarlov, A. R. (Eds.) (1991). *Disability in America: Toward a national agenda for prevention.* Washington: National Academy Press.

Schweitzer, S. O., Atchison, K. A., Lubben, J. E., Mayer-Oakes, S. A., De-Jong, F. J., & Matthias, R. E. (1994). Health promotion and disease prevention for older adults: Opportunity for change or preaching to the converted? *American Journal of Preventive Medicine, 10*(4), 223–229.

Stuck, A., Aronow, H., Steiner, A., Alessi, C., Bula, C., Gold, M., Yuhas, K., Nisenbaum, R., Rubenstein, L., & Beck, J. (1995). A trial of annual in-home comprehensive geriatric assessments for elderly people living in the community. *The New England Journal of Medicine, 333*(18), 1184–1186.

Travis, J. W., & Ryan, R. (1988). *Wellness workbook.* Berkley: TenSpeed Press.

U. S. Preventive Services Task Force Guide to Clinical Preventive Services (1989). Baltimore: Williams and Wilkins.

Vladeck, B. C. (1996). Recommendations regarding future directions in the Medicare program: Hearing before the Subcommittee on Health of the Committee on Ways and Means, House of Representatives, One Hundred Fourth Congress, second session, April 30, 1996.

Wagner, E. H., LaCroix, A. Z., Gothamus, L., Leveille, S. G., Hecht, J. A., Artz, K., Odle, K., & Buchner, D. M. (1994). Preventing disability and falls in older adults: A population-based randomized trial. *American Journal of Public Health, 84*(11), 1800–1806.

Ware, J. E., Jr., Bayliss, M. S., Rogers, W. H., Kosinski, M., & Tarlov, A. (1996). Differences in 4-year health outcomes for elderly and poor, chronically ill patients treated in HMO and fee-for-service systems. *Journal of the American Medical Association, 276*(13), 1039–1047.

Wolinsky, F. D., Stump, T. E., & Clark, D. O. (1995). Antecedents and consequences of physical activity and exercise among older adults. *Gerontologist, 35*(4), 451–462.

Zazove, P., Mehr, D. R., Ruffin, M. T., Klinckman, M. S., Peggs, J. F., & Davies, T. C. (1992). A criterion-based review of preventive health care in the elderly. Part 2: A geriatric health maintenance program. *Journal of Family Practice, 34*(3), 320–347.

CHAPTER 13

The Public Health Paradigm and Aging Research

Robert L. Kane

THE PUBLIC HEALTH PARADIGM

Interest in prevention as it applies to aging populations can be addressed in the more general paradigm applied to public health issues or it can follow a more individualized clinical approach. Each has its strengths and its limitations. The Institute of Medicine has defined the mission of public health as, "The fulfillment of society's interest in assuring conditions under which people can be healthy" (Institute of Medicine, 1988, p. 7). Such a broad definition can be readily applied to older persons, but not without some careful examination. The same committee also described the substance of public health as, "Organized community efforts aimed at the prevention of disease and promotion of health (p. 41)." Public health draws on many disciplines but it builds on epidemiology.

The basic public health paradigm involves the following components:

- It is population based. A group is identified by one or another means, usually geopolitically (e.g., residents in a community), but the group could also be defined by enrollment in an HMO, for example.
- Public health has a fundamental role in protecting the commons (Hiatt, 1975). Some areas of life are not easily distributed among the population (e.g., air and water quality).

Society cannot look to each member to do his fair share. In fact, the actions of those who are responsible will benefit those who are not. Hence, a collective enterprise is needed.

- Public health is closely tied to prevention, especially primary and secondary prevention. Prevention is often trichotomized into primary prevention (i.e., the minimization of risk factors that are believed to create circumstances that increase the likelihood of developing disease), secondary prevention (i.e., early detection and treatment before the disease becomes clinically detectable), and tertiary prevention (i.e., effective clinical care to prevent exacerbations and adverse consequences).

- By default, public health agencies often become the last refuge for service to underserved groups. For some time, older people were viewed as an underserved group, but the tide of opinion has changed with the passage of Medicare and Medicaid. The elderly population is now the only subgroup in this country universally covered by health insurance (Hayward, Shapiro, Freeman, & Corey, 1988).

The basic components of public health have been defined by the Institute of Medicine as assessment, policy development, and assurance. Assessment includes surveillance to determine the health status of a population (which can be expressed in terms of disease rates, disability rates, or even utilization rates). It connotes a function of identifying unmet needs and analyzing the causes of disease and disability. Assessment involves collecting and interpreting data, case finding, monitoring and forecasting trends, research into the determinants of health, and evaluating the outcomes of various interventions.

Policy development covers such tasks as planning, priority setting, and policy leadership advocacy. Successful performance includes the ability to recognize barriers, convene interest groups, negotiate, and broker among them. It can extend into mobilizing resources, training and constituency building, providing public information, and encouraging public and private sector action through incentives and persuasion.

The assurance role of public health covers monitoring, encouraging the private sector (through persuasion and requirements, and sometimes by direct purchase of services), providing services (either because no one else will or in competition), and regulation.

No part of the health care system is more heavily regulated than the nursing home industry, which suffers from a checkered past (Mendelson, 1974; Moss & Halamandaris, 1977; Vladeck, 1980).

CHRONIC DISEASE

Many of these functions can influence an approach to the older population, who use a disproportionate share of health services and still have many unmet needs (Gornick, Warren, Eggers, Lubitz, DeLew et al., 1996). The problems of addressing the health concerns of older persons are complicated by the predominant role of chronic disease. The shift from an acute disease model to one that addresses chronic disease has many implications (Hoffman, Rice, & Sung, 1996). Chronic diseases are less likely attributable to a single cause. Hence, efforts to prevent them cannot address a single action or even a single locus of activity. Because the lag time between the occurrence of a risk factor and the presentation of disease may be many decades, advocates for prevention in older persons may confront a paradox. It may be more efficient to address such actions in those who are still much younger. Such a strategy implies, in effect, transferring resources to a younger generation. Advocates may thus be faced with advocating that funds intended for older persons be used to address health problems in their juniors.

The long lag time poses problems in demonstrating the effectiveness of interventions. Because definitive data is often absent, preventive strategies must often proceed in its absence (Office of Technology Assessment, 1988, 1990). Such conditions leave the field open to advocates on both sides. Prevention enthusiasts are quick to push for actions. More cautious respondents can find ample cause for hesitation.

The era of chronic disease requires a new conceptual framework. The World Health Organization (WHO) proposed a model by which to examine various points of intervention (WHO, 1980). It features a transition from disease to impairment to disability to handicap. An impairment refers to decrease in organ performance. A disability implies a problem with functioning as a whole unit or person in some aspect of usual performance. This functional deficit is transformed into a handicap by social and physical environmental forces that influence a person's ability to perform his or her social roles.

The public health paradigm affects the chronic disease model as one debates the suitability of a population-based approach or a more individual direct services approach. Efforts to base preventive efforts for older people on evidence of effectiveness face a Catch-22. Ironically, although older persons experience more disease, they had until recently been systematically excluded from most large scale trials of community interventions. Hence, there could be little evidence of effectiveness, because there was little evidence at all. The pressing policy question is then how does one proceed in the absence of clear information pointing one way or the other. Most of the recommendations in regard to older persons in the report of the U.S. Task Force on Preventive Services, for example, rely on professional judgment (U.S. Preventive Services Task Force, 1989).

The public health approach preferentially addresses risk factors, but undifferentiated preventive efforts can be very expensive, especially when everyone is seen as being at risk. For example, many efforts have been made to prevent unnecessary admissions to nursing homes. Although many risk factors have been identified as being significantly associated with nursing home admission, it has proven extremely difficult to identify a population at sufficiently high risk to warrant the costs of the interventions (Carcagno & Kemper, 1988; Murtaugh, Kemper, & Spillman, 1990; Weissert, 1986, 1988).

Enthusiasm for screening programs must separate the yield for first time efforts, which reap the effects of prevalence, from those of repeated efforts, whose yields are driven by usually much lower incidence rates. Indeed, the recommendations of many professional groups about the use of screening in older persons now recognizes that a pattern of negative findings in an individual argues for much less frequent subsequent screening.

Decisions about the cost-effectiveness of prevention must recognize the implications of how concepts are applied. It has become quite fashionable of late to employ measures like quality adjusted life years (QALYs) in analyzing the cost-effectiveness of care. However, such measures may pose special problems for older persons (Avorn, 1984). Not only do they rely heavily on survival, they usually address dysfunction as though it were irreversible. Hence, anyone who is disabled has already lost any access to benefit.

PREVENTION AND CHRONIC DISEASE

The trichotomous prevention classification system can be applied to the WHO chronic disease model as shown in the following diagram.

(1)   (2)   (3)   (4)

disease------------➤impairment------------➤disability------------➤handicap

The numbers in parentheses refer to primary (1), secondary (2), and tertiary (3) preventive actions that are possible at various stages.

Primary prevention is still possible in older persons. Perhaps the most familiar components are immunizations (i.e., annual flu shots, pneumonococcal vaccines, and tetanus). However, there is evidence of positive benefits from behavioral changes as well. Stopping smoking is associated with relatively re-assumption of non-smokers' risks (Hermanson, Omenn, Kronmal, & Gersh, 1988; Jaijich, Ostfeld, & Freeman, 1984). Exercise is seen as offering a variety of benefits (Fiatarone, O'Neill, Ryan, Clements, Solares et al., 1994; King, Oman, Brassington, Bliwise, & Haskell, 1997; Larson, 1991). Likewise, estrogen is being hailed as a potential risk reducer for many problems (Paganini-Hill & Henderson, 1996; PEPI, 1996; Schneider, Barrett-Connor, & Morton, 1997). Control of hypertension is actively advocated (Applegate & Rutan, 1992; Lapalio, 1995; SHEP Cooperative Research Group, 1991). Social support is viewed as a protective device (Berkman, Leo-Summers, & Horowitz, 1992; Colantonio, Kasl, Ostfeld, & Berkman, 1993; Wan & Weissert, 1981). Perhaps the most significant, and overlooked, primary preventable problem for older persons is iatrogenic disease (Gorbien, Bishop, Beers, Norman, Osterweil et al., 1992; Lefevre, Feinglass, Potts, Soglin, Yarnold et al., 1992). Inappropriate or unnecessary or excessive care may readily create health problems.

The enthusiasm for screening must be tempered by the appreciation that at least some of the benefit attributed to screening may be attributed to detection bias. Figure 13.1 illustrates how detection bias can occur. The first line represents the natural course of a disease. The second line shows the apparent survival time if it is detected by some preclinical screening. This post-detection survival period seems much longer than the survival time after symptoms shown on the third line, but that benefit can be artificial. Not

detection   symptoms   death

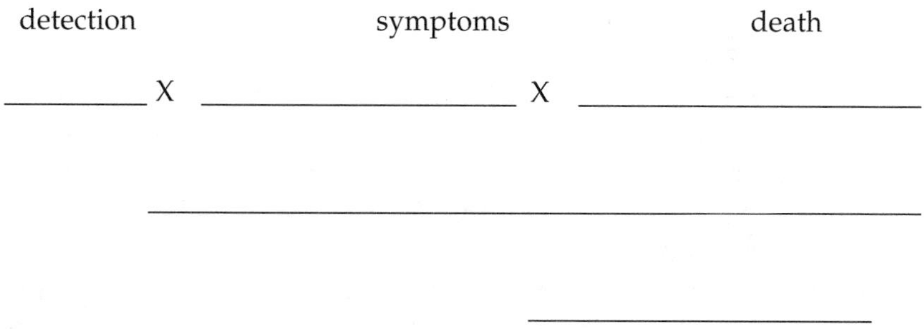

_____ X _____ X _____

_____

_____

Figure 13.1 Potential Survival Bias from Screening. The upper line shows the natural course of a hypothetical disease. The middle line shows the perceived clinical course if the condition is detected early, but the detection has no real effect on the outcome of the disease. The bottom line shows the apparent clinical course if the disease is not detected until it becomes symptomatic. The difference in the apparent survival time after detection in the last two lines is called "detection bias." In effect, one is aware of the condition longer and hence has the misimpression of a longer survival time.

all benefit from screening is illusory, but the only true test of such benefit is to compare the death rates in populations where active screening occurs and those where it does not.

A number of conditions common in older persons can be screened for. Familiar examples are mammograms and pap smears. In both cases, recommendations have been tempered by cost concerns and an appreciation that the development of cancer in older persons may proceed differently than in younger people. The recommendations place upper limits on the ages for screening and reduce the frequency of efforts in those with histories of previously normal tests. A condition that meets the criteria for screening in older persons (i.e., inexpensive detection and benefit from treatment) is depression. Too often this problem is overlooked either because the clinician fails to recognize the symptoms or incorrectly attributes them to the inevitable consequences of aging (Anderson, Malmgren, Cater, & Patrick, 1994). Other simple screening tests may address problems of vision and hearing, where correction can profoundly affect function. Other areas are more controversial. For example, the benefit of the prostate screening antigen (PSA) test remains unresolved (Woolf, 1995).

Tertiary prevention has special salience for the care of older persons. Much of the preventive effort can be usefully directed at better, more aggressive treatment aimed at preventing the onset or worsening of disability. Comprehensive geriatric assessment has been shown to produce substantial benefits (Stuck, Siu, Wieland, Adams, & Rubenstein, 1993). Ironically it works with both targeted and untargeted populations (Stuck, Aronow, Steiner, Alessi, Bula et al., 1995). More aggressive rehabilitation can also change the course for older patients, reducing the incidence or impact of disability (Keith, Wilson, & Gutierrez, 1995; Kramer, Steiner, Schlenker, Eilertsen, Hrincevich et al., 1997; Melin, Hakansson, & Bygren, 1993). Another form of tertiary prevention may involve minimizing the transition from disability to handicap through such efforts as home modifications or the provision of prosthetic equipment.

The relationship between disease and disability serves as the basis for many preventive strategies. Unfortunately, the epidemiological evidence to support this relationship is weak. Salive and Guralnik (1997) reviewed the extent to which various chronic diseases were associated with disability in a number of major epidemiologic studies and found a pattern rife with discrepancies. For example, diabetes was specifically not associated with disability in the Framingham Study (Pinsky, Branch, Jette, Haynes, Feinleib et al., 1985), but is associated with disability in the Longitudinal Study on Aging (Mor, Murphy, Masterson-Allen, Wiley, Razmpour et al., 1989). These inconsistencies may be due to differences in how the diseases were assessed or in how disability was measured. Nonetheless, the inconsistent findings make it difficult to develop a rational strategy for attacking disability through attention to specific diseases.

AGE BIAS

Efforts to promote prevention in older persons must recognize the importance of prior beliefs about older people (Palmore, 1988). Stereotypes about aging as representing inevitable decline must be addressed. There is growing evidence that at least some of the phenomena associated with aging can be delayed or reversed by active processes (Fries, Bloch, Harrington, Richardson, & Beck, 1993). There persists an active debate between those who maintain that medical advances have created a pool of more disabled persons who will raise the costs of care (Isaacs, Livingstone, & Neville, 1972), and those who maintain that it is possible to extend years of active life (Fries & Crapo, 1981).

The truth likely lies somewhere between these two poles. Dismissing efforts at prevention in older people would be foolish, especially at a time when we are developing growing evidence that even very disabled persons can benefit from active interventions designed to improve their function (Fiatarone et al., 1994). At the same time, we must appreciate that even positive scenarios that involve decreased incidence of chronic disease may have adverse implications on the overall levels of disability in the population (Boult, Altmann, Gilbertson, Yu, & Kane, 1996).

EXAMPLES OF PREVENTIVE PROGRAMS

One area where efforts to demonstrate the malleability of functioning in older people that has attracted substantial attention lately is around exercise and its general benefits, as well as its role in preventing falls. Mary Tinetti has probably contributed more than any other investigator to our knowledge about falls in the elderly. She views falls as preventable. Table 13.1 is based on the results of a study she conducted to test the effects of a targeted intervention to reduce the rate of falls (Tinetti, Baker, McAvay, Claus, Garrett et al., 1994). Compared to the control group, fewer of those receiving the intervention had falls, but there was no significant difference in the number of falls or the rate of serious falls.

A meta-analysis of the findings from seven of the eight sites that participated in the FICSIT trials examined the overall effects (Province, Hadley, Hornbrook, Lipsitz, Miller et al., 1995). The statistically significant results of the association between various types of preventive strategies and falls and injurious falls are summarized in Table 13.2. In only two cases was the association significant. Exercise and balance training were associated with significant reductions in falls, but not in falls with injuries. Further analysis suggested that balance training was likely the most effective intervention.

The benefits of balance training and Tai Chi in preventing falls were tested against an educational control group. Compared to the

TABLE 13.1   Tinetti's Targeted Intervention

	Intervention Group (N = 147)	Control Group (N = 144)
% fallers	35	47 p = <.05
No. of falls	94	164
% needing medical care	14	18
% with serious injury	8	10

Tinetti et al., 1991

group receiving only education about falls, the Tai Chi group had a significantly longer time experiencing a fall, but there was no significant difference in the time to a serious fall; nor was there any significant benefit from balance training (Wolfson, Whipple, Derby, Judge, King et al., 1996).

In a study done through the Group Health Cooperative two strategies were compared to a control group. The first included disability and fall prevention; the second focused exclusively on chronic disease prevention. At 1 year, the falls prevention strategy showed a significant advantage in reducing the rate of falls and injurious falls, but the gains disappeared by the second year (See Table 13.3). In a study directed specifically at older persons with osteoarthritis of the knee, researchers tested the effects of simple exercise and resistance exercise. Both produced significant functional benefits (Ettinger, Burns, Messier, Applegate, Rejeski et al., 1997).

Although there may be demonstrable benefits from exercise, the clinical trials used to establish these benefits have ended up working

TABLE 13.2   FICSIT Meta-Analysis (7/8 sites)

	Association (p value)	
	Falls	Injurious Falls
Exercise	.04	.35
Resistance	.59	.48
Balance	.03	.77
Endurance	.87	.35
Flexibility	.29	.26

Province et al., 1995

TABLE 13.3   GHC Fall Intervention Study

	Fall prevention	Chronic disease prevention	Control
% falls yr. 1	27.5	29.6	36.8 p < .01
% falls yr. 2	31.4	29.3	29.2
% injurious falls yr. 1	9.9	10.1	14.5 p < .01
% injurious falls yr. 2	13.4	9.2	10.1

Wagner et al., 1994

with very selected groups. Pacala traced the sample loss for one FICSIT site and found that of 7191 older people contacted from the list of registered voters, only 411 were interested in participating in the study, and only 274 were deemed eligible. Of these, only 110 eventually participated (Pacala, Judge, & Boult, 1996). While this selection may not affect the internal validity of the comparisons, it makes generalizations to the broader population of older people tenuous at best and raises real questions about how to entice the vast majority to even attempt such exercise programs.

A group of researchers at the University of Washington developed a more comprehensive approach to addressing prevention and health promotion in older persons. Working closely with community groups, they attempted to identify the issues that were salient to their potential audience. Focus groups and community-level discussion uncovered four areas to target, which represented a compromise between those most important to the older persons and those which the investigators believe would benefit their clients: physical activity, social integration, physical security fears, and transportation. A multi-factorial interventional program was created to respond to all four of these areas. Benefits were assessed by three subscales from the SF-36. In fact, the experimental groups had significantly more decline in three factors (physical functioning, emotional role functioning, and social functioning) than the control group (Omenn, Beresford, Buchner, LaCroix, Martin et al., 1997).

CONCLUSIONS

Several points emerge from this exploration. While preventive efforts have a real role in improving the health status of older people, excessive zeal must be kept in check. Many questions remain to be resolved. In some cases, there seem to be clear indications that simple and obvious actions are not being taken. For example, the immunization rate is still low. Clinicians fail to recognize depression, when even a simple single question (i.e., "Are you depressed?") would identify substantial potential cases. Exercise certainly seems to benefit some people, including the very frail. Part of the benefit of exercise programs may lie in the way such people are treated. If they are seen as having potential for improvement, their overall care may change. The concept of simply identifying risk factors and attempting to modify them may prove less fruitful and ultimately excessively expensive. Targeted interventions based on strong conceptual and empirically verified models are more likely to work. However, interventions can be hard to sustain. Short-term benefits need not promise long-term results.

The research for effective prevention in older persons agenda includes the following activities:

- We need more studies that will test interventions. In conducting these studies investigators should monitor progress closely to assure that the intervention is occurring as planned. Interventions should include efforts to increase meaningful social activity and build on the strengths of older persons.
- A major challenge will be translating the results of experiments conducted on highly selected samples to the general population. How can one achieve wider participation? How can such activities be incorporated into everyday clinical practice?
- Ageism is still prevalent. Both the general public and clinicians need to be educated about the potential older people possess for change and improvement. Incorrect beliefs about the inevitability of functional decline stultify efforts to mount positive programs.

REFERENCES

Anderson, E. M., Malmgren, J. A., Carter, W. B., & Patrick, D. L. (1994). Screening for depression in well older adults: Evaluation of a short form of the CES-D. *American Journal of Preventive Medicine, 10*(2), 77–84.

Applegate, W. B., & Rutan, G. H. (1992). Advances in management of hypertension in older persons. *Journal of the American Geriatrics Society, 40*(11), 1164–1174.

Avorn, J. (1984). Benefit and cost analysis in geriatric care: Turning age discrimination into health policy. *New England Journal of Medicine, 310*(20), 1294–1301.

Berkman, L. F., Leo-Summers, L., & Horowitz, R. I. (1992). Emotional support and survival after myocardial infarction. *Annals of Internal Medicine, 117*(12), 1003–1009.

Boult, C., Altmann, M., Gilbertson, D., Yu, C., & Kane, R. L. (1996). Decreasing disability in the 21st century: The future effects of controlling six fatal and nonfatal conditions. *American Journal of Public Health, 86*(10), 1388–1393.

Carcagno, G. J., & Kemper, P. (1988). The evaluation of the national long term care demonstration: An overview of the channeling demonstration and its evaluation. *Health Services Research, 23*(1), 1–22.

Colantonio, A., Kasl, S. V., Ostfeld, A. M., & Berkman, L. F. (1993). Psychosocial predictors of stroke outcomes in an elderly population. *Journal of Gerontology, 48*(5), S261–S268.

Ettinger, W. H., Jr., Burns, R., Messier, S. P., Applegate, W., Rejeski, W. J., Morgan, T., Shumaker, S., Berry, M. J., O'Toole, M., Monu, J., & Craven, T. (1997). A randomized trial comparing aerobic exercise and resistance exercise with a health education program in older adults with knee osteoarthritis: The fitness arthritis and seniors trial (FAST). *Journal of the American Medical Association, 277*(1), 25–31.

Fiatarone, M. A., O'Neill, E. F., Ryan, N. D., Clements, K. M., Solares, G. R., Nelson, M. E., Roberts, S. B., Kehayias, J. J., Lipsitz, L. A., & Evans, W. J. (1994). Exercise training and nutritional supplementation for physical frailty in very elderly people. *New England Journal of Medicine, 330*(25), 1769–1775.

Fries, J. F., Bloch, D. A., Harrington, H., Richardson, N., & Beck, R. (1993). Two-year results of a randomized controlled trial of a health promotion program in a retiree population: The Bank of America study. *The American Journal of Medicine, 94*(5), 455–462.

Fries, J. F., & Crapo, L. M. (1981). *Vitality and aging.* San Francisco: W. H. Freeman and Company.

Gorbien, M. J., Bishop, J., Beers, M., Norman, D., Osterweil, D., & Rubenstein, L. Z. (1992). Iatrogenic illness in hospitalized elderly people. *Journal of the American Geriatrics Society, 40*(10), 1031–1042.

Gornick, M. E., Warren, J. L., Eggers, P. W., Lubitz, J. D., DeLew, N., & Cooper, B. S. (1996). Thirty years of Medicare: Impact on the covered population. *Health Care Financing Review, 18*(2), 179–237.

Hayward, R. A., Shapiro, M. F., Freeman, H. E., & Corey, C. R. (1988).

Inequities in health services among insured Americans: Do working-age adults have less access to medical care than the elderly? *New England Journal of Medicine, 318*(23), 1507–1511.

Hermanson, B., Omenn, G. S., Kronmal, R. A., & Gersh, B. J. (1988). Beneficial six-year outcome of smoking cessation in older men and women with coronary artery disease. *New England Journal of Medicine, 319*(21), 1365–1369.

Hiatt, H. H. (1975). Protecting the medical commons: Who is responsible. *New England Journal of Medicine, 293*(5), 235–241.

Hoffman, C., Rice, D., & Sung, H.-Y. (1996). Persons with chronic conditions: Their prevalence and costs. *Journal of the American Medical Association, 276*(18), 1473–1479.

Institute of Medicine. (1988). *The future of public health*. Washington, DC: National Academy Press.

Isaacs, B., Livingstone, M., & Neville, Y. (1972). *Survival of the unfittest*. London: Routledge and K. Paul.

Jaijich, C. L., Ostfeld, A. M., & Freeman, D. H. (1984). Smoking and coronary heart disease mortality in the elderly. *Journal of American Medical Association, 252*(20), 2831–2834.

Keith, R. A., Wilson, D. B., & Gutierrez, P. (1995). Acute and subacute rehabilitation for stroke: A comparison. *Archives of Physical Medicine and Rehabilitation, 76*(6), 495–500.

King, A. C., Oman, R. F., Brassington, G. S., Bliwise, D. L., & Haskell, W. L. (1997). Moderate-intensity exercise and self-rated quality of sleep in older adults: A randomized controlled trial. *Journal of the American Medical Association, 277*(1), 32–37.

Kramer, A. M., Steiner, J. F., Schlenker, R. E., Eilertsen, T. B., Hrincevich, C. A., Tropea, D. A., Ahmad, L. A., & Eckhoff, D. G. (1997). Outcomes and costs after hip fracture and stroke: A comparison of rehabilitation settings. *Journal of the American Medical Association, 277*(5), 396–404.

Lapalio, L. R. (1995). Hypertension in the elderly. *American Family Physician, 52*(4), 1161–1165.

Larson, E. B. (1991). Exercise, functional decline, and frailty. *Journal of the American Geriatrics Society, 39*(6), 635–636.

Lefevre, F., Feinglass, J., Potts, S., Soglin, L., Yarnold, P., Martin, G. J., & Webster, J. R. (1992). Iatrogenic complications in high-risk, elderly patients. *Archives of Internal Medicine, 152*(10), 2074–2080.

Melin, A. L., Hakansson, S., & Bygren, L.O. (1993). The cost-effectiveness of rehabilitation in the home: A study of Swedish elderly. *American Journal of Public Health, 83*(3), 356–362.

Mendelson, M. A. (1974). *Tender loving greed*. New York: Alfred A. Knopf.

Mor, V., Murphy, J., Masterson-Allen, S., Wiley, C., Razmpour, A., Jackson, M. E., Greer, D., & Katz, S. (1989). Risk of functional decline among well elders. *Journal of Clinical Epidemiology, 42*(9), 895–904.

Moss, F. E., & Halamandaris, V. J. (1977). *Too old, too sick, too bad: Nursing homes in America.* Germantown, MD: Aspen Systems Corp.

Murtaugh, C. M., Kemper, P., & Spillman, B. C. (1990). The risk of nursing home use in later life. *Medical Care, 28*(10), 952–962.

Office of Technology Assessment (OTA) (1988). *Preventive health services under Medicare: Screening for open-angle glaucoma in the elderly* (Paper 1). Washington, DC: Congress of the United States, Office of Technology Assessment.

Office of Technology Assessment (OTA) (1990). *Preventive health services under Medicare: Costs and effectiveness of cholesterol screening in the elderly* (Paper 3). Washington, DC: Congress of the United States, Office of Technology Assessment.

Omenn, G. S., Beresford, S. M., Buchner, D. M., LaCroix, A., Martin, M., Patrick, D. L., Wallace, J. I., & Wagner, E. H. (1997). Evidence of modifiable risk factors in older adults as a basis for health promotion/disease prevention programs. In T. Hickey, M. A. Speers, & T. R. Prohaska (Eds.), *Public health and aging* (pp. 107–127). Baltimore, MD: The Johns Hopkins University Press.

Pacala, J. T., Judge, J. O., & Boult, C. (1996). Factors affecting sample selection in a randomized trial of balance enhancement: The FICSIT Study. *JAGS, 44*(5), 377–382.

Paganini-Hill, A., & Henderson, V. W. (1996). Estrogen replacement therapy and risk of Alzheimer disease. *Archives of Internal Medicine, 156*(19), 2213–2217.

Palmore, E. B. (1988). *The facts of aging quiz: A handbook of uses and results* (Vol. 21). New York: Springer Publishing Company.

PEPI investigators (1996). Effects of hormone therapy on bone mineral density: Results from the postmenopausal estrogen/progestin intervention (PEPI) trial. *Journal of the American Medical Association, 276*(17), 1389–1396.

Pinsky, J. L., Branch, L. G., Jette, A. M., Haynes, S. G., Feinleib, M., Cornoni-Huntley, J. C., & Bailey, K. R. (1985). Framingham disability study: Relationship of disability to cardiovascular risk factors among persons free of diagnosed cardiovascular disease. *American Journal of Epidemiology, 122*(4), 644–656.

Province, M. A., Hadley, E. C., Hornbrook, M. C., Lipsitz, L. A., Miller, J. P., Mulrow, C. D., Ory, M. G., Sattin, R. W., Tinetti, M. E., & Wolf, S. L. (1995). The effects of exercise on falls in elderly patients: A preplanned meta-analysis of the FICSIT trials. *JAMA, 273*(17), 1341–1347.

Salive, M. E., & Guralnik, J. M. (1997). Disability outcomes of chronic disease and their implications for public health. In T. Hickey, M. A. Speers, & T. R. Prohaska (Eds.), *Public Health and Aging* (pp. 87–106). Baltimore, MD: The Johns Hopkins University Press.

Schneider, D. L., Barrett-Connor, E. L., & Morton, D. J. (1997). Timing of postmenopausal estrogen for optimal bone mineral density: The Rancho Bernado study. *American Journal of Public Health, 277*(7), 543–547.

SHEP Cooperative Research Group (1991). Prevention of stroke by anti-hypertensive drug treatment in older persons with isolated systolic hypertension: Final results of the Systolic Hypertension in the Elderly Program. *Journal of the American Medical Association, 265*(24), 3255–3264.

Stuck, A. E., Aronow, H. U., Steiner, A., Alessi, C. A., Bula, C. J., Gold, M. N., Yuhas, K. E., Nisenbaum, R., Rubenstein, L. Z., & Beck, J. C. (1995). A trial of annual in-home comprehensive geriatric assessments for elderly people living in the community. *New England Journal of Medicine, 333*(18), 1184–1189.

Stuck, A. E., Siu, A. L., Wieland, G. D., Adams, J., & Rubenstein, L. Z. (1993). Comprehensive geriatric assessment: A meta-analysis of controlled trials. *Lancet, 342*(8878), 1032–1036.

Tinetti, M., Baker, D. I., McAvay, G., Claus, E. B., Garrett, P., Gottschalk, M., Koch, M. L., Trainor, K., & Horwitz, R. I. (1994). A multifactorial intervention to reduce the risk of falling among elderly people living in the community. *New England Journal of Medicine, 331*(13), 821–827.

Tinetti, M. E., Liu, W. L., Marottoli, R. A., & Ginter, S. F. (1991). Mechanical restraint use among residents of skilled nursing facilities. *Journal of the American Medical Association, 265*(4), 468–471.

U. S. Preventive Services Task Force (1989). *Guide to clinical preventive services: Report of the United States Services Task Force* (2nd ed.). Baltimore, MD: Williams and Wilkins.

Vladeck, B. G. (1980). *Unloving care: The nursing home tragedy.* New York: Basic Books.

Wagner, E. H., LaCroix, A. Z., Grothaus, L. Leveille, S. G., Hecht, J. A., Artz, K., Odle, K., & Buchner, D. M. (1994). Preventing disability and falls in older adults: A population-based randomized trial. *American Journal of Public Health, 84*(11), 1800–1806.

Wan, T., & Weissert, W. (1981). Social support networks, patient status and institutionalization. *Research on Aging, 3*(2), 240–256.

Weissert, W. G. (1986). Hard choices: Targeting long-term care to the "at risk" aged. *Journal of Health Politics, Policy and Law, 11*(3), 463–481.

Weissert, W. G. (1988). The national channeling demonstration: What we knew, know now, and still need to know. *Health Services Research, 23*(1), 175–187.

World Health Organization (WHO) (1980). *International classification of impairments, disabilities, and handicaps: A manual of classification relating to the consequences of disease.* Geneva: World Health Organization.

Wolfson, L., Whipple, R., Derby, C., Judge, J., King, M., Amerman, P., Schmidt, J., & Symers, D. (1996). Balance and strength training in older adults: Intervention gains and Tai Chi maintenance. *Journal of American Geriatrics Society, 44*(5), 498–506.

Woolf, S. H. (1995). Screening for prostate cancer with prostate-specific antigen: An examination of the evidence. *New England Journal of Medicine, 333*(21), 1401–1405.

Index

Arthritis self-management
(ASMP) studies
assumptions, 56–57
in Australia, 72–73
building block approach, 67–68
in Canada, 73–76
comprehensive written material,
65–66
content *vs.* process, 59–60, 64–65
effectiveness, search for, 58
future directions for, 76–77
group sharing, 67
lay instructors, 70–71
lay led *vs.* health professional
led programs, 61
long-term outcomes and
cost-effectiveness, 60–61
overview, 57–58
patient education, 62, 67,
69–70
patient problem solving and
decision making, 68–69
problems and concerns of
patients, 62–63
public health model, 64
reinforcement study, 60
rituals, 68
self-efficacy, 66–67
self-management characteristics,
62–71
skills for working with health
professionals, 69
social support, 61–62
Spanish, 76
theory, search for, 58–59
in the United States, 71–72
versions, shorter *vs.* longer, 62
Assessment, 243
Assurance, public health role,
243–244
Australia, arthritis self-management (ASMP) studies in,
72–73

Balance training
defined, 3, 23
exercise recommendations, 25
literature review, 23–25
outcomes, 26
Ballistic stretch, 8
Bedrails, 140
Behavioral Risk Factor
Surveillance System
Survey, 189
Behavioral theories, of smoking,
112
Beta-carotene, 149
Bladder cancer, 150
Bladder control problems, *see*
Urinary incontinence
Body weight, 149
Bone density screening, 152
Borg scale, 5
Bowel management, 142
Breast cancer, 146, 149–150, 156
British Columbia Arthritis Society,
74
Bupropion hydrochloride, 109
Bursitis, 19
Bypass surgery, 166

Calcium intake, 50, 149
Calisthenics, 18
Canada, arthritis self-management
(ASMP) studies in, 73–76
Cancer
aging biology and, 147–148
preclinical symptoms, 153
prevalence of, 146
primary prevention, 148–150
risk factors, 43, 45, 90, 103,
105–107, 147, 149–150
screening, 150–151
secondary prevention, 150–152
tertiary prevention, 152
vitality and, 148–149, 153
Candida albicans, 89

Osteoarthritis, 58
Ovarian cancer, 150

PACE (Program for All Inclusive
    Care of the Elderly), 228
Pain, post-operative, 139
Pain management techniques,
    58
Palliation, 237
Pancreatic cancer, 150
Pap smears, 103, 150
Paratelic states, 113–114
Parenteral nutrition therapy, 47
Partial continence, 134–135
Patient compliance, 191
Patient education
    arthritis, 62, 67, 69–70
    diabetics', 207–208, 210, 213
    health promotion programs,
        231–232, 234
    immunizations, 193
    managed care and, 224
    urinary incontinence, 140
Patterned urge response toileting
    (PURT), 141
Peer education, 142
Pelvic muscle exercises, 142
Periodontal disease (gum disease),
    85–87, 91
Periodontist, role of, 87
Personal assistance, 230
Physical activity, nutrition and, 52;
    see also Exercise/training
Physical therapy, 230
Physicians, role in oral health, 94
Plasma triglycerides (TG), 158
Pneumococal vaccination 180–184,
    186, 188
Pneumonia, 192
Preventive services, evaluation
    criteria, 236
Primary care physician, 164,
    186–187, 227–228

Primary prevention, *see specific
    types of conditions/diseases*
Private insurance, 226
Problem-solving skills,
    self-management
    interventions, 68–69
Progressive muscle relaxation, 68
Progressive resistance exercises, 16
Project Independence, 125
Proprioceptive neuromuscular
    facilitation (PNF), 8
Prostate screening antigen (PSA),
    247
Psychosocial Adjustment to Illness
    Scale (PAIS), 207
Psychosocial support, importance
    of, 237
Public health model,
    self-management
    interventions, 64
Public health paradigm
    age bias, 248–249
    characteristics of, 242–244
    chronic disease, 244–246
    disease prevention, 246–248
    prevention programs, examples
        of, 249–251
Public policy, 243

Quality adjusted life years
    (QALYs), 245
Quality of care, 220, 237

Racial differences
    in coronary heart disease
        (CHD), 161, 166
    immunization rates, 188
Recommended Dietary
    Allowances (RDA), 44, 50
Rehabilitation, exercise training, 6–7
Rehospitalization, 192
Relative perceived exertion (RPE),
    5

Respiratory illness, 192
Respiratory infection, 107
Restraints, use of, 140
Reversal theory, 112–113
Reversible incontinence, 141
Rheumatoid arthritis, 58
Rheumatologist, role of, 66
Rimer, Barbara, 103
Risk containment, 230
Risk factors, *see specific conditions/diseases*
  malnutrition, 47
  nutrition-related problems, 44
Rituals, in self-management interventions, 68
Rowing, 2, 18
Running, 2

Screening and Health Promotion Clinic (SHPC), 226
Screening tests, generally, 227, 229, 247
Secondary prevention, *see specific types of conditions/diseases*
Sedentary lifestyle, 32, 160, 163
Self-care management, 233
Self-Efficacy Theory, 59, 66–67
Self-help movement, 62
Self-help programs, smoking cessation, 110
Self-talk, 68
Self-toileting, 139
Senior meals programs, 50
Seniors Independence Program, Canada, 73–74
Sensory Organization Test, 24
Serum cholesterol, 161
Service utilization, *see* Utilization
Shame, 132
SHMO (Social Health Maintenance Organizations), 228
Sibling studies, premature coronary heart disease
  African American population, 166
  detection of risk and incidence, 166
  nurse management, primary care compared with, 166–167
  participants, characteristics of, 168
  prevalence of risk factors, 165, 169
  risk factor knowledge and attitude, 165
  white population, 166
Skills mastery, 66
Skin cancer, 148
Smoking
  cancer and, 148
  cessation of, *see* Smoking cessation
  coronary heart disease (CHD) and, 159–160
  depression and, 107
  health effects, 52–53, 103–105, 148
  hypertension and, 162
  incidence of, 103
  pharmacological agents and, 103
  quality of life and, 104–105
  sibling studies, 165
Smoking cessation
  age at, 105–107
  benefits of, 107
  coping responses, 110
  intervention programs, 107–111, 162, 164
  pharmacological aids, 108
  rates of, 111
  relapse, 111–115
  theories of, 111–115
Social continence, 136
Socioeconomics, nutrition and, 50–51

Utilization
cultural barriers/differences,
151, 204
dental health services, 82–84
disease-prevention services,
266
health care, generally, 124
health promotion programs
and, 226
holistic approach to, 220

Vaccination guidelines, 180; *see
also* Immunization; *specific
types of vaccinations*
Venous pooling, 5
Visualization, 68
Vitality, 148–149, 153
Vitamin A, 50
Vitamin B$_{12}$, 46, 50
Vitamin C, 52
Vitamin D, 50, 149
Vitamins, generally, *see specific
types of vitamins and
supplements*
deficiency, oral health and, 88
importance of, 148
supplements, 149
Voiding patterns, urinary
continence strategies,
135, 141
Vulnerability, 140

Walking, 2, 18, 22

Warm-up
in endurance training, 17
in exercise prescription, 5
Water exercises, 22, 24–25
Watson, Nancy, 133
Weight loss, 204
Weights, in strength training, 17
Well-being, health effects, 161
Wheelchair wheeling, 18
Women's health issues
bone density screening, 152
breast cancer, 146, 149–150, 156
endometrial cancer, 149
mammography, 150
menopause, 161
obesity in, generally, 149
ovarian cancer, 150
pap smears, 103, 150
uterine cervical cancer, 150
Workplace carcinogens, 148
World Health Organization
(WHO), 244, 246

X-rays, 148
Xerostomia, 90, 94

Yale Frailty and Injury:
Cooperative Studies of
Intervention Trials
methodology, 120–122
purpose of, 120
results of, 122–124
Yoga, 2